Secure
Relating

Secure
Relating

Holding Your Own
in an Insecure World

Sue Marriott, LCSW, CGP
& Ann Kelley, PhD

An Imprint of HarperCollinsPublishers

The characters in this book are entirely fictional and used solely for illustrative purposes. The therapeutic insights shared are for educational purposes and are not intended to replace personalized, professional guidance, which is encouraged for optimal support. The authors and publisher assume no liability for consequences that may occur as a result of applying the information presented.

HarperCollins books may be purchased for educational, business, or sales promotional use. For information, please email the Special Markets Department at SPsales@harpercollins.com.

FIRST EDITION

All original illustrations by Ashley Cruz, finalized by Deena Warner.

Designed by Bonni Leon-Berman

Library of Congress Cataloging-in-Publication Data has been applied for.

ISBN 978-0-06-333455-7

24 25 26 27 28 LBC 5 4 3 2 1

Dedicated to all the sturdy survivors out there who have shouldered the care for those who weren't able to care enough for themselves.

Contents

Acknowledgments

This book would not exist without the legacy of attachment researchers Mary Ainsworth and John Bowlby and all those who followed, as well as those whose tireless and groundbreaking life's work has established and reinforced the clinical link between hard neuroscience and psychology, namely Dan Siegel, Allan Schore, and Steve Porges.

We've had the massive honor to sit with and directly learn from some of the most prominent expert guests in this area. A few of these conversations or relationships have especially shaped our thinking and clarity: Sue Carter, Jill Bolte Taylor, Stephen Porges, Dan Siegel, Bruce Perry, Lou Cozolino, and Joseph LeDoux (neuroscientists); Carol George, Patricia Crittenden, Alan Sroufe (legend attachment researchers); and cutting-edge clinicians or relational researchers Deb Dana, Lori Gottlieb, Bonnie Badenoch, Pat Ogden, Tina Payne Bryson, Nancy McWilliams, Arielle Schwartz, Esther Perel, Elizabeth Stanley, Sarah Peyton, Laurel Parnell, Kristin Neff, David Elliott, Dan Brown (late), Frank Anderson, Stan Tatkin, Dacher Keltner, Bruce Ecker, and Steve Finn. We especially appreciate and hope you tune in to the conversations with *cultural movers and shakers* Gliceria Pérez, Debra Chatman-Finley, Linda Thai, Liz Plank, Loretta Ross, Jessica Fern, Melody Li, shena young, Jeff Lutes, Doug Braun-Harvey, Sharon Lambert, and Trey Ratcliff.

We are especially thankful for our **content experts** who carefully reviewed and critiqued chapters: Alan Sroufe, Carol George, Stephen Porges, Gliceria Pérez, Debra Chatman-Finley, Susan Ansorge, and Mason Marriott-Voss. This feedback specifically makes the book better and more inclusive.

This book would not have happened without the podcast, and so we send love to talented therapist and jig-dancer Patty Olwell, who started the podcast with us and helped launch the fruitful ecosystem that it is today. Without Catherine Mulder, Ashley Cruz, and Jack Anderson, our long-term core team, we could not have kept the show going.

Bethany Saltman's writing support and connection was critical, as it led to our relationship with Eryn Kalavsky, our literary agent. Eryn's belief in us from the start and careful shepherding transformed our collection of ideas and made them come alive with coherence and clarity. We appreciate the patient and detailed literary guidance of Rachel Bertsche, and our publishers at HarperCollins, Karen Rinaldi and Rachel Kambury, who steered us to the finish line. Julie Will—thank you for recognizing the book for what it could be and championing us to Harper.

Also thank you to all the workers without which this book would not have gotten into your hands: prepress technicians, interns, papermill workers, delivery drivers, bookstore staff, and all the non-visible labor required to get us to this moment together.

Sue thanks the whole group of founders of Austin IN Connection, especially Kat Scherer, and all the members of Austin Group Psychotherapy Society. She credits these organizations for helping to "raise her" professionally.

Holy moly our friends and family are saints! They've helped us long-labor this book into existence. So many celebrations and encouragement through the ups and downs and for excusing us from events and not taking it personally when we were missing things, heads down, researching and writing. We are so grateful to each of you and glad you are still standing with us! Let's play!

Probably the most influential in our thinking and inspiration about the book is our clients, especially our long-haulers whose trust and shared exploration have touched us so deeply. This is also true in a different way for our dedicated podcast listeners and especially our Neuronerd online community, who stepped up and hand-held us through the years.

And finally, to our heart—our three adult children, Sydney, Cade, and Mason. We are not overstating it to say you have been an integral part in pushing our brains to expand and our hearts to grow and change. These beautiful young humans make us hopeful about the generations to come!

Introduction

We invite you to join us on a transformative journey—a pilgrimage really—that will deepen security inside yourself and with your favorite (and least favorite) people.

At our core as human beings, the very foundation of our neural wiring causes us to crave love and belonging. From the moment we enter the world we seek connection—it's our very first and most basic survival strategy. This innate drive continuously influences how we engage in relationships, build communities, and find meaning in our lives. We are most inspired toward our best self when we feel grounded and experience a deep sense of security inside ourselves and in the relationships around us. In fact, when we feel secure, we are compassionate, flexible, benevolent, and connected to the well-being of the collective—whether that's the "we" in our primary relationships or the "we" in humanity.

It is also true that our core biology is designed to automatically switch into a focused self-protective mode when we feel threatened, and oh, do we feel threatened. Our nervous system is being stoked into alarm and we have a lot of reasons to feel shaky these days. This free-floating anxiety causes us to unconsciously armor up and lose access to the goodwill we mentioned above. Connection goes by the wayside when we are focused on defending ourselves or those we love.

Secure Relating is about stabilizing and protecting your most evolved and grounded sense of self, especially when we are being incited to regress to the most primitive parts of our nature. In the chapters ahead, you'll learn to build and sustain a competence fueled by security that will benefit everyone: you of course, but also your kids, romantic partner(s), friends, family, colleagues and your community. You'll discover strategies to help you better *co-regulate* (instead of *co-dysregulate*), communicate more effectively, and even respond to conflict with a modicum of grace.

To do this, you'll need to discover more about your unconscious defensive patterns and ways to transform them into conscious strengths. However, this isn't just a feel-good self-improvement guide meant for personal growth alone. As you'll discover, *Secure Relating* is also a call for collective action. If each of us were to build our capacity to stay in our most secure state of mind, we could resist the seductive pull toward emotional cutoffs and malignant polarization that is being created inside us and around us.

This is urgent because if we allow ourselves to sink into chronic emotional activation, we fuel the problem rather than being an active part of the solution. *Blame, cynical mistrust, and hopelessness are contagious.* They corrode our interpersonal relationships and can be exceptionally destructive when unleashed on a larger scale. Our bodies aren't wrong—chronic arguing or ongoing disconnection with those closest to us is painful and a cause for alarm. The horrors of war, environmental devastation, and racial violence *should* activate us; but staying in a chronic state of alarm doesn't help. In fact, it diminishes our collective strength.

When we are unconsciously defensively activated, we lose access to discernment and nuance and are prone to jump into action, a quirk that gets intentionally used against us. It's a familiar strategy in politics—igniting fear and mistrust surpasses evoking hope and inspiration in its effectiveness to galvanize us to pick sides, rally, and show up to vote. Marketers and media outlets also strategically employ the concept of scarcity and our own insecurity to seize our attention, move us to act, and thus bolster their financial gains. Add to that social media algorithms and relentless news cycles that narrow our worldview and amplify our differences, inflaming our mistrust and exaggerating our need for self-protection—a cycle that demands our ongoing vigilance and alarm.

From this insecure and defended state of mind, criticism evokes defensiveness, blame invites childlike counter-blame, and relational bitterness and resentment become accepted as "normal." To cope, we may isolate, band together in collective hate, or mobilize against those "others" we are being directed to fear. This self-focused armored dance becomes a cycle reinforced by others stirred up and in the same boat, a toxic loop perpetuating itself.

Fortunately, this isn't the whole story, and it's definitely not where this story ends.

These destructive and sometimes paranoid behaviors flourish in an environment of scarcity and threat. However, lower that high sense of danger and you'll begin to see something very different emerge. **Mindful attention evokes connection, understanding invites intimacy, and care fosters warmth and generosity.**

A secure state of mind enables you to care about, advocate for, and be generous with people close to you and those you'll never meet. In this way, making the deliberate choice to prioritize secure functioning over myopic self-preservation is a powerful action that can disrupt, and even reverse, the unrelenting fear and pain that creates the defensive activation cycle we see spinning around us today.

Protecting our more secure state of mind and helping others do the same enable us to become a meaningful part in something greater than ourselves. This isn't about being "nice" or settling for something less than you deserve; it's quite the opposite. *Secure relating is about gathering the full force of our understandable fury and collecting our wits to act effectively rather than adding fuel to the fire with impotent rage.* From our more resourced mind we can better care for ourselves and hang on to others even if they are totally regressed and acting out from their own self-protective armor.

Think about it.

If the person you are fighting with shifts even slightly toward compassion and connection, it makes a subtle difference inside of us even if we don't want it to. It's a superpower we can cultivate. These tiny ripples of security contain ingredients to transform shaky relationships, and collectively, they can make a difference in this pained, insecure world.

Honing Your Superpower

The problem is, even when we know better, we don't always do better. It takes honest and often uncomfortable self-examination, and you'll need support to traverse the depths and learn to unstick yourself from these patterns. This is probably not your first rodeo—you've likely worked on these things before and even gotten better, but before long you drift back into more automated, unproductive, and sometimes destructive habits. It's hard to hold your own when there are underlying forces inside you and around you holding you back.

This book is dedicated to unraveling *why* and *when* you lose access to your secure functioning, *what* your particular obstacles are, and *how* you can help the best parts of yourself stick around and stay in charge.

Modern Attachment

Truly understanding what motivates and discourages us will take more than a five-steps-to-change process. It's a journey that requires honest self-examination and an understanding of how humans develop and navigate close relationships as adults. That is why we've incorporated decades of clinical experience and the most important findings from various relational science disciplines. Of these, *attachment*, the psychobiological foundation of one's sense of self that impacts how we relate as adults, stands out as one of the most crucial strands of study and is among the most researched and influential psychological concepts to date.

It refers to a mostly unconscious evaluation of oneself and one's faith in the world. People tend to think of attachment as a category and thus a static personality trait, but in reality, we are highly complex and contradictory creatures who defy simple labels and who learn and evolve based on cumulative and current relational conditions. In this book we focus on states of security and defensiveness, not just categories, and we emphasize how to cultivate that wiser and fiercely compassionate sense of self no matter your diagnosis or personal history.

In *Secure Relating*, we incorporate and update more than a half century of research on attachment with the more recent findings from studies that show how our minds work and impact one another (relational neuroscience). We bring in the important elements of historical context, class, and culture that differ from attachment but have similar biopsychosocial impacts, and ground the ideas on a base of intersubjective psychotherapy in a concept referred to as *Modern Attachment*. Finally, and most importantly, we translate all this complexity into an easy-to-understand framework designed for practical application in your life today.

High Investment, High Reward

We need insulation from the strong gravitational pull toward reactive anger, apathy, groupthink, shared mistrust, hopelessness, and the pervasive paranoia that has led to our current polarization and division. Secure relating starts with quieting the noise within you so you can engage in an honest reexamination of your assumptions about yourself, the stories you carry, and the policies you've adopted when it comes to dealing with other people. This practice will give you needed skills to hold on to your best self as you deal with your spirited child, angry partner, or your own reactions as you take in the latest distressing world news.

We will deliver the hows and whys, but ultimately, what you gain from this work will depend on the interpersonal risks you are willing to take. We are built to resist questioning our own story, and, by definition, we aren't conscious of the unconscious forces that are mucking about in our sense of self and trust in others. We wish merely reading would bring about profound, lasting change on its own—we've tried! Actual experience and measured interpersonal risks create real change: high investment, high reward.

Why Us?

For more than three decades, we've studied what works in healing humans. As professional therapists, we've had the privilege of walking beside a variety of people on their highly individualized journeys toward authenticity: adults, adolescents, couples, thruples, families, peer groups, and decades of interpersonal process groups (these are therapy groups where members openly discuss their thoughts, feelings, and experiences—particularly as they relate to others in the group). A back-of-the-envelope good guess is that combined, we've clocked more than forty thousand hours of sitting with beautiful souls as they work deeply to emerge from real suffering and begin to make meaning of their time on this spinning planet. These experiences have filled us with hope.

Dr. Ann Kelley is a licensed clinical psychologist specializing in relational work with individuals and couples, while Sue Marriott is a licensed clinical social worker, certified group psychotherapist, and a geeky enthusiast for group therapy. We are not bashful about saying that we love our clients and are enriched by these deeply intimate relationships.

Our passion for bridging the psychological sciences beyond the scope of our clinical practices led us to start our podcast, *Therapist Uncensored*, in 2015. The show's success has surprised us—with more than eight million downloads in 270 countries, we've come to realize that many people are interested in the science of relationships and are especially eager for help using the most relevant findings in their daily lives. This platform has brought us into expansive and meaningful conversations with a range of highly respected scientists, clinicians, cultural leaders, and interdisciplinary experts in various fields. See appendix 1 for a list of just some of the leaders who have deeply informed our thinking, work, and lives and who have joined us for in-depth interviews on our podcast. We aim to bridge those unaware of these resources with the originators of the work, so these and many other interviews related to attachment, trauma, and relational neuroscience are freely available for readers wanting to nerd-out with a deeper dive at www.therapistuncensored.com.

To be sure, it's with earned humility that we join you on this journey. We know the messy pitfalls of intimacy personally because besides being cohosts and coauthors, we are a married couple working together, living, loving, laughing, arguing, and raising a menagerie of kids, nieces, nephews, pets, and plants together. We know what works to bring back closeness in times of conflict, but that doesn't mean the intellectual knowledge always saves us during challenging relational moments from reacting in embarrassing ways—just like the best of us.

To add important context: We are a same-sex married couple raising kids in a blended family with a rainbow of people that make up our full family, and, like so many who have come before us, we've been on the front lines in LBGTQ+ advocacy. However, as white, cisgender, middle-aged (and still sassy!) women who can easily blend into the straight majority (aka pass), we are aware we have built-in advantages and unearned privileges that shape our perspectives. We are dedicated to actively supporting and uplifting those whose skin color, body, or gender expression diverge from the social norm, and we commit to continuing to recognize and work to dismantle the oppressive beliefs and harmful attitudes we've absorbed and continue to benefit from. One of our aims within these pages and through our platform is to use our privileges to amplify the perspectives and voices of individuals who have historically been overlooked and underrepresented.

This pilgrimage toward building greater internal security can be unsettling, but it delivers. In therapy-speak it's referred to as "earning security." As witnesses of many who have tried and succeeded on their quest toward earning more relational security, we can attest—if you stick with it, you will change and grow, and it's worth the effort! So, no matter your age or life experience, we assure you that it *is* possible to heal and change—starting right now.

The Science That Won't Make Your Eyes Cross

When it comes to the science of relating, what we have is a digestion problem, not a supply problem. Researchers and clinicians are constantly advancing our understanding, but distilling these findings into something practical and accessible for ordinary life is challenging. It's difficult to find resources that don't oversimplify the beautiful complexities of attachment and human development or that aren't meant for clinicians or researchers. Those conversations can make the information seem inaccessible or, at the very least, not all that helpful to the average person.

That's where we come in.

We've spent years refining how to translate these rich resources. In this book, we are delivering what we think will be the most useful information in a way that we hope maintains the integrity of the science but can also be applied directly in everyday life and relationships.

The Plan

The book is divided into three sections that roughly mirror how real change happens, a process called the *3-R healing spiral of change: recognizing, reflecting, and rewiring.*

Part I: The Power of Awareness

This is the "brainy" part of the book.

Besides learning about how our brains impact one another and catching up with contemporary attachment science, in this first section you'll find a framework called the *Modern Attachment–Regulation Spectrum* (MARS for short) that integrates the most essential need-to-know components into visuals that are easy to understand. You'll grasp how powerfully we're impacted moment-to-moment by the implicit neural networks formed in our earliest years and how that does—and does not—play out in our adult relationships.

You'll also meet a few lively characters who will help you realistically see how these dynamics play out in real life as we follow them through parts of their secure relating journey on the pages ahead. Finally, you'll see how systems, not individuals, are responsible for creating inequity and insecurity and how culture and context impacts us on a biological level.

This takes you on the first portion of the healing spiral, ***Recognition***, because well, sometimes . . . we just don't.

Part II: Building Agency

Here we get practical and apply all that brainy material you learned in part I. This is where it gets more fun, and some of you may want to skip straight to this section for the more direct deliverables. We collect your lightbulb "aha" moments and look for patterns and reexamine stories about ourselves and other people. ***Reflection*** is the part of the healing spiral where you actively explore your own triggers and look for your part in stuck patterns of thinking or fighting.

Rather than resting in the certainty of our position, we engage in curiosity and exploration. This part is about kicking the tires and getting at what's underneath. During this phase, you're open to looking more deeply at your own assumptions and expectations and are secure enough so that you can question what you think you know.

Each chapter in this section goes more deeply into the gradations of coping trends we cover in part I. We look at how the different styles of defenses interact, and it's where you'll get more exploration of why you are the way you are and how best to build and hold on to your most secure functioning when others around you are not.

Part III: Creating Deep Change

Rewiring goes beyond just intellectual understanding or the lightbulbs of insight and is where significant and sustained change takes place. To rewire our nervous system (which we literally can do), it requires some interpersonal risks and new experiences, such as taking in the love we usually let bounce off, learning to actually listen and let someone influence us, or trusting ourselves to speak up.

Rewiring is ultimately experiential and somatic and requires a good dose of vulnerability. It is often the avoidance of the pain rather than the experience of it that blocks us from our most enlivened self, so we will push you a little to get out of your comfort zone because we assure you, the payoff can be nothing short of life-altering.

Each chapter in part III is a deep dive into healing. We start with healing as an individual, then move to healing interpersonally, and end with a chapter on rewiring toward a healthy community.

It's Not Me, It's My Amygdala!

We say on the podcast, "It's not me, it's my amygdala." It's a humorous one-liner referring to the part of our brain that causes us to lose our rational mind at times, but more importantly, it conveys a serious and valuable perspective shift. You aren't "intentionally" choosing to act in ways that seem needy or push away your loved ones—it's truly your brain doing its job. From a social or community perspective, you might try this with whatever group is driving you crazy right now: *It's not them, it's their amygdalae.* The solution for the amygdala is always the same: increasing felt safety.

This book continues in that direction, helping to de-shame human folly while lifting and challenging us to step out of the muck and into our full adult human functioning. It can be helpful to know you aren't alone; there are many of us fighting to hold on (or quickly get back) to our secure selves no matter what rapids we hit as we go. This is a journey we take together.

Let's do this!

Part I

Recognition— The Power of Awareness

1

The Earning
Security Journey

Imagine with us for a moment: You're sitting on your couch engrossed in your screen when a slight movement on the wall to your right catches your attention. Your gaze instinctively shifts and falls on something you've never seen before—a strange, rather elegant insect. Its unusual shape captivates you, so you lean in closer for a better look. Its long, graceful antennae extend from its head and remind you of a butterfly, but its iridescent shell is more beetle-like, glistening with an array of captivating colors. You are mesmerized by this otherworldly creature and are struck that you've not encountered anything like it before. Then you remember your cat, who loves to stalk and capture bugs, so you consider catching this little guy to take it outside to protect it.

Your reverie is interrupted, however, as it lifts its head and fixes its large eyes on yours, causing a wave of uneasiness to wash over you. Its body twitches as those eyes remain fixed on you, intensifying the sensation that this encounter is taking an unnerving turn. Neither of you move; it's as if you are suddenly in a stand-off.

In an unexpected burst of movement the insect takes action. It either jumps or flies—you can't tell which—and quickly whirs by your ear, landing on a spot behind you.

Your startle was comical. Embarrassed by your cartoonish involuntary flinch, new thoughts flow through your mind—what if it sprays some crazy bug chemical at you, or jump-flies at your face again!

Your hand flies out and reflexively smacks the insect to the floor. You consider fetching that jar to take it outside, but the damn thing recovers quickly and begins to fast-crawl in your direction. You definitely don't like this weird thing after all! Not only did it infiltrate your house, but what if it's the first of many? What if it scurries under the couch and has a bunch of creepy babies? You cringe only slightly as you hear its carapace snap under your shoe.

This multilegged stranger went from being a fascinating creature you were enjoying and wanting to protect to an invader you squashed in just a matter of seconds. With the slightest (perceived) provocation, your underlying defense circuit hijacked your interest and reverie.

But you aren't a bug hater; you were quite drawn to it. So how did you end up squashing the poor little guy, and what does that have to do with secure relating?

Protection and Connection Circuits

This, in a nutshell, is how two essential circuits within our nervous system influence our daily interactions and experiences. The first, the *connection circuit*, draws us toward exploration, bonding, and belonging. The second, the *protection circuit*, helps us recognize potential dangers and respond accordingly.

When you first encountered the bug, your connection circuit sparked to life, and curiosity popped forward, guiding you to a pleasant exploration of this alien being. You enjoyed a sense of excitement and wonder. However, it took only a bit of creepy eye contact and a twitch for the protection system to kick in. Then, when the bug started moving toward you, it felt like a full-blown problem. The alert signals in your body *changed your perception* of the creature dramatically. What was once a curious discovery became an invading threat, justifying its abrupt, brutal end.

These same reactions can happen in our everyday interactions with people (minus the brutal ending of course). Everything is smooth sailing in the connecting state of mind, but then something makes us uncomfortable, and it's as if scary music turns on in the background. We see things differently and interpret events with squinty eyes as we erect a shield so as not to get hurt. However, all this happens outside of our awareness—we think we're being totally rational, and the problem is out *there*—the bug—rather than within, which is shaped by our own interpretations and perceptions.

What Is Secure Relating?

Secure relating refers to a state of mind, a healthy and balanced way of connecting and interacting with yourself and others in relationships. It is not a description of personality; *it is a verb describing a way of interacting with the world that comes from a grounded place of agency, connection, and self-awareness.* In a secure state, your mind can hum along, enjoying its natural proclivity to be close, and your nervous system isn't distracted, readying to defend against an incoming threat. Communication comes freely, and you are receptive to the needs of others.

When you are in a secure state of mind you don't necessarily feel secure, but you are aware of your own internal activation and can be curious about it. At the same time, you are aware of others as separate and distinct from you, with their own insecurities and sense of self that is important but different than you. When in a secure state of mind, it feels calming to you and others and is physiologically a healthy place to hang out. However, it's a destination you aim for and, when not there, paddle toward. It is not a place you find and just move into.

For those who enjoy lists, here are a few characteristics that describe when you are in that well-rounded, balanced secure state of mind:

Emotional Regulation: You are less likely to lose your mind when stressed and can generally express feelings and needs without being overwhelmed by intense emotions in yourself or others.
Autonomy: You can usually be close and connected to others without feeling trapped, and you are generally comfortable on your own.
Empathy and Compassion: You have general access to care and can express it—for both you and others. You don't lose yourself to it and are likely able to take it in and value it when it comes your way.

Effective Communication: You are relatively transparent and say what you mean with care.

Trust and Reliability: You have confidence in others' reliability and trustworthiness, and others find you safe to turn toward emotionally.

Adaptability: You can be flexible and open to compromise and problem-solving without feeling like or becoming a doormat.

Boundaries: You can generally set and hold them with respect for yourself and others.

Conflict: You are in touch with your ability to confront with care and accept feedback constructively.

We like to say that you are your *right size*. Rather than trying to shrink yourself to protect someone else's ego or puff up and seem bigger than you really feel, secure relating is about being *your* right size—just your right size, nothing more and nothing less. When you are your right size, you can handle much of what comes your way or you can ask for help with it without your ego getting in the way. You can also shift comfortably from solitude to connection and back again.

That said, being in a secure state of mind does not mean always *feeling* secure. You still experience the difficult emotions that come with the slight from a friend or a slammed door from your teenager, but you can generally maintain your thinking and connections despite feeling unsettled. You can recognize that you are being reactive, slow down, and move to a more deliberate position to reflect and hear the other side.

Here's a good one: in a secure state of mind you can embrace someone else's idea and not feel diminished, and you can let people lend you a hand whether or not you actually "need it." Generally, it's the balance between thinking and feeling and being connected to yourself and others simultaneously that are hallmarks of a secure state of mind.

It's easy to describe but, unfortunately, not so easy to maintain.

We tend to save our worst selves for our closest others. We can be stubbornly zipped up, disregard how we're affecting others, ruminate on what others may think, shut down, feel overwhelmed, collapse, attack those we feel hurt us, and hate righteously. Even if we already have a healthy, nurturing, significant relationship, maintaining it at a secure base level is challenging because much of what goes wrong between two humans is driven from below conscious awareness. Our very human but highly problematic tendency to defend and blame operates deep inside the brain, causing us to double down on a common fatal flaw: a certainty, when we are defensively activated, that we are right and the other person is wrong.

Let's say Sue is "in a mood." What do you think Sue does if Ann gives her feedback that she's being short and a bit dismissive—thank her for her accurate and keen insight? Very doubtful.

Like most of us, if Sue's already in a dismissive mind-set, she probably isn't especially open to unsolicited feedback at that moment; her protection circuit is running and is content to stay slightly defended. However, if she were in a more secure state of mind, Sue would likely be much more receptive to Ann's pointing that she was acting moody. She'd be able to pause and perhaps consider what Ann said. She'd be capable of wondering, *Maybe Ann's on to something, good to know.* Or maybe Ann is off base and instead, it's more a signal that she needs something different from Sue. No skin off Sue's back either way. Because she's in a secure state of mind, she's open to getting to the real issue: Ann wants or needs something different from her.

When you are functioning securely, complaints from your partner are much less threatening, the stakes are much lower, and you know you have the resources to manage whatever comes next. Importantly, relating from a secure place of connection creates safety, and makes communication more open and pleasant for everyone. And it changes us at the biological level, bathing important body systems in nutrients that help them function at their best.

Learning to operate from the possibilities of authentic connection and realistic hope (in other words, relating securely) rather than automatically engaging from a place of unconscious defensiveness (or relating "insecurely") can create a powerful cascade of positive change. If Ann complains to Sue about something, and Sue genuinely catches it and responds with some modicum of skill, guess what happens to Ann? Even if she was riled up before, this type of kindness and feeling of being understood comforts her and takes the wind out of her sails. Just like negativity builds on itself, so does felt safety.

Even though it can bring out the best in others, secure relating is a state of mind that emerges inside you and doesn't require anyone else to be different. Others can cooperate and relate in this flow with you—or not. The more practiced you are at gaining this grounded sense, the better you will be able to hold your own with increasing strength no matter the circus around you. While this can sound easy, grounding ourselves first takes awareness of our patterns in the connection and protection systems and how they are showing up in our everyday relationships.

Secure Relating Versus Secure Attachment

As you can see, secure relating is not a diagnosis or a set of techniques. It is not dependent on any childhood experience and is not the same thing as secure attachment. Attachment is a pivotal concept in human development that emphasizes the profound impact of close relationships throughout our lives—especially the caregiver-infant bond. *Secure attachment* is a category from attachment research associated with having a trusting relationship with early caregivers and patterns of trust in oneself and others in adulthood.

Secure relating goes beyond early attachment research categories. In fact, we don't just fall neatly into one category in all relationships, we continue to evolve and develop throughout our lives. This is great news for us because *anyone* can relate securely, no matter their history, because secure relating is a *state of mind* that can be fostered and practiced. Yes, those fortunate enough to have a secure attachment history have an edge up on resilience, but no one lives there all the time—there are plenty of times they won't be relating securely, either. And even the most relationally injured adults can access a secure state of mind; it's a learnable skill and is accessible to everyone! This practice of developing a more consistent style of secure relating is often referred to as *earning security.**

---

*   Mary Main, a key figure in developmental attachment, first used the term *earned secure* to describe those who did not come from a secure past but who had resolved their early experiences. We say *earning security* because it is an ongoing process. The *earning security bus* is the journey. You are invited to join with us!

Rather than thinking, *Sue is securely attached* (she's on that earning security bus and is working on it!), instead consider whether or not Sue is in a secure state of mind. Granted, that actual language is a little therapist-y, but the concept is face-saving and, frankly, more accurate. After all, people don't identify exclusively as one thing or stay in only one state of mind—we are complicated. And this way, when we slip out of this grounded, wise state of being, it's okay, we can learn how we fell off and get better at knowing how to get back there.

Hustling toward a secure state of mind is an ongoing process. It's a forgiving dance that involves consciously scooting back to feelings of connection, safety, and trust once you notice that you've drifted into a more defensive stance. Sometimes things are too stirred up, and the path back to connection might seem intractable. When someone gives their side of a story, for instance, and they leave out essential details from your perspective, how do you let them just keep going? Surely it would feel better to jump in and give them the more accurate accounting of events so they can see how unnecessary their feelings of disappointment really are?

Secure relating includes recognizing that you're feeling defensive, dealing with your own activation, and making room for others even when it is challenging. In this case, it would look like catching yourself before butting in to add your perspective—a master move! It might involve clarifying that you will share your perspective afterward so you can settle into listening, or recognizing you can't listen right now and asking for some time to settle down before continuing the conversation. It's flexible and imperfect, which is wonderful.

For each of us, this will look different because we all operate with unique neurology and physical and emotional abilities. Secure relating involves learning your own unique history and abilities and deepening your understanding of others'. For some, closeness with others is not the end-all for feeling safe, especially for many whose brains may function differently than the majority, such as those with autism or attention deficit disorder or severely traumatized individuals. People in marginalized communities have had their healthy adaptive patterns pathologized because they were different from the so-called neuro-normative, Western standard. And if your community is oppressed and unprotected, growing up vigilant is adaptive, not dysfunctional. So, context always matters.

Nevertheless, it is safe to say that a secure state of mind involves relating from a foundation rooted in biologically determined feelings of capability and trust in yourself and safe others.

You Can't Do This Alone

Confidence is often overrated. Just because you feel confident doesn't necessarily mean you are in a secure state of mind. In fact, overconfidence can blind us from self- and other awareness as our "I know best" thinking is comfortable but probably not as true as we'd like to think. When we are coming from a place of security, we recognize our need for others. We need them to question us, help us see what we miss, support us, and build upon our strengths and weaknesses.

From a base of security, it's not hard to recognize that we didn't get here by ourselves. We owe our progress to the support of countless individuals and communities who have buoyed us—extended family, friends, teachers, spiritual guides, coaches, and countless others. They may have shielded us from the subtle and overt threats to our self-worth, or have worked the other way—eroding or even over-elevating our sense of worth. Our development is a mosaic, a sum of many intricate people and shaped by the world around us.

Remember, humans evolved with wiring that yearns to be close, belong, and feel part of something larger than ourselves. Now it's just a matter of clearing the rubble that covers that natural space and learning to protect it so that we can hang out there more freely.

As you learn the science behind emotional regulation and interpersonal closeness, we will help you recognize your personal signs of activation so you can identify when your protective circuit is juicing up. Do this enough, and you'll begin to become aware of your patterned defenses and the stories that keep them strong. With time and practice, you can interrupt the old, harmful stories that keep you stuck and rewire them into more updated, accurate, and compassionate stories about who you are and what you have a right to expect of others.

What Is Modern Attachment?

Numerous researchers and clinicians have come before us and made decades of invaluable contributions to our understanding of attachment (see appendix 3). As it has evolved, so has appreciation for how attachment shapes our brain and nervous system and how class, culture, and community impact human development. We have woven together the threads of attachment research, both old and new, with the most important insights from relational neuroscience to capture the essence of Modern Attachment. This comprehensive perspective allows us to understand how our attachment patterns shape our stress response system. The hard science and technical interventions alone would be just techniques if not rounded out with depth psychology.

It's easy to make the mistake of getting excited about what we've learned and then providing psychoeducation about the brain or attachment, but that handout or mini-lecture is not always automatically therapeutic. The base of our ideas on attachment are grounded in years of depth relational psychotherapy and informed by respected psychoanalytical clinicians such as Phil Bromberg, Carol Gilligan, Irvin Yalom, Stephen Mitchell, Lew Aron, Nancy McWilliams, and Jessica Benjamin. For us, it is important not to dilute depth therapy. The danger there is that it can become about what the therapist knows (keeping us as therapists comfortable and feeling "helpful," a feeling we love) rather than what the client more deeply needs at that moment.

Our framework is based on the idea that experiences in therapy are cocreated with the therapist and the patient each influencing the other. This can be hard, because therapists also have an unconscious, but when you get two people together willing to be mutually impacted, then you have a wonderful recipe for growth and healing. Change that lasts is rarely only intellectual; it requires close emotional connection on the nonverbal realm that you'll learn much more about soon when we introduce relational neurobiology led by Dr. Dan Siegel and the important clinical work of Dr. Allan Schore in chapter 3.

Finally, from our perspective the concept of Modern Attachment goes well beyond the focus on the mother, the first eighteen months of life, and Western child-rearing norms. This more current perspective respects and acknowledges the diversity of individual experiences and expressions. It also encompasses a wide range of family constellations, highlights the strengths and vulnerabilities within different subcommunities and cultures, considers historical precedents that influence child development, and sheds light on the effects of institutionalized discrimination in marginalized communities.

The Modern Attachment–Regulation Spectrum (MARS)

As mentioned in the introduction, the Modern Attachment–Regulation Spectrum (MARS) is a framework that enables you to apply relational science to your personal life and specific relationships. It's an easy-to-use visual model that represents the complex and relevant aspects of attachment and relational neuroscience accessible to people who may otherwise not come across it.

The visual images start out very basic and then build in layers of complexity, incorporating up-to-date research and clinical theory on attachment across one's life span. It weaves in how our early history shows up in the way we view ourselves and the world, how we manage our emotions, how we interpret information coming from within and around us and how we impact and are impacted by our various relationships. For the clinicians and neuronerds, this means we include *implicit relating, internal working models, emotional state regulation, information processing distortions, unresolved trauma, co-regulation*, and *context*. But don't be intimidated if these terms are unfamiliar; we keep things pretty straightforward and walk you through it all.

Once you get the hang of it, MARS will help you identify yours and others' state of mind in the moment as well as understand what is going on inside you and how to shift back to a more connected place. It gets really enjoyable once we start working on it with close others and seeing how states dynamically interact with one another (part II).

Figure 1 below depicts the primary framework of MARS. As we go, we will continue to break down the individual components, starting first with the spectrum itself. We will expand and deepen each of these concepts in the chapters ahead, and the last half of the book will be dedicated to applying these concepts to your everyday life and relationships.

A note about illustrations: we refer to colors throughout the book as a way of helping you envision the ideas. You'll find color versions in the insert and black-and-white images embedded in the text. Please refer to the color images initially so that you have a mental map to refer to as you go. Also, find citations referenced in the endnotes.

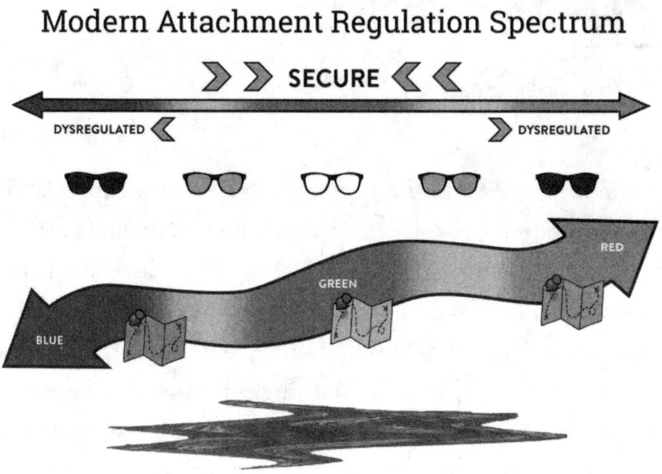

Modern Attachment Regulation Spectrum

Figure 1: Modern Attachment Regulation Spectrum (MARS)

The Spectrum (States of Mind)

The central feature in MARS is the spectrum itself, a bidirectional arrow with an array of color variations. The colors represent how our emotions and body fluctuate throughout the day, depending on how safe, excited, or activated we feel at any given moment. Our bodies respond to threat in predictable ways, and we will dive more deeply into these patterns in the next chapter. The spectrum illustrates the nuance of in-the-moment flow of individual states of mind and emotional activation or deactivation. We use colors to illustrate the natural flow through these states with the varying shades to represent increasing and decreasing intensity. See Figure 2.

The Spectrum

Figure 2: The Basic Spectrum

The middle of the spectrum is green—this is our secure relating sweet spot! Being in the *green zone* means that your body and mind perceive things as safe enough, and you're okay to "go on being." You can relax whether alone or with someone, and you can do nothing, be highly productive, work on solving that difficult work problem, or simply self-reflect. This doesn't mean you can't feel stirred up, though. You might ruminate or be petty or feel angry or sad or lonely, but you are still operating with your higher thinking intact and have access to your whole, wise, and caring mind.

A key feature of secure relating is emotional regulation, so identifying if you are in the green zone or not is a first step, and frankly, it's harder than it sounds. When we are defensive, we often don't think we are defensive—we are "right" and they are wrong, end of story. You don't need to know yet exactly how you are activated or why, but just learning the specifics of your green zone experience will help.

Figure 3 shows all we need to know so far—you are either operating from your green zone, the connection system—or you are not. So ask yourself, what are signs that you are in your green zone, how can you tell?

Connection System (felt safety) or Protection System (felt threat)

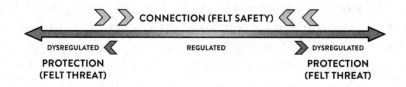

Figure 3: Connection System (Felt Safety) or Protection System (Felt Threat)

Dr. Dan Siegel, clinical professor of psychiatry at UCLA, is considered the father of interpersonal neurobiology. He astounded therapists by proving the linkage between neuroscience and psychology with his epic textbook, *The Developing Mind*. He also introduced the idea of a *window of tolerance*. This is a widely used concept in the therapy world popularized further by trauma therapist and director of the Sensorimotor Psychotherapy Institute Dr. Pat Ogden. The concept of a window of tolerance refers to the optimal emotional arousal a person can tolerate without becoming overwhelmed. You'll also hear the term *dysregulated*, which means we've left the regulated green zone connection circuit and have shifted into our protection circuit. Figure 4 is an adaption of the window of tolerance along the spectrum.

Learning to hang out most often in our most secure-related self involves expanding our green zone capacity—growing our window of tolerance—

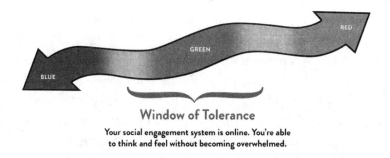

Window of Tolerance

Your social engagement system is online. You're able to think and feel without becoming overwhelmed.

Figure 4: Window of Tolerance (Adapted from Siegel, 1999)

by enhancing our capacity to tolerate the reality of our immediate experience without our protection circuit kicking in.

The range of your green zone is influenced by many factors, including your attachment history, your developmental stage, your cumulative life experiences, and your current circumstances. You can grow your green zone by engaging with your internal world; avoiding our inner life maintains or contracts our current window of tolerance. When we focus on our ability to tolerate distress, engage with it, and experience it with openness and curiosity, we send the message to our mind and body that we can handle what is happening and are open to discomfort. By protecting our green zone and spending as much time as we can operating out of this state of mind, it grows and keeps our protection circuit offline until it's actually needed.

If we believe we aren't supposed to feel discomfort, we will naturally try to avoid it. However, by giving ourselves permission to have distress and cultivating pride in being able to tolerate it without losing our thinking, we are more likely to be able to sit in discomfort and explore it. This practice helps make unfamiliar and complex emotions less threatening and fosters our ability to stay in charge of our responses.

We no longer have to dodge and weave around interpersonal unfamiliarity. It's like going into the sunshine—if you rarely get exposed, you burn easily, but once you learn what you can handle and what protection you need, you can enjoy the outdoors. As you keep facing challenges and learn to understand all the emotional information being conveyed, you build up a kind of emotional skin. So to be clear, tolerating distress isn't about shutting down your feelings or pretending everything's fine; it's about really feeling what you're going through, understanding it, and accepting that it's all part of being human.

Being in the green means we can tap into what is happening inside us and be interested in what's happening to the other person simultaneously. This is relating securely—we don't have to drop ourselves to connect with the (perceived) wants of others, nor do we cut off or forget about the other person. Instead, we simultaneously hold a connection to them and ourselves. Being able to feel feelings for the person across from us *and* for ourselves is a great green zone description.

Moving Out of Secure Relating

Okay, but what about when our protection circuit kicks us out of the green zone?

It's natural for life and relationships to kick up a sense of threat and for us to lose access to our more friendly ease of relating. The bigger the feelings, the further away from the green zone you will slide. Which direction you slide and how far out you go now becomes what we want to track.

As your protection circuit activates, your body begins to rely on well-learned strategies to regulate your emotions and protect you from the sense of threat you are experiencing. Based on history and your circumstance, you are likely to favor one side of the spectrum more than the other.

Red Zone Activation

Moving right on the spectrum represents an uptick in emotional activation depicted by shifts in color gradients from green to red with many shades in between (this is more clearly represented in the color insert). The shades darken as you move right and upward along the spectrum arrow. It can be amusing to imagine the color of your nervous system as it moves up the spectrum—from greenish to something akin to amber, terra-cotta, pink, maroon, crimson, and then fiery hot scarlet red. This is *not* meant to be technical or exact, but instead to give you a feeling for changes in your state of openness. Being able to name a feeling or visualize a dynamic state of mind in the moment builds your green zone.

Shifting to the right on the spectrum means that your brain is perceiving threat and your (unconscious) strategy to handle that is to intensify your attention, emotions, and actions toward others. Your nervous system revs up to attend to the threat, which is often referred to as *upregulating*. Rather than intellectualizing and avoiding feelings when you are at this end of the spectrum, you become more emotionally alert and expressive. As you move further to the right, this uptick into higher emotionality can be experienced by others as exaggerated and somewhat intimidating. You may not be aware of it at the time, but likely deeper down you sense the threat of losing something important.

The higher intensity of red zone activation causes difficulty in letting go of negative experiences and an urgency to resolve discomfort. This can lead to either conflict avoidance or a compulsion to run toward conflict in a desire to settle it quickly. Ann can really relate to this, as she is more of a red leaner during conflict. The temporary emotional distance that often occurs in an argument can be especially challenging for red leaners. For example, Ann's discomfort with distance during conflict can cause her to press Sue to talk through things when neither is ready. While she may believe she is "the relational one" at the moment, simply trying to resolve the conflict like normal people are supposed to do, her urgency and insistence belies her red-tinged activation. This intensity and rush does little to signal to either of them that they can relax and safely connect.

Another aspect of reddish activation is avoiding the risk of increasing distance by avoiding conflict altogether. This might look like walking on eggshells to avoid someone's anticipated reaction. When we are on our tiptoes, we typically feel justified and are focused on the other person's potential reaction being the problem, missing the fact that we are having a big reaction ourselves—we are the ones tiptoeing! Remember, when you find a more secure state of mind, you can be your right size and say what you need to say while holding yourself and the other person in mind.* If the eggshells break, so be it, you know you will be able to handle what comes next. You don't work to coax someone to feel or not feel a particular way, and if they are out of bounds in their reactivity you can take action to set boundaries or otherwise take care of yourself.

Tracking your level of activation is the same thing as caring about your sense of safety. Noticing when and why you uptick will help you recognize your blooming pinkish activation more quickly and help you make choices about what to do about it. These insights propel conscious shifts in states and, if practiced, eventually can become naturally occurring traits of our rich, untidy personalities.

You'll find much more detail on red-zone relating in chapter 9, so hang tight, we've got you!

---

* This assumes a certain level of basic relational safety and no threat of physical danger, of course. We will say more about how to tell the difference in the next chapter.

Blue Zone Activation

We can also have well-worn strategies aimed at *deactivating*, or cutting off, our emotions. This is represented by the color blue, as we sometimes become a bit cooler, even cold. As defensive deactivation intensifies, this is represented by the colors turning from green and darkening as we slide left down the spectrum toward dark blue. This blue-tilted progression represents withdrawal into oneself, emotional disengagement, and a heavier reliance on thinking over feeling.

Like everything, we are breaking free of categories, so we don't just jump from green to blue, we go through variations such as aqua, turquoise, indigo, sapphire, and eventually to that very cold and dry navy blue. The point is to recognize your changing hues early and often—have fun with it!

Blue zone activation generally reduces expressiveness and moves us away from feelings, also called *down-regulation*, and the primary goal is to avoid vulnerability. Shifting toward the blue side means that you are (mostly unconsciously) motivated to avoid emotions and to pull more inside yourself at that moment. Seeking emotional distance does not make you mean or withholding, it's simply been encoded in your mind and body that avoiding emotion and vulnerability is the right way to stay safe.

Shifting toward the blue zone has the underlying goal of moving away from or shutting down emotional experiences in yourself and others. Most often it's a pretty clear move toward avoidance, but the blue zone isn't limited to withdrawal. It may also look like an uptick in anger to stop an interaction (versus anger to engage more actively over on the other side of the spectrum), quick dismissal of the topic, or moving into action via hyperrationality. Notice they all have the underlying intent of shutting down someone else's emotional expression or our own so that we can become more comfortable again.

When we lean blue, protecting our identity and avoiding the feelings around making mistakes can be of utmost importance. Logic and facts are useful cooling-off tools. However, research shows that shutting down or stonewalling is one of the worst things you can do in an argument. This really caught Sue's attention because she trends bluish under duress and can use intellect to manage emotionality. She is happy to remind you that she is also colorfully diverse, so she can become hypervigilant too, especially with her closest people. So, all of you intellectualizers, stay tuned so that we can help you remain emotionally engaged and manage dicey situations with more agility.

Your attempts to avoid vulnerability may read like irritability, but it's hard to know how somebody in the blue zone feels or what they need because they often don't know themselves. If you've shifted blue, you will rely too heavily on your own instincts and not trust others as much. You may even act disparagingly toward someone who is more in touch with their emotional needs because you experience their emotions as blame or an unnecessary burden.

Making your way back toward green will require accessing your body and feelings and getting your heart back online. If we do not realize that we have shut down, we are likely to remain in a deactivated state for long periods of time to avoid potential conflict. Simply recognizing that you are traveling down the blue spectrum can be an important step for blue leaners in their journey toward secure relating. You don't have to be able to change this yet; noticing is a great first step.

Whether you are the blue leaner or you are close to a blue-tinged soul, we have much more help for you to come in chapter 8, but we encourage you to learn more about the brain in this section to make the best use of the applied strategies.

Using the Spectrum in the Moment

By identifying where you are in any given moment—either by noticing if you tend to activate or deactivate, tracking color variations over time, or just noticing small shifts to the right or left—you are already building secure relating capacity! You don't need to know more about your overall attachment patterns or your unconscious narratives. By just recognizing your state in the moment and focusing on moving toward green, you can immediately impact your relatability in the moment, which is good for everyone involved.

In Figure 5, you'll find the basic spectrum with colors indicated that loosely represent what parts of your nervous system are activated. Below the spectrum are quick descriptors of the ranges of these states of mind.

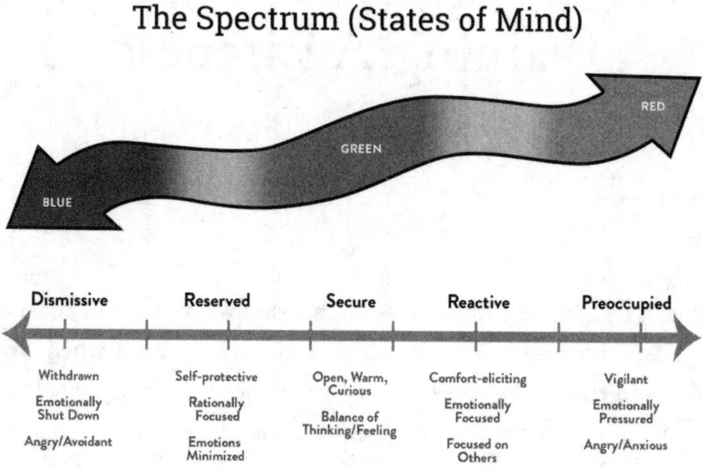

The Spectrum (States of Mind)

Dismissive	Reserved	Secure	Reactive	Preoccupied
Withdrawn	Self-protective	Open, Warm, Curious	Comfort-eliciting	Vigilant
Emotionally Shut Down	Rationally Focused	Balance of Thinking/Feeling	Emotionally Focused	Emotionally Pressured
Angry/Avoidant	Emotions Minimized		Focused on Others	Angry/Anxious

Figure 5: The Spectrum (States of Mind)

In short, if you are juiced up in the red zone, you'll want to slow down, question your pressure to act, and regain access to nonurgent thinking. If you are tuned down and hanging out way over there in the blue zone, you'll doubt that you are activated at all because you've turned down access and interest in emotions. If you find yourself stiff and detached, your best move is to look for your heart. It is those caring feelings that will warm you back toward green, and the dreaded v-word, *vulnerability*. It's scary but way better for you than being iced-out in isolation over in that dark blue zone.

2

Gaining Awareness

Trouble in our relationships brews not because we sometimes get snarky, clingy, demanding, or eye roll-y. The real problems arise when we feel justified and righteous, unaware that we are defensively activated or uncaring about the impact on those close to us. It's when we refuse to be aware and vulnerable.

Rather than justifying that dismissive eye roll or snarky comment based on someone else's behavior, stop and ask yourself, *What am I feeling?* Look for a nonintellectual word, or at most a short phrase—not a paragraph explanation or intellectual description. Feelings sound simple, like mad, sad, or glad, but as you get more discerning, you'll recognize many more feeling flavors, such as relaxed, content, disheartened, discouraged, sullen, troubled, restless, lively, mellow, and so on. If you tend to struggle recognizing and naming your feelings, don't hesitate to use a feelings chart or an app to help you. This neural rewiring is serious business, and many of us have had little training in this, so there is no shame whatsoever in getting help naming feelings. Being the detective and neutrally observing your feelings helps you identify the nuances of defensive activation, which will help you stay grounded in the green zone even when you are churning with uncomfortable feelings. Practicing mental check-ins and self-reflection and expanding your feeling vocabulary builds your green zone capacity. Put in the reps to grow!

Like a good trainer, once you get that down we encourage you to go further than merely noticing you have a feeling. Get curious about what triggered the response inside you *beyond what the other person just did.* Instead of "I'm mad because she keeps making a big deal about small things," ask yourself: *Why does hearing about small things bother me so much? What feelings does it stir and why?* The answers to these questions may not be as obvious as they seem on the surface.

When upset you might push further. It can be helpful to remember that not everyone will have the same reaction to whatever just happened. You are having *your* particular reaction at the specific volume you have it, and that is your focus first. Your boyfriend is being rude, and you think he's acting like a jerk. Maybe your reaction is spot-on and he's being selfish or uncaring, but what volume are you experiencing your feelings? Not everyone would have the same volume and accompanying internal chatter about it. So, how do you know what is true? This is where gaining awareness of your internal stories and how your body tends to protect itself really comes in. We aren't saying don't trust yourself and instead question all your feelings—it's quite the opposite. Learn to know and trust yourself so much that you recognize what parts of you to listen to and when, and what parts may be whispering in your ear and steering you wrong.

Record-Scratch— What About Abusive Relationships?

Being activated can also mean that we ignore or deny actions that are, in fact, hurtful or abusive and blame ourselves or make excuses for their behavior. We may feel it too threatening to lose someone, confront someone, or let in negative qualities that are incongruent with our image of who the person is. It may even be dangerous to show your grounded, secure self—if you resonate with that, trust yourself. As you gain more awareness of what you are feeling, we implore you—believe you! We are primarily discussing safe-enough relationships where all parties are open to influence and working on themselves.

People who feel fundamentally safe don't have to wonder if they are in a dangerous and abusive situation even if they don't like what's going on. Get yourself in a safe environment and you'll get clearer. You shouldn't do this on your own, so reach out for support—friends, coworkers, or domestic violence services—find what feels like your right next *safe* step.

Research shows that one of the most risky and dangerous acts a woman can do is leaving a partner who is violent. Anyone in a situation that feels it too dangerous to exit is dealing with many factors that impact that decision. If you or someone you love is in a dangerous situation, build a support network that can help prepare a safety plan and find a secure environment for everyone involved. It's not up to anyone else to dictate what is right for you. Remember, we are about security, and too often that means we need to focus on our physical safety first. The main message here is to listen to your sense of danger and take it seriously; get support that helps you recognize how important you are and that your well-being matters.

Deepening Your Secure Relating Skills

Assuming a safe-enough, mutual relationship, finding your authentic voice is an important, yet often challenging step. The good news about authenticity is that it doesn't require you to be right, accurate, or fair. Finding your authentic feelings starts with reflection and curiosity. This reflection can be explored together. For instance, why do you feel anxious every time she goes out with friends? Rather than jumping to fix the problem and eradicate the uncomfortable feeling, take some time to first explore what emerges for you.

With practice, this earning security journey will help you take yourself and your instincts very seriously and get the respect you deserve.

Don't Focus Only on the Bug (Poor Bug)
Let's think back to our innocent bug from chapter 1.

When we're stirred up, we tend to blame the bug (or, more specifically, the person "out there" causing our uncomfortable feelings or keeping us stuck in overwhelm). We focus on the bug and then try to make sense of our experience—this could range anywhere from warm, pleasant feelings (*What a sweet creature*) to aversive feelings of disgust (*Invading insect!*). The bug didn't do anything wrong; it was being a bug. Our feelings toward it changed when threat and fear were introduced, which led to the deliberate bug murder. It's uncomfortable to look just at our side of things: we want to explain ourselves based on the bug's behavior, but in fact we killed it because we had an uncomfortable feeling. Since the most important action is happening *inside us*, we must learn how to direct our attention inward rather than focusing on others as the cause of or the cure for relating securely.

That's quite the task, though.

Most of us don't walk around interested in our inner thoughts and feelings, much less are we any good at managing them. When we have uncomfortable feelings in our body, we want them to go away as quickly as possible—heaven forbid that we move *toward* them. Plus, even if we want to pay more attention to what's happening inside, it's hard to discern without practice. We must learn what to look for.

How Can We Be "Self-Aware" of Things Outside Our Awareness?

Perfect question. Once we solve this problem, everything gets easier.

You know how you don't know you've fallen asleep until you wake up? That's how slippery defensive activation is. It's often only after the fact, like by the light of the next morning, that we can see things more fully and clearly—and from a wiser, more secure, and less defensively activated perspective.

Secure relating means we are working from the inside out.

When in high defense, we are working outside in, but the process of secure relating is learning to work inside out: tracking our reactions and responding intentionally rather than reacting to what's going on out there or pulling away because of what feels threatening to us. The point is to focus on what's happening in here, right now, in this moment.

While the human nervous system evolved over time to protect and connect, each person's nervous system is unique. From the get-go, we each learn whether or not to expect people to be there for us, how they'll show up, how to avoid rejection, how to disarm hostility, and how to get our needs met through our specific caregivers, with our specific temperament, in our specific family, neighborhood, community, and culture. And all of this is embedded in deep personal history that matters now. No one escapes this truth, whether you are aware of these factors impacting you now or not, because it all begins before we know we are learning.

Let's investigate how these patterns unfold by meeting Derek, a sweet six-month-old who's just trying to find his way in the world. He can't think in words because babies don't yet have language, but he sure can learn. When he's hungry and crying, his body feels better once he hears his mama shuffling toward him because he knows it means food and comfort. However, when he's just fussy and she can't fix it, Mama gets impatient, and he can feel it.

She knows what to *do* when he needs something concrete, such as feeding, changing his diaper, and keeping him warm, but she gets flustered when his needs are less concrete, emotionally driven, and not easily resolved. Over time, Mama becomes more stern, and eventually Derek learns that it is not helpful to cry unless there is "good reason." When Derek's content, Mama is right there, but when he's whining, she communicates subtle disapproval, scowling or turning away if he becomes too needy or tries to crawl up in her lap.

Derek understands fast. Not only does he learn to resist crying, but crying and the accompanying feelings are quickly associated with the painful feeling of parental disapproval and emotional distancing. Over time Derek develops an unconscious aversion to his negative "needy" feelings. If they threaten to emerge, he shuts them down so fast that he doesn't even notice them.

You can see where this is going. Know any Dereks in your life?

Developing Core Narratives

Like Derek, as we adapt to our early environment, we internalize many life lessons. Up to this moment, you, the reader, have accumulated a lifetime of experiences that have created an internal template of what you expect from the world and how you view yourself and others. These experiences have literally shaped how your mind develops; what brings you comfort or anxiety; what you tend to focus on or ignore; your underlying assumptions, values, and beliefs; and the deep knowing of what your body deems safe or threatening. No two templates are alike—it's part of what makes you uniquely you. This is your attachment system in 3-D.

Do you believe talking helps, or would you rather poke your eyes out than share a feeling with someone? Is showing emotion and vulnerability a way to bond, or done in haste because you just can't help yourself? Do you usually rely on yourself as an independent agent, or are you comfortable turning to others for support? Do you doubt your own ability to make the right decisions, so you rely on other's instincts rather than your own? Answers to questions such as these can crystalize awareness of your personal template, adding insight into how your body is wired, what unconscious learning and assumptions have been stored, and what strategies you draw on to keep yourself safe and comfortable. This represents deep early learning that is stored in the lower, more primitive part of your brain and goes into your quick-and-easy conscious answers.

Unpacking your own story and forming a map of how you have learned to protect yourself is important to create and maintain a sense of stable security, but how can you see something that, by definition, you can't see because it's unconscious?

It's not easy! In fact, we are typically more tuned in to the feelings of others than we are to ourselves. Since it's often easier to recognize patterns in others, let's meet DJ and Mia, a couple with small children who are mostly happily married and each other's best friend on their good days. This particular day is not one of those.

As you read their story of a date night gone bad, pay attention to any cues of each partner's internalized narrative and the in-the-moment reactions that cocreate the conflict. Keep track of your thoughts and feelings as the story unfolds; you'd be surprised how different people respond to the same story.

DJ and Mia

Mia hurries to finish briefing her sister-in-law, Tia, on what homework is required before the kids can get screen time. She's grateful for the help tonight but knows that Aunt Tia is too easy on the kids, acting more like a friend than an authority figure.

Mia and DJ have planned dinner out sans kids for the first time in months. She doesn't want to start the night off with his impatience, so she rushes to join him as he waits for her in the Jeep. Scrambling as she climbs in, she quickly realizes she doesn't need to rush after all. He's lost in thought, head down and texting, and he doesn't look up to greet her. She settles herself, closes the car door decisively, and then waits, intentionally silent. There is more than one way to make a point.

Finally, DJ snaps the phone closed and glances at Mia. She tries to catch those brown-flecked eyes that used to flip her stomach but misses. Instead, he puts the car in reverse and backs out of the driveway wordlessly.

Eventually he side-glances her way—something seems to be bothering her, but he has no idea what. He takes inventory and is confident he hasn't done anything to anger his wife, so it must be something else. He sure doesn't want to start anything at the beginning of their date. He turns his mind back to the problem at work he'd been Rubik's Cube-ing, assuming she'll relax once they get to dinner.

As they drive, Mia is internally planning for the night ahead. She wants it to be nice but is disappointed already. DJ seems lost in his thoughts, and she wonders if, once again, she will have to carry the bulk of the conversation between them. As she looks out the window, she is ruminating about how distracted he has seemed, then slides into thoughts about Daniel, their eight-year-old son, and his tendency to stay home after school rather than play with the boys in the neighborhood. She wishes she felt more comfortable sharing her worries with her husband.

Once at the restaurant, Mia turns cheery, ignoring the earlier tension and chatting with their waiter, Anthony. She asks him about recommendations, how long he's worked at the restaurant, and the various menu options. He tells her about the fresh food sources, and they go over possible substitutions. Mia studied the menu for some time, but she still isn't yet sure what to order, so DJ asks the waiter for a few more minutes.

When Anthony returns for their order, Mia cringes: she still hasn't decided. Everything sounds so good! Mia wants the date to be perfect, and the food is part of the date. She also likes to order complementary dishes to try more than one thing. So, Anthony fields more questions and points out the most popular dishes on the menu.

DJ doesn't understand why his wife always seems to take so long to make simple decisions. He always knows what he wants; why does she complicate things? Despite his self-confidence, DJ doesn't recognize that underneath his certainty and growing impatience, he's feeling uncomfortable and even embarrassed by what he perceives as Mia's indecisiveness and need for help in ordering. He imagines that the waiter is internally rolling his eyes, and he really doesn't want to be "that table."

"Should we share something?" Mia asks DJ.

He glances at the waiter, conveying a subtle "Can you believe this?" message.

Mia tilts her head down, peering through her eyeglasses at the menu again, and says to no one in particular, "Well, shoot, I just don't know. What's your favorite dish, Anthony?"

After he answers, there's another silence long enough to be uncomfortable as DJ and the waiter give Mia time to think. She's unaware of the feelings she's creating and takes her time. By now, DJ is visibly irritated.

Rather than finally making her selection, Mia asks, "What are you going to order, babe?"

DJ gives in to the suppressed eye roll with an exasperated "Good God, Mia! He has other tables, you know. Just decide already!"

Let's pause for one second to perform a quick internal-awareness scan. What thoughts are you having toward Mia and DJ? Which of them do you relate to more? Who turns you off?

Interrupting and asking these questions as you read is important because sensing your state of mind while engaged relationally with something or someone else is an important emotional regulation skill. Consider this hands-on practice.

Some of you will identify with Mia and even feel protective of her; others will sympathize with DJ. Some may be irritated at the rather stereotyped gender dynamics at play, while others will bounce along, not noticing such details. While it will seem obvious to you how to feel about the situation, your perception isn't the "truth," and it gets most interesting by being curious.

After DJ snaps at her, Mia looks up, surprised by her husband's tone. She's embarrassed by his comment but quickly manages her discomfort by seeing it from his perspective. Her indecisiveness *is* irritating, she thinks, but she just can't help it. She quickly orders the dish that Anthony first recommended.

Mia wants to let this pass, but she can't. She has been trying to dodge a series of DJ-related disappointments over the days, weeks, and months leading up to this date. She subtly tracks a running list of slights, and her list of resentments toward him is impressive. However, she's afraid of angering him, so she tries to keep it at bay in herself as much as possible. She knows he's been under a lot of pressure at work and she doesn't want to add to it. She would do better to push back a little as things come so DJ would get a read on how he is coming across, but she usually doesn't until it's too late, and she lashes out.

For his part, DJ isn't even aware that there's an issue brewing. He isn't attuned to Mia's vulnerability, and without her being more explicit, it's easy for him to miss her signals and focus on the more concrete issue at hand.

Deep down, her outward neediness threatens him, though he would deny feeling threatened because he doesn't know he's stirred up. Instead, DJ would say that he just doesn't like indecisiveness or neediness. If pressed, he might say he's turned off, maybe even vaguely disgusted, by what he considers "too much" need. Because of that, he's quick to fix things or dismiss feelings as unnecessary, even silly. When someone is "too" emotional and not looking for a rational solution, he might internally ridicule the other person—without realizing that doing so means he has big feelings himself.

DJ's comment hurt Mia's feelings, and the fact that he didn't even notice that she quickly retreated into herself made her feel even lonelier. At this point, neither partner recognizes how much is roiling under the surface. Instead, they continue with their evening and superficially seem to relax more as time passes.

Mia has been considering how to bring up a subject that she anticipates may be a bit loaded between them. Mia is determined to pull DJ away from work and get the time together they want as a family, but she also knows how much stress he has been under recently. They are a drink and a half in, and dinner is served when she makes her move and brings up the family trip she wants to discuss.

"I'm so ready for spring break," she says. "I'm looking forward to our vacation! The hotel is one block from the beach, it has a pool—"

"Vacation?" DJ stops chewing and looks at Mia warily.

"Yes, vacation. You know, the trip with the kids to Port Aransas. We discussed the plan together over a month ago."

Shaking his head, DJ responds quickly, "No, *we* didn't plan anything."

He wipes his mouth with his napkin. "Did you book it?!" He delivers the question as an accusation because he knows the answer, and Mia's hurt stare only aggravates him more.

"You did that on your own, Mia. I know you brought it up, but I remember telling you I wasn't sure if it would work. I didn't know you had *booked* something. Did you already pay for it?" DJ's voice is rising.

Mia's voice also pitches up—she hates that but can't help it.

"We had to grab a reservation, or everything would be booked! We agreed that we needed it. The kids need it, too. They need us to–"

"*They* need?" DJ interrupts. "They are kids, Mia. They are fine! You know that work is crazy right now. What about me? I'm swamped, and taking time off would only worsen it. This was your plan, not 'ours,'" he says, making finger quotes in the air.

DJ's pulse has taken a sharp upturn, but he's not aware of this physical change. His body learned a long time ago to bypass threatening emotional information and to rely on his thinking, which it could trust more easily. He thinks he's "fine" and is just being accurate and direct. Still, his body now has a good dose of the stress hormones coursing through his bloodstream, and he's on guard to protect himself, which biologically overrides his motivation to connect with Mia.

If DJ were truly "fine" and in a regulated, secure state, he would have room to slow down and care about his partner's perspective. He'd be curious about what just went wrong in their communication rather than rushing to be "right." If he were grounded in himself, DJ would feel confident in his perspective and yet also be aware of his impact on his partner. He might even feel bad about letting Mia down or be open to working together to find a solution. But right now, his defense system is activated, and he is emotionally stiff. Unfortunately, the disavowal of his discomfort only adds to the disconnection and hurt.

Mia, on the other hand, is also swimming in cortisol. She can't think clearly and feels hurt by DJ's rejection of the trip. Truth be told, she *knew* her husband was not fully on board with the vacation, yet she presented it as if they'd agreed to the trip rather than simply advocating for what she wanted. She often hopes DJ will see what's important to her without her having to ask for it expressly. She justified booking the trip "because the kids need a vacation," a good example of how she often expresses her needs and wants indirectly.

"This is not my fault, Mia," DJ continues, hoping to prove his innocence. "Why do you always do this to me—make me feel guilty for just trying to work and . . ." He continues to assert his perspective, but neither partner registers his words. Mia looks up from her plate and sees the red blotching DJ's cheeks and neck.

Although she's registering her husband's anger, Mia is more overwhelmed by the anticipation of his rejection. To her, fighting is better than distance, and it's what she expects, but her partner rejecting her entirely is another story.

She's thinking: *He has no interest in going anywhere with me. He's not invested in the family at all. He's so selfish; doesn't care about anyone but himself. Why have I put up with this so long?*

Notice the rage building in Mia and how she converts that hurt into feeling actively angry, a common mistake when we get activated.

"Of course, work comes first yet again!" She is hurt, but it comes out indignant.

"I'm working my ass off to get us out of debt, and you are booking beach hotels?" DJ continues between bites.

Mia's voice begins to carry across the restaurant patio. "You can't take one week off to be with us?! The kids miss you, DJ. Do you want me to tell them you can't get off work once again to be with us?"

"Oh, come on, that isn't fair! I know I didn't agree to go because I never wanted to go in the first place." It all comes spilling out now. "I hate traveling with you when you're like this, and I can't stand how you treat the kids—like they are a bunch of . . . *babies*!" He spits the word *babies* as if it is an insult.

Mia was ready for some resistance but is taken aback by his force. Her brain heard "I hate you," or something like that. She isn't sure. She doesn't care. Her eyes are back on her lap, and her heart is racing. She can no longer pretend they are doing okay, that DJ was just distracted by work, or that he didn't mean what he said. She's tired of this! She is convinced he doesn't care and is just going through the motions. She lets that sink in, unaware that these are *her* insecure feelings she's projecting as if they are coming from *him*.

DJ is also upset about the misunderstanding but believes his wife's wounded feelings are totally unjust. He is on full autopilot: determined to stop this conflict by clarifying the details. Does she not realize he's a good guy working his butt off and would never go back on an agreement?

"Look, you know I never go back on my word. If I had agreed—"

Mia stands up and is already a few steps away before DJ registers what's going on. She makes it across the outdoor patio in giant steps and is inside the restaurant before he turns his head to watch her leave. By the time he finishes a long exhale, she is out the front door and storming to the car, where they both know she will remain until he joins her.

Making Sense of It All

Mia and DJ think they're fighting about a vacation, but if they kept arguing, they would likely spiral downward to complaints about what one or the other "always does." Mia would be upset that DJ focuses on work and might call out his neglect of her and the kids. She would point out how often he is distracted and rarely seems aware of all that she does, to which DJ would counter with his frustrations about Mia being upset and disappointed way too often. He especially is tired of her indirectness and getting mad at him for not giving her things she hadn't asked for. He feels under-recognized for all he does—after all, he's working toward eventually becoming a project manager and he needs to be focused on keeping the team on budget, yet he took the night off for their date when a bid was due the next day. And, of course, there's Mia's obvious immediate infraction: planning the vacation without really including him. Now he has to be the bad guy—as usual.

These are probably not new complaints between Mia and DJ. When couples shift from fighting about immediate content to overarching patterns—"You never do this" or "You always do that"—things become entrenched and repetitive: same song, different verse. Instead of looking at the surface content, we need to begin to understand the unconscious patterns between them.

It's not hard to see that this fight isn't solely about the vacation. It's also not about DJ's preoccupation with work or Mia's tendency to cater to the children. It's about the disconnect between how each partner seeks connection and security.

DJ and Mia could go back and forth forever about who agreed to what, but no sorting through the details or giving each other a more accurate picture of what happened will solve a problem when you're stuck in the kind of fight that's really about emotional security. Even if you had a video recording to "prove your point," until you're each de-escalated, it would be hard to see the other side with compassion.

Remember when we talked about knowing better versus doing better? We can tell ourselves that we'll sit down, calm down, and follow all the right steps to positive communication, and *still* end up fuming alone in the car like Mia, when all we really want is to feel close and enjoy time with our partner. Our higher relational mind wants closeness but cannot get it as long as the lower defensive circuit hijacks the relational boat.

So how do we make inroads to actual change? An important first step is understanding the differences in what each partner perceives as a threat, what the threat represents, and how our bodies respond. This is what the journey of secure relating is all about.

Unconscious Dynamics

Any defensive reaction—blame, silence, or anything in between—is meant to help you move out of distress toward relief. It's not an intellectual decision; it's a physiological response.

Learning your special and highly personal activation cues will sharpen your ability to recognize your state in the moment and help you gain the agency to shift those stuck patterns toward more secure functioning. Your protective circuit activation shows up in the body through increased heart rate and verbal pace, heightened attention, and a sense of urgency. You might notice other clues, such as a pressure to "do" something (walking away or rolling your eyes) in reaction to a comment, or you might avoid important topics or try to one-up the other person to win a conflict or freeze the action.

Let's take a look at Mia.

On the surface, it might seem like she had it all together and became activated only once she got into the car and DJ didn't look up from his phone. After all, she had rushed on his behalf! But if you dig a little deeper, it becomes clear that her protective system was activated before she even walked out of the house. For one thing, she didn't ask or expect her husband to stay and help. Instead, she found herself rushing to avoid his irritability.

Once in the car, Mia expressed her frustration passively with the light door slam rather than talking about it. Given what you know about red and blue activation, where do you think Mia was? Her ongoing focus on DJ in her inner dialogue, the tallying of the frustrations and disappointments that have been simmering under the surface for some time, and even her notable difficulty deciding what to order for dinner could be signs of preoccupation or running in the red. Staying in uncertainty can be a way of hiding your true sense of self, or a sign of a disconnection to it. Remember, though, this isn't to label her; she's not one thing. Right now we have a lens specifically looking for these issues, we are not looking for the complexity in her, tracking her over time, or asking her what she thinks—all things you would actually do in real life.

Let's take a look at DJ.

We'll use DJ now as an example of blue activation, but certainly, he up-regulates as well, and Mia can slide up and down the emotional regulation spectrum like all of us. It's not labeling a person; it is labeling a behavior that can indicate different types of defensive activation.

Surprise: we met DJ earlier when we met baby Derek. That was Derek Jr., later called DJ because he hated the tie to his absent dad. Knowing some of DJ's early life helps us make sense of his patterns now. Like most of us during an argument, there are long patterns at play that DJ is not even thinking about, and that early learning with his mother is part of his struggle tonight.

Before the evening even began, DJ was already somewhat emotionally distant, indicating that not only does he defend at the moment by withdrawing, but he likely has a pattern of a high need for "independence," as he thinks of it. This is *pseudo-security*: a claim of being secure when his actual needs and vulnerability are absent.

Signs of dismissing activation included his choice to go to the car to avoid engaging with the chaos of readying to leave and saying good-bye to the kids, focusing on his phone and work, and failing to pick up on his wife's distress. There was also his inability to reach out to learn more about what was going on with Mia that moment in the car when he noticed something was wrong, and his escalating need to be "rational." DJ was insensitive toward Mia's insecurity when ordering dinner, which, based on her surprised reaction, was unusual for him—in other words, he's not just a jerk. He amplified his focus on accuracy ("I remember telling you I wasn't sure if it would work") and zeroed in on protecting himself ("This is not my fault!").

The more he did all this, the less he tuned in to his relationship with Mia.

Changing the Lens

When reading DJ and Mia's story, it might have been tempting to think of DJ as selfish or Mia as indecisive or weak. However, looking through a lens of secure relating, you might find a more compassionate and accurate understanding of both of them.

DJ's shortness with Mia was his admittedly misguided but not un-caring way of trying to keep things from escalating. On the other hand, Mia's storming out of the restaurant was a sign of overwhelm and pain over the disconnection with DJ—also misguided but rooted in the pain of disconnection and the desire for connection. She'd learned from past quarrels that once they got upset to a certain level it was best for her to stop the action, in this case, by retreating to the car. Both she and DJ knew her reason for bolting; likewise, both felt secure that they would talk things out later. If Mia's leaving alarmed you, notice that you didn't have the whole story. By staying clear in yourself and curious, we can continue to learn what's really going on here and hold the whole perspec-tive. It's hard, but we have to find out from the person directly involved what these actions mean and not just interpret meaning based on what we might do in the same situation.

Sometimes, when trapped in an argument we want desperately to end, the pressure we feel just keeps making it worse. As DJ and Mia reacted to each other, they were *co-dysregulating*, each making it a little worse rather than better. And, as they shifted further away from the green zone, they went in the patterned direction that they'd learned early on to protect themselves: Mia gets more activated when in conflict and DJ zips up. Remember, the further you get from the balanced green, the more rigid you become. Neither of them was happy about the conflict, so they behaved in the same old ways they knew for trying to manage the discomfort of their escalating defenses.

Finding compassion and understanding underneath our patterned conflict does not mean standing by passively and allowing others to hurt us. Quite the opposite: the clarity and insight from secure relating includes caring for yourself and setting limits when needed without blowing up bridges and those close to you.

Compassion and insight can be two of the biggest motivators for change, while withdrawal and righteous anger keep us suspended in our negative beliefs and dysfunctional patterns. As we continue on this path we will add solid science about what's going on underneath to help you get better and better at the compassion and insight parts. By the end of the next chapter you will be able to see even more subtly about this fight and recognize DJ's and Mia's underlying defensive biology.

3

Relational Neuroscience 201

Old friends Priya and Naomi haven't seen each other in a while and make plans two weeks in advance to have lunch together. As usual, Priya arrives at the coffeehouse early and grabs a table. They'd agreed to meet at noon, so about five after, Priya checks her phone for a text from Naomi perhaps alerting her that she is running late. Since there was no note, Priya texts her friend to say that she is already at the restaurant, adding, "You on your way?" Nothing.

As the minutes pass, she picks up her phone several times, despite knowing full well that the ringer is on, so she'd have heard the distinctive ping of an incoming message. It's not long before Priya is convinced that something is terribly wrong. At this point, Naomi is only about ten minutes late, but since Priya has been there for twenty, it feels like a much longer time to her.

Priya's leg is rhythmically bouncing up and down, and she is picking at her cuticles while her thoughts churn. She conjures stories of what has happened to Naomi. Had she just forgot her and the lunch? Had she been in a car wreck? She doesn't hear sirens, which is good—but maybe they aren't on the scene yet. She gets up and peers through a nearby window, searching the parking lot for Naomi's car. At a quarter after twelve, she sees Naomi pull up, and Priya is flooded with both relief and irritation. Naomi rushes inside to join her, explaining apologetically that she'd been stuck in traffic on the freeway and couldn't text. Although Priya knows on one level that this is a normal occurrence, she feels rattled, and it's hard for her to shake her discomfort and ease into the meal with her old friend.

Right Channel, Wrong Volume

It is normal to feel concern or irritation if someone is late, but for Priya, Naomi being just fifteen minutes late caused enough distress to affect her ability to enjoy their lunch. She filled in the blank with fear and insecurity rather than trusting that Naomi was coming or that she'd hear from her soon. This overreaction is a pattern for Priya. Someone else may have hardly noticed the lateness or filled in the blank with anger or personal offense. For Priya, other people's lateness is a trigger that provokes a reaction bigger than the situation warrants. It's like she's tuned in to the *right channel* (Naomi *is* late), but the *volume is too high*. Priya's worry and bodily reaction (quickened pulse, tightening chest) were pretty high for such a short delay.

Triggers are often a sign that our protection circuit threw a threat signal when there was no actual danger, and Priya was triggered. They usually trip something in our unconscious, causing implicit or explicit stories from our past to leak into the present. Had Priya not been triggered, she would have quickly recovered once Naomi arrived and they had a pleasant lunch. Focusing on her feelings rather than the person out there (the bug) could help Priya recognize her patterned response is out of proportion. The underlying fear can then more likely be recognized and thus increase the chance she'll get the comfort that part of her needs.

That's where relational neurobiology comes into play. It's all about understanding what's happening to throw the system off and learning how to clear the cache so that our brains are operating on accurate, updated information rather than default to outdated programming. Noticing what triggers you can be a way of scanning for hitches in the system. This understanding empowers us to navigate triggers and regulate our responses effectively.

Components of Modern Attachment

Let's start by taking a high-level look at human development and unpack how you became the person who is reading this book today. Neuroscience is the first piece of a larger puzzle, and secure relating comes from the ability to fit all those pieces together.

Research has made huge strides in discovering how neuroscience, infant attachment, childhood working models, and adult attachment relationships are interwoven and flow together. We use the acronym BAMA (biology, attachment, maps, adult attachment) to explain the various components and evolution of the concept of attachment, which together help us figure out how we have learned to show up in our current relationships.

Over the next three chapters, we will cover each of these components as they apply directly to building your secure relating capacity, beginning with the biology that undergirds attachment.

Biology of Attachment (B in BAMA)

Starting during pregnancy but especially in the last few months before birth and continuing throughout your life, your stress response patterns create a physiological scaffold that frames ongoing development. This scaffold—the relational neurobiology we cover in this chapter—sets up the neural patterning that manifests later as attachment behaviors.

Attachment (A)

Between six to eighteen months, as early experiences become repeated and circuits become more patterned, an infant and toddler's attachment behavior becomes observable and predictable. In this case, *attachment* refers specifically to relational behaviors in infancy, sometimes called *developmental attachment*. The science here is fascinating, as you will see when we dig into it in chapter 4.

Maps (M)

The third letter in BAMA refers to *attachment maps*. They include our *internal working models* (IWMs), which are speculated to begin to form in our unconscious by year one, while more stable mental imagery emerges around three to four years of age and organize how we see ourselves and what we expect from the world. We call them attachment maps to include IWMs but also the biological markings, behaviors, and proclivities that we inherit from the culture and context in which we grew up. Maps are partially conscious and accessible with language, and partially unconscious, embodied templates.

In chapter 5 we will focus on understanding and moving our attachment maps because they are critical in how attachment insecurity gets carried forward.

Adult Attachment Styles (A)

The last *A* in BAMA stands for *adult attachment* and refers to a significantly different body of research than developmental attachment in infancy. Adult attachment is influenced by infant attachment, but it's not the same thing. Instead, it refers to a line of research focused primarily on conscious beliefs around adult relationships, as you'll see in chapter 4.

Figure 6, Modern Attachment Components: BAMA Chart, on the next page, summarizes these different components and tracks the language used and primary disciplines of those who studied it. Some of the detail included is a preview of where we are going in the next few chapters and is not exhaustive, but a good general pointer.

BAMA + the Context Umbrella

Modern Attachment includes all the BAMA components plus the context umbrella.

The culture and context in which we live is inextricably linked to how we develop our sense of self, which leads us to the *context umbrella*. Just like BAMA, each of these contextual factors has lifelong impacts on our sense of self.

Each spoke of the context umbrella represents one of the many important factors that impact us throughout our lives: our cultural identity

BAMA	Development Window	Primary Discipline	Common Assessment	Key Ideas	Common Nomenclature
B Biology of Attachment	Prenatal - Lifetime	Affective Neuroscience / Interpersonal Neurobiology	fMRI cortisol/oxytocin heart rate variability	Protection/connection systems, polyvagal theory implicit memory, right-to-right relating	amygdala HPA Axis hippocampus prefrontal cortex
A Attachment Patterns (child)	3 Months - 18 Months	Developmental Psychology	Strange Situation	Behavioral attachment patterns, caregiver/infant relationship, not individually diagnostic, relationship strategies	Secure Insecure/Resistant Insecure/Avoidant Disorganized
M Maps - Attachment Maps	3/4 Years - Lifetime	Developmental & Clinical Psychology	AAI Adult Attachment Interview and AAP Adult Attachment Projective	Internal Working Models IWM + embodied culture & context	Secure Preoccupied Dismissing Disorganized/Unresolved
A Adult Attachment Styles	Adult - Lifetime	Social Psychology +	Experiences in Close Relationships - Revised (ECR-R)	Adult Attachment Styles Anxiety/Avoidance dimensional measures Self-report	Secure Dismissive/Avoidant Preoccupied Fearful/Avoidant

Figure 6: Modern Attachment Components: BAMA Chart

and the strengths and vulnerabilities that come with that, internalized religious teachings, community protections or aggressions, religious and political affiliations, social and economic status, geography, and all the systemic -isms, especially institutionalized racism, antisemitism, Islamophobia, misogyny, LBGTQ+phobia, ageism, and ablism.

The context umbrella is also informed by deep cultural histories and the strengths and traumas of those who came before us, called *epigenetics*.[*] This context umbrella represents the frame under which we are developing our brains, minds, hearts, and narratives about ourselves and the world around us. As we will see as we continue, this umbrella continues to impact us positively or negatively throughout our lives.

We will dive much more deeply into culture and context related to attachment in chapter 7.

---

[*]   Epigenetics demonstrates how our genes can be influenced by external factors and experiences, impacting our health and biological markers.

Relational Neurobiology—The Need to Know

Humans are highly social and persistently interdependent mammals. One reason we all get so worked up at times is that we need one another, and our bodies know it. True independence is a fantasy—no one would be here without years of care from others, no matter how subpar your early care may have been.

As bothersome as this may be, we aren't in charge. Cooperation and coordination are key to our survival, not only around us, but also internally within us. We have vulnerable bodies with internal systems and subsystems that are constantly communicating and working together. For example, the digestive system affects the immune system, which coordinates with the stress response system. We even have entire colonies of tiny creatures we depend on for normal functioning called our microbiome: hundreds of trillions of little microorganisms that influence metabolism and brain function without our awareness. Far from anyone standing alone, it's more accurate to think of us as a complex ecosystem embedded in a wider web of other ecosystems.

In an exciting twist, the more you know about these interactive systems, the more agency you have to impact each of them. Let's revisit what you already know.

The co-coordinator of these systems mentioned above is the brain, which is an extension of our physical body. Our brain is an incredible miracle in itself. According to the life work of Dr. Siegel, it is a specialized physical and social organ that regulates and is regulated by the body and the environment. It constructs mental states and imaginings out of the feeling states the body is signaling in a complex collaboration that includes biochemistry and bioelectrical activity.

It's interesting to think about the difference between the brain and the mind. Dr. Siegel suggests that the mind is a self-organizing process that emerges from the flow of energy and activity of our brain, and then acts together with our body to bring us consciousness—all the thoughts, feelings, and perceptions one would expect. The trifecta of the brain, mind, and body interplay so deeply that, again according to Dr. Siegel, as you shift your mind (reading this book, having new experiences, and partaking in close relationships, for example), you are literally changing the structure of your brain, which, in turn, changes the structure of your body.

That is why we have so much certainty and hope about secure relating—the impact of security can be seen on an fMRI!

A DOSE of Musical Metaphor

The key brain chemicals involved in interpersonal relating can be remembered by the acronym DOSE: *dopamine* (energy, movement, and anticipation of reward), *oxytocin* (the bonding and attachment molecule), *serotonin* (mood, satiation, and well-being), and *endorphins* (natural opiates). These neurotransmitters and neuropeptides are chemical messengers that transmit signals between neurons (nerve cells) in the brain and the rest of your nervous system.

They work together to deliver an experience that can be thought of like music from an orchestra. Let's think of these neurochemicals as sections working together toward the whole of your listening experience—they certainly aren't supposed to be on at the same intensity and at the same time; that would be chaos.

Serotonin serves as the base of the music with melody and rhythm, providing background stability and gently guiding us toward tranquility and contentment. Dopamine creates the excitement—it is that crescendo that builds from the base and delivers powerful feelings of surprise and pleasure. It emerges and recedes to add to the experience, but trying to stay there throughout the piece would wear us out and fall flat. Oxytocin is the harmonizer, bringing us a feeling of warmth and connection, adding to the notes that are already there. Think of a beautiful duet that envelopes you like a pleasurable embrace. And those natural endorphins are like the back beat—the percussion driving and adding to the overall enjoyment of the music. When in a secure state these sections work peacefully in coordination, rising and falling, with the balance being the full integrated orchestra.

The other important class of chemical couriers are hormones that don't emerge from your brain at all. *Cortisol* and *adrenaline* (epinephrine) are released from your adrenal gland, which sits atop each of your two kidneys. They are called *stress hormones* because they mobilize the body to respond to excitement and danger. This is an important point as our body can respond to stress without our brain fully registering a conscious threat. More on this later.

Going back to that orchestra (how long can this metaphor continue, we all may be wondering), cortisol is the conductor with the baton; when it rises the orchestra pays attention and is ready to execute whatever signal is next. It keeps the music on track, coordinating the different sections. When something is off, cortisol revs up the metronome or it can tell a section to stop. As cortisol slows back down, the orchestra can re-regulate, allowing everyone to get back in sync. Finally, epinephrine would be like the burst of a trumpet cutting through the composition with a rush of urgency. Under too much stress these hormones are more like sour notes—disrupting continuity and calling all the attention to themselves. (Phew, we made it to the end of this stretched metaphor pretty well, we think!)

This is a long way of saying we aren't supposed to be happy all the time. Or connected. Instead, we simply want this biological orchestra coordinated and integrated, responding to one another fluidly. The goal is not to have constant serotonin satisfaction or only to experience dopamine pleasure, for example. Chasing one note, or working to avoid the others, dilutes the experience, and fortunately it doesn't work that way by design. We need variation, movement, disruption, and synchronicity. The whole ecosystem working together.

Now, let's turn to the brain itself and deepen our understanding of the physical structures that coordinate the neurochemicals. Note again that no one part of the brain acts alone or does just one thing; the relational brain is an intricate and coordinated web. However, it will help us to highlight a few main parts of our anatomy—the big relational players that will help all this complexity make sense. We've narrowed it down for simplicity.

Three Key Relational Brain Regions

We are going to get brainy for just a second because we have found it quite useful as clinicians when clients develop a deeper understanding of what is going on inside of them when they get upset. We have seen firsthand how much compassion and empowerment this understanding can bring and how much shame it can alleviate.

The more you can understand how these areas interact and impact one another, the more competent you can be in learning to manage big emotions, keep your cool under fire, and stay close to those you love under stress. But learning to relate more securely does not require all these details, so if this gets too in the weeds for you, it's fine to bounce on over to the next chapter or even to part II, where all this science gets directly applied to real life.

The amygdala, the hippocampus, and the pre-frontal cortex are three critical interpersonal brain regions that make you uniquely you.

The Fussy Amygdala

Our small, almond-shaped *amygdala* is part of the neural network that mediates many aspects of our memory, motivation, and especially our emotions. The protection circuit we've been discussing is managed by our amygdala. Well, it actually operates in conjunction with the *hypothalamus*, the *pituitary gland*, and the aforementioned adrenal gland—referred to collectively as the *HPA axis*—to manage our stress response system, but we will stick with the amygdala for simplicity.

One of the amygdala's primary jobs is to detect threats and trigger a response quickly, without requiring our slower, thinking brain to be involved. It is so fast that it processes emotions and facial expressions well before we become consciously aware that something is happening. If someone unexpectedly slams a book shut behind you or you almost step on a snake, you will jump first (amygdala) and then figure out what happened.

Interestingly, we have two amygdalae, one on each side of the brain. They reside deep in a more primitive section you'll hear referred to as *lower limbic* or old brain (from an evolutionary perspective) or our *emotional center*. Each amygdala processes pain, emotions, and other people's facial expressions a little differently and anatomically are not quite the same. This bilateral structure and its connections with other brain regions contribute to the speed and complexity of our emotional experiences. Humans would have never survived if we had to rely on our slower, conscious, thinking mind to analyze something and decide what to do.

But here's the problem. Our threat-detecting amygdala is online and active even in the womb. As a matter of fact, the stress response system is the only neural circuit immediately working at full charge at birth. As a result, our amygdala is fussy—it will sound the alarm bells at the slightest provocation, but it can't turn off the sirens by itself.

In essence, *we are born with a sensitive alarm system with no off switch or volume control*.

This fundamental design quirk makes it hard to be a young child and is why our attachment system and those early caregiver relationships are so critical. We require the help of a more mature nervous system nearby to evaluate, make sense of, and soothe our distress at a time when our little brains are in an intense process of rapid growth and learning.

Suppose that during this time, when your amygdala sounds the distress alarm, your caregiver mostly responds and effectively calms you down, bringing relief. (We say *mostly* because we don't have to be—and never will be—perfect in giving or receiving care.) Having our distress relieved helps our developing stress response system generally understand that emotions can be managed because it has "learned" that comfort typically follows the expression of distress. We anticipate that someone will respond to us and even begin to anticipate that the presence of other people brings pleasure and relief. As we mature, our caregiver's responsiveness helps our developing mind form a healthy and balanced stress response system that responds accurately to threat. It plays well with the rest of the orchestra.

This early limbic learning sets the foundation for the extremely important secure relating skill of emotional regulation.

The Smart Hippocampus

Like the amygdala, there are two hippocampi on each side deep in the limbic brain, but the *hippocampus* sits up higher (closer to the cortex) and is less primitive. It is responsible for various pro-social abilities, including memory and learning, exploration, imagination, creativity, decision-making, character judgments, making and keeping social bonds, empathy, and language.

The hippocampus is an area of our mind we want to protect because it helps us engage with our wiser, more secure functioning selves. It creates *explicit memories*, which are the conscious and intentional information you can recall about events or experiences in your past. If you stop to think about where you went to elementary school, you are accessing your explicit autobiographical memory. This is part of your conscious self-awareness and sense of self over time.

Think of the hippocampus as a film editor.

As you engage in the world, taking in events and experiences, the hippocampus helps encode and consolidate all of these experiences into a coherent story. It integrates all the small clips and emotional experiences into a larger narrative that makes sense of your life. Without the hippocampus, our experiences would be like scattered frames of a movie, full of chaos, with no way to tie things together in a meaningful, whole way. But with the hippocampus online, you can store experiences that will then turn into stories about your present and past. **Later, it's the hippocampus that helps us learn and update those old models into more accurate and compassionate models of the present.**

Basically, it helps us learn what different signals mean and how not to be stuck in loud alarm bells. This is important because context, history, and memory impact us in subtle but important ways in our everyday relationships. Let's say you're an architect meeting with a potential client about your latest creative endeavor. He says he likes it, but his face and eyes are flat, and he doesn't convey any other signals one way or the other. The difference between his words and his affect catches the attention of your stress response system and makes you anxious and suddenly self-conscious. Then you remember that you've met the guy before, and he's just naturally pokerfaced. Your hippocampus is using explicit memory and fine-tuning emotional input: the blank expression that so unnerved you at first has nothing to do with the merits of your creative idea. Now you can smile to yourself, knowing that he probably has the same effect on everyone and likely does like your design.

The hippocampus serves as a hinge between the more reactive, lower-limbic-amygdala stress response system and our higher conscious thinking mind: the prefrontal cortex. *The hippocampus thrives when it is bathed in oxytocin, and it can continue to grow and develop as we age with proper exposure to warmth and compassion.*

Think of secure relating as a way to feed your little seahorse-shaped structure; the hippocampus loves the nutrients of safety, predictability, and responsiveness. Remember, those three feelings promote green zone security, which is a goal in itself.

The Wise Prefrontal Cortex

The *prefrontal cortex* (PFC) sits in the upper section of your brain, the cortex, behind your forehead and takes a long time to fully develop. It is effectively the last part of your brain to come online. It also has a right side and a left side, which work together to manage all the instincts and urges of the lower, more primitive functions in the brain and nervous system. If you're a parent, you may know already that the prefrontal cortex doesn't finish maturing until adulthood—you have this undeveloped PFC to thank for your young child's temper tantrums and resistance to reason, and the impulsivity of your adolescent. (But you have their hippocampus to thank for getting you out of the terrible two- and three-year-old stage!)

The prefrontal cortex acts as a wise elder, keeping our more primitive urges and impulses in check. You might want to get sarcastic with your boss, but your prefrontal cortex helps you know better. However, when our brain and body are inundated with stress hormones (remember the conductor, cortisol?), the power of the PFC gets turned down in favor of the older parts of the brain. This is called the *amygdala hijack*.

In especially stressful situations, as our amygdala and the stress response system take over, we can lose complete access to the hippocampus and prefrontal cortex. This is high activation and dysregulation. Without the hippocampus to remember past and future, there is the sense that whatever we feel is all there is and all there will ever be. Most importantly, we lose the feeling of caring and are more likely to snap at our favorite people or re-vert to old indulgences such as smoking more pot than usual, drinking too much, or using sex, shopping, or food for comfort. As you can see, these are all the more primitive, non-relational ways we cope, and they may work in the moment but generally don't bring sustained relief.

The brain is so interwoven and critically involved in relationship secu-rity that recent studies have found that individuals raised in relationally responsive environments have plump hippocampi and pre-cortical volume, which helps them keep their hands on the wheel and increases emotional regulation. Unfortunately, these studies also indicate that in nonoptimal environments, the reverse is true: ongoing cortisol secretion due to chronic high stress appears to impact the development and function of these higher brain structures by decreasing their size and elasticity. It can restrict their development to begin with or impact otherwise healthy brain functioning later. For example, post-traumatic stress disorder (PTSD), in which an in-dividual experiences distressing trauma-related symptoms long after the trauma occurred, is reliably associated with reductions in hippocampal and amygdala volume, resulting in heightened sensitivity to threat and stress and decreased capacity to manage big feelings.

The good news is that research shows that we can nurture and grow these areas needed to help better manage our stress response. Thanks to author and neuroscientist Dr. Jill Bolte Taylor's suggestion to name and call upon the different parts of your PFC and limbic system, Sue inspires herself into higher relating by calling upon Dame Yoda, the af-fectionate nickname for her right PFC. By visualizing and giving areas of your brain a name, you can more consciously activate higher areas of your brain needed for recall and imagination, which pulls you out of lower-brain reactivity. Just the act of picturing the part of your mind that you could use more of right now fires up your PFC, calming the stress response system, and giving you more access to your full resourced mind.[*]

---

[*]   There are many other examples to enjoy in our interviews with Jill Bolte Taylor, episodes 164 and 195, www.therapistuncensored.com.

Nervous System Activation 2.0

We've covered the main neurochemicals (DOSE), the stress hormones, and the anatomy of the relational brain. Now let's turn to the nervous system itself, which will bring all these components together.

Dr. Stephen Porges, a highly influential neuroscientist and professor of psychiatry, developed *polyvagal theory*, which has come to be accepted as a direct link between hard neuroscience and applied psychological clinical practice in the 1990s. It starts with an idea he calls "neuroception" to describe how our lower-brain neural circuits determine whether a person or situation is safe, dangerous, or life-threatening. Think of it as a personal sonar system that scans your surroundings, then responds to what it detects by initiating neurochemical adjustments outside your awareness that direct your actions or reactions accordingly, be it distance, closeness, openness, or defensiveness.

We like to think of these neuroceptive sonar sweeps as creating unconscious background music that helps us know what to expect from the world. The tone of the music depends on our body's current perception of threat. Imagine how you feel when you hear the music in Steven Spielberg's 1975 thriller *Jaws*. Those ominous chords that increase with intensity: Da-dum . . . *Da-dum* . . . *Dadumdadumdadum*. (Notice how the music suggests the sound of an increasingly racing heartbeat.) Hear those chords enough and your vigilance increases in anticipation of an incoming threat. When warning background music plays for your nervous system, it impacts how you perceive the world and predisposes your reactions in real time. In *Jaws*, the foreboding soundtrack transforms a normally tranquil ocean-water scene into a source of threat and defensive activation.

In contrast, let's say your face is relaxed, your eyes are soft, your breath and heart rate are steady, your limbs are loose, and your environment is as expected. Your brain plays your favorite background music, signaling, "All is well. Keep on keeping on." Your eyes will remain soft, you will have wide peripheral vision, you can hear subtle sounds if you tune into them, and your breath will remain slow and steady. This is the state of security and the connection system—you are humming along in the green zone.

Now, this sonar is always scanning in two directions: one for external signals from your environment and the other for internal signals from within your own body. Importantly, people tend to overestimate the external environment when trying to understand our reactions, which is why it's especially tempting to point to our partner or child—or the bug—as the reason we raised our voices or lost our temper. This contrasts with first considering our own perceptions and internal stories as being the driver of our reactivity.

Think about the implications of this for a moment. In reality, information collected especially from our gut but also the rest of our body combines to generate *80 percent* of what we respond to at any given moment.

Emotion Regulation: Green Zone Living from the Inside Out

Let's play this out in real life.

Your ten-year-old refuses to brush her teeth and get in bed as you've asked her repeatedly. If you've worked all day at a job that makes you feel undervalued and overlooked, you bring home that warning background music. Your inner voice may then say, *I will* not *be treated this way in my own home!* and respond as many people would when faced with behavior interpreted as defiant and disrespectful. On the other hand, if you've spent the day alone and feel a need for attention and affection, you might indulge her procrastination and enjoy the extra snuggle time. The point is that your *inner state* impacts your interpretation of your daughter's conduct more than the objective behavior itself. The good news in this example is that as we learn to recognize and analyze our emotions, we become better able to continue steering toward our emotionally regulated green zone and not veer into the wrong lane.

Because emotional regulation is so important, let's dig a little deeper to learn about the imaginary disc jockey spinning the background music in our mind. Our *autonomic nervous system* (ANS) determines whether or not we sense threat (ominous music) or safety (chill music). The rock star of emotional regulation is the *vagus nerve*, the longest of twelve pairs of cranial nerves, and we think the most interesting nerve in the body. It works like high-speed internet, conveying almost instantaneous signals back and forth from various parts of the body to the brain and back again. This nerve is involuntary, meaning it works without us knowing it or being able to control it, and it wanders through our face, lungs, neck, and torso, monitoring any changes in our heart rhythm, breath, gut, ears, face, and vocal tone and looking for changes in our immediate environment. It is part of our parasympathetic branch of our nervous system, which works as a brake alongside our sympathetic branch, which works as our accelerator.

When our energy is balanced and all seems stable and well, therapists call this calm from perceived safety *ventral vagal activation*. Think about lying chest to chest (front to front) with your partner, your puppy, or your baby sleeping on her tummy lying heavily on your chest—a lovely feeling, isn't it? That is ventral vagal activation! This means that the senses in your body feel safe and open, your muscles can relax, and your digestive system can do its job. When hanging out in ventral vagal, you feel safe and are in a secure state of mind.

Being in ventral vagal means your brain and body are nourished with feel-good neurotransmitters that help you experience pleasure, contentment, and empathy. In this state of mind, we are at our most generous, flexible, and compassionate. Ventral vagal activation feels good whether you enjoy solitude or are connecting with someone else. If you are in this relaxed state when your body detects a mild to moderate threat, you are less likely to become defensively activated and, instead, will keep your thinking online, enabling you to respond rather than react. (See why we promote the idea of secure relating?) You can feel your strong spine and open heart and face the incoming challenge without making yourself too big or too small.

Together, ventral vagal activation, PFC, hippocampal and amygdala balance, and a little oxytocin for good measure coordinate to establish green zone relating. That is why the green zone is your North Star. When lost, think of your best self and paddle in that direction.

Leaving the Green Zone

Speaking of getting lost: it's fairly easy to drift out of this more secure, open green zone activation. When a creepy guy stares at you too long, or your boss summons you for an unexpected meeting, or national legislation targets the rights of people like you—really, anything that's perceived as threatening—your body kicks into gear as designed.* If being friendly or social engagement can't manage the situation (ventral vagal), then the *sympathetic branch* (accelerator) of your nervous system perks up.

First it mobilizes your attention (activates) and quickly orients by gathering information to assess the level of threat and what to do next. If it can, it'll have you simply slide out of harm's way (flight—hide or be hurt). However, if that isn't going to work, it may move you to confront the problem (fight—hurt or be hurt). But remember, these states of mind are not an on/off switch. They are more like a dimmer switch that works in degrees (i.e., gradations in color on the spectrum). That's why you may be activated but not quite leave your green zone if you can maintain your thinking and feeling and care.

As the perception of threat increases and you do leave the green zone, you are "activated," and your protection system is now driving. You defend yourself by either sliding up (mobilization, red) or down (conserving energy, blue) depending on the situation and largely dependent on your learned patterns. Over the course of our lives, we have likely developed predictable patterns and strategies for protecting ourselves and regulating our emotional and physical threat experience, so you likely have a tendency to trend red (up-regulate) or blue (down-regulate).

Dr. Porges has identified a twist to the commonly understood fight-or-flight perspective: if the sense of threat persists, and, in the moment, you lack sufficient resources to protect yourself, your protection system can downshift out of fight-flight to the more serious freeze-or-flop state. By activating the parasympathetic brake more intensely, the back of the

---

*   We are focusing on stress and emotional regulation, but sympathetic and parasympathetic activation doesn't necessarily mean you are in danger. Lovemaking (sympathetic) and collapse afterward (parasympathetic) are good examples of activation while safe.

vagus nerve, known as the *dorsal vagal*, is in charge of our last resort to protect ourselves.

Imagine a mouse dangling from a cat's mouth. Since it cannot fight or escape, its only chance of survival is to "go dorsal," or limp. He is not pretending, his body responds involuntarily by physiologically shutting down. Similarly, we may drop into dorsal vagal activation when our neuroceptive sonar perceives a serious threat with no escape, generating sheer terror.

Whereas in sympathetic *fight*, we tend to become bigger and louder, and sympathetic *flight* causes us to avoid, run, and actively attempt to escape, our parasympathetic nervous system is our ultimate protector when escape is not a perceived option or fear has overwhelmed our system. In this state, we go small and perhaps, like the mouse, slow down our system or shut down entirely.

If you experience this dorsal vagal nervous system overwhelm, you probably aren't feeling big emotions anymore. As a matter of fact, you will likely lose your sense of interest and investment in just about anything, your own well-being included. Your respiration and heart rate will drop, and endorphins will be coursing through your body to prevent pain and anesthetize you to what is coming.

Unfortunately, many of us have endured horrible stress and trauma that led us to freeze or flop in the face of a crisis. Remember, however, that when this happens, it is not a conscious decision. As therapists, it makes our blood boil when we hear of crime victims being grilled about why they didn't fight back, as if this implies consent or ambivalence rather than being recognized as a sign of feeling one's life being threatened. Until you know otherwise, respect the science and understand that not fleeing or fighting back during an assault conveys *terror*—the opposite of consent. And no matter what you think, until it happens to you, you can't know how you would respond to something your protection system considers terrifying.

Falling into a dorsal vagal shutdown doesn't always mean we shut off completely like the dangling mouse. If we have been experiencing severe chronic overwhelm from work or a relationship, for instance, our body may go into this type of physiological conservation mode to save our energy. In this space, we can feel numb, dissociate from what is happening around us, and emotionally or physically distance from those right next to us. In chapter 6 we will dive more deeply into how experiences of overwhelm and trauma can lead to living in chronic states of self-protection and disconnection.

Neural Wi-Fi

Like wireless speakers searching to sync up with an invisible connection, our neurons ping back and forth as they seek connection. This unconscious syncing up of our bioelectrical nervous systems is a mutual dance, part of neural Wi-Fi. Fortunately, it's not just you that has neural Wi-Fi running in the background, continually reading, adjusting, and fine-tuning—so does everyone else. *Co-regulation* is a natural extension of neuroception. It turns out that as babies, this neural Wi-Fi dance with our caregiver is our first experience of co-regulation.

Human brains are so specifically designed for this task that most of us are far better at reading other people's emotions than our own. This is possible because of our *mirror neuron system*, a network of brain regions that work together to enable mirroring-like responses when observing others' actions or emotions. These cells react to other people's intentions as if they are our own and are considered the basis for empathy. Think of tearing up while viewing a movie with a close-up of someone crying; that isn't *your* sadness, but it feels like it is.

Notice any shifts in your face and body as you think of watching a football game on TV and see the receiver go down, his knee bending in the wrong direction as he falls. Or how about the way your face and body mirrors that of someone who is vomiting? (Extra points if we can make your mirror neurons fire right now—across time and space—just sit with the previous example for a bit.) That's your brain firing—feeling the other person's pain as if this were happening to you. By feeling things so specifically and intensely, we have a window into what the other person is experiencing—the basis of empathy.

Understanding this is important relationally and helps us manage our emotions. If you've ever been around an anxious person, one of two things will likely happen. Either your nervous system metronome will amp up, and you'll become anxious yourself, or your chill background music will hold, and you'll keep your metronome at its moderate, steady pace. With some time, the anxious person will likely sync with you, becoming less anxious as they "borrow" your nervous system to calm down.

Lullabies Are Co-Regulation in Action.

The combination of rocking and singing helps parents to regulate their own distress at their child's upset feelings. Singing steadies their breath and helps their voice maintain a calming tone. The soft melody sends a reassuring message to the baby's nervous system that they are safe, all is well, and they are protected. Slowly their amygdala realizes they can turn off the alarm and relax in relief in their caregivers' arms. This is using your more mature nervous system to soothe theirs, and you direct their system to sync up with your steady, calm music.

Unfortunately, *co-dysregulation* is also a thing.

Rather than settling down, two upset people can progressively spur each other into more and more dysregulation. We saw this in the last chapter with Mia and DJ. Mia's body-brain sonar quickly picked up DJ's coolness and emotional distance when she got in the car. This registered as a low-level threat to her amygdala. In response, her protection circuit sent out a minor warning to pay attention—a squirt of stress chemicals that served as the background music—which impacted Mia's perceptions and behaviors. (Everything seems more threatening with shark music.)

Behaviorally, Mia looked out the car window instead of engaging DJ, gaining emotional distance herself. She probably wasn't aware of her own activation, but the background music was signaling danger and thus tilting her toward negative interpretations of even innocent actions. She might have been aware that she was upset with and avoiding DJ, but she would have rationalized her behavior by convincing herself that "he should have acknowledged me when I opened the door to get in."

DJ couldn't help but notice his wife's chilliness, so his protection system kicked in too, without his being aware of it. If you asked him why he was being so silent, he'd attribute it to Mia: *she* seemed uninterested in him; *she* appeared to be upset about something but wouldn't talk about it. However, DJ's retreat into his own thoughts served to turn down his sense of threat. By not reaching out, despite sensing that Mia was upset, he was equally responsible for their mutual toddling down the road toward dysregulation. By shutting out thoughts of an upset partner, he relieved his tension and defensively avoided her—even in the privacy of his mind. Neither partner noticed how they were reinforcing their own—and their partner's—mutual withdrawal.

Had DJ held Mia's eyes in the beginning, had she reached for his hand instead of withdrawing, had they each given voice to their feelings or been able to let themselves feel and show their longing to be closer—all of these co-regulating actions could have profoundly soothed the other person's nervous system. Had that happened, one partner would have recognized the other as safe enough, which would have activated relaxing neurochemicals such as serotonin or oxytocin, helping to shift both partners toward more open stances.

This is what we mean about moving toward the green. A gentle touch, a caring expression, and a kind word are powerful tools in the neural Wi-Fi co-regulation dance.

Implicit Right-to-Right Relating

This is our favorite interpersonal neuroscience concept. This one idea brings together everything in this chapter and will point to answers to difficult questions such as "All this happened a long time ago; can we do anything now if the damage is already done?" Or: "If we can, how do we heal all this early learning we don't even know we have?"

There is great news here and a heart-opening answer to those questions: yes, there is *absolutely* hope, no matter your age or your history. How? We will use the same mechanism that caused the problem, rewiring through surprising new implicit and explicit experiences.

Grab some popcorn and let us explain.

Implicit memory, an unconscious process present at birth, becomes important here. As babies develop, they need a way to store what is working and what isn't working, what is pleasurable and what is aversive, and so on.

These very real memories of experiences are lodged deep in their limbic system, without words. In contrast, *explicit memory* is consciously accessible and comes to us in organized thoughts that we can understand and articulate.

Implicit memory can be harder to grasp because it is expressed through actions or sensed through feelings. Riding a bike or tying your shoes, for example, requires your remembering how to do it, but you do so subconsciously; you don't realize that you are retrieving the information.

Ann teases Sue that she ties her shoes weird, with the bow on the side and going up and down instead of side to side. Despite plenty of effort, Sue simply can't seem to unlearn it. (In addition, she takes pride in being weird.) Once a belief or attitude gets lodged in your implicit memory, it can be difficult to see it as anything other than "normal" and especially challenging to unlearn.

How does this relate to security as adults? If you were like baby Derek, and crying or neediness caused your caregiver to get anxious, pull away or scowl, you likely learned to resist crying before you even knew what tears were. If, on the other hand, your parents ignored you unless you demanded attention, you might have learned to express distress freely— and with flair!—because it brought your caregiver close.

This doesn't mean that you consciously hold back emotionally or that you purposely cue waterworks for attention: the memory is stored implicitly yet impacts how you relate today. This is good news for those raised in oxytocin-rich, nurturing environments full of warmth and emotional attunement. Positive early learning stored in your implicit memory is why you have a healthy entitlement to love and affection from others as well as generally trusting others to do right by you. However, it works both ways: thus, early experiences involving misattunement, disconnection, and an unpredictable parental presence are also stored in implicit memory.

Brain lateralization is complex and the details are beyond the scope of this book, but if at all interested, we highly recommend a short YouTube video by psychiatrist Iain McGilchrist, "RSA Animate: The Divided Brain,"* As we've emphasized, no part of the brain does one thing and

---

* Iain McGilchrist, "RSA Animate: The Divided Brain," RSA, 11:47, uploaded to YouTube October 21, 2011, https://www.youtube.com/watch?v=dFs9WO2B8uI.

it's easy to oversimplify the complexities, but there are important differences in the hemispheres that relate to our secure relating journey. Most simply, think of the left side doing everything, but with a specialization in the literal, logical, linear, and linguistic side of relating. It forms words and has language. Think of our urge to quickly explain things we actually don't understand that well—this satisfies the left side of our mind. The right, on the other hand, specializes in getting the gist of a situation, facial and emotional recognition, and your sense of self. It uses parallel processing instead of linear processing, so it understands experiences much faster than the left. It takes in the whole of the information but doesn't have language to explain. It's where we create from, how we recognize what art represents, and is alive when playing or hearing truly improvisational music.

Dr. Allan Schore, a highly distinguished neuropsychologist who is considered one of the primary contributors to applied relational neuroscience, emphasizes the importance of implicit, "right-to-right" connections between infants and caregivers. He particularly underscores the pivotal role of the right brain in regulating emotions and providing our sense of connection and belonging. His research delves into the importance of unconscious nonverbal communication and resonance between the caregiver and the child. His work points to the rather unsettling idea that your first sense of self comes from the unconscious of your mother (or primary caretaker).

Right-to-right relating is about *being* with one another. It is also a vehicle for real change and growth and is how we can access and heal those hearts that have difficult early memories stored so deeply. Like a parent who "just knows" if their child's cry is communicating fever or fatigue and responds accordingly, implicit relating encompasses nonverbal communication such as pitch, tone, eye contact, and emphasis of speech, plus facial expressions and hand gestures. It's how you can tell if another person is expressing sarcasm, boredom, or uncertainty; or the disturbed feeling a child feels when they sense that their mother's smile is inauthentic. Right-to-right connection is *attunement*: a meaningful connection that goes much deeper than words and cannot be faked even if you want to.

This is how change often happens in deep *relational therapy* (psycho-therapy with an emphasis on the healing power of the relationship between client and therapist). The cumulative experience of attuned, safe connection is established, and over time, this sense of security is then broadened. The storing of new safe experience happens below conscious awareness. It's like if you bring us your car that has a noise—we can lift the hood and maybe fix the noise, and if so, great, you are done in therapy. However, if it's more complicated and we tinker around together working collaboratively to figure it out, that is building a relationship. The experience of having help fixing your car becomes as important as whatever specific problem we were trying to solve.

Humorously, sometimes you and your therapist have to figure out what to talk about while that deeper implicit right-to-right syncing and relating takes hold. So, when it comes to healing attachment difficulties, it isn't sage advice but the actual relationship between the therapist and client itself that is healing. This is true in everyday relationships as well. When we seek support from our partner, parent, sibling, or friend, we are most often seeking a right-to-right implicit feeling of being seen rather than the unsolicited advice that is so tempting to give.

How does this translate into real life?

If your partner says, "I *did* hear you, you said . . ." (a literal, left brain–dominant response) and recites verbatim in a stiff voice what you said, will you *feel* heard? Or if they say, "I *did* apologize. Look at the text message I sent you; it's right there!" will you feel that satisfying catch of being understood? Doubtful.

Your partner's Excel-spreadsheet answer might be technically correct (left brain=literal), but it will most certainly miss your plea to feel understood (right brain=gist). This left-brain miss is a common point of relational frustration. When your partner is in their secure, connected green zone self, you will implicitly *feel* understood and *know* they are sorry because of that clear feeling of being felt that comes with right-to-right communication. Feeling felt means knowing the person really gets you; it's more than words, it's an inner knowing.

This is also why we are feeding your left brain with an explanation right now, so that it will be more motivated to move over for your right brain experience-dependent responses. We promise this will be much more effective in connecting to those you love. Connection first, then sort things out intellectually.

It's Never Too Late . . .

We've saved the best thing about the human brain for last: *neuroplasticity*.

Brain cells in the hippocampus are especially capable of new neural growth; in fact, they can continue to develop throughout adulthood. Returning to our story about longtime friends Naomi and Priya, just because Naomi's lateness triggered Priya on this occasion doesn't mean that other people's lateness will always make her irritable and anxious. Likewise, just because Mia's chronic indecisiveness turned off DJ on their all-too-rare date night doesn't mean that he can't learn to become more accepting and compassionate of this comparatively minor personality quirk. Rather than believing that our defenses are just who we are (i.e., I'm just not emotional), we can dive deeper to understand why and open up parts of ourselves that felt too threatening before.

We wouldn't be out here working so hard to share all this information if there wasn't real hope. Yes, it's daunting to think your brain can be impacted by trauma for the rest of your life! But thanks to neuroplasticity and our basic wiring for connection, safe relationships also impact our brain for the rest of our life. And you have a lot of life left.

Therapy grows new neural connections, as does reading this book and learning anything new, really. Safe relationships literally grow new neural capacities. Being vulnerable with someone and it going well gets stored as a new path in your brain cells. Mindfulness, meditation, and physical exercise grow new connections.

As we round out this brainy chapter, don't worry one second about remembering everything or if it was just too much to absorb. A single working mother of five can raise secure kids without knowing anything about the brain, just as a neuroscientist can know everything about the prefrontal cortex but not be working primarily from her connection circuitry.

The fact is you made it through the book's hardest science section. Nice work! It's worth it because all this learning will give your PFC an advantage, helping you to outsmart your nervous system when it throws shark music on the soundtrack.

4

Attachment Theory's Coming-of-Age Story

The spectrum concept of green, red, and blue leanings (and a tie-dye mixed color, as we'll elaborate) is a clinical interpretation, grounded in the rich world of attachment science. We will get into much more detail about the kinds of activations represented by colors and how they interact with one another in chapters 8, 9, and 10, but first we have to sort out what *attachment* really means. The term is often used ambiguously and over the decades has been diluted from the careful descriptions of the original research.

Attachment theory has indeed evolved and expanded to encompass a broader understanding of how our early relationships with caregivers profoundly influence our adult relationships. It has a rich history spanning more than seventy years, yet it has recently experienced a surge in popularity. Influencers on Instagram and TikTok have gained massive followings by sharing quizzes and making short videos on attachment. In fact, hashtags related to attachment on TikTok alone have accumulated hundreds of millions of views. As therapists, we find it heartening to see these concepts gaining such recognition, and it is inspiring to see so many individuals eager to explore how their early attachment experiences are influencing their adult relationships. Our aim is to channel this enthusiasm toward a more profound and precise understanding of this research and theory, while also dispelling the misconceptions that naturally arise from its complexity.

For example, categorizing attachment strategies as solely "positive" or "negative," trying to quantify their "strengths," or equating them with love demonstrates a misunderstanding of the concept. This isn't surprising because it is easy to miss the scientific underpinnings of attachment theory and oversimplify its intricate nature. As you'll see, even using the term *attachment* as a single, all-encompassing idea can lead to misconceptions. To truly understand how attachment shapes our lives and affects intergenerational patterns, we need a balanced and nuanced comprehension of this highly influential theory.

What follows is the beautiful intergenerational story of the beloved theory with a few of the key people who have shaped it. There are three main branches—what we will call generations—and by the end of this chapter, you may know more about attachment than your therapist!

First Generation

Attachment

The father of attachment theory, John Bowlby (1907–1990), was a British psychoanalyst and psychiatrist who played a crucial role in reshaping our understanding of the profound impact of early childhood experiences on our emotional and social development. Although some of his findings may appear obvious today, Bowlby's emphasis on the importance of infant-caregiver relationships during the late 1950s stirred resistance from the professional community. His insights posed a direct challenge to conventional psychoanalytic theory, which historically focused on an individual's inner psychic realm over the consideration of real-life experiences and interpersonal connections. Bowlby's ideas also presented a counterpoint to classical behaviorism, a school of thought that tended to place observable behaviors in the foreground, often at the expense of understanding the intricacies of mental processes.

Dr. Bowlby's dissatisfaction with these conventional theories, punctuated by his family history in evolutionary biology, motivated him to explore new perspectives. He drew insights from diverse fields such as evolutionary biology, ethology (the study of animals, especially their social behavior in natural settings), developmental psychology, cognitive science, and control systems theory. He developed a groundbreaking proposition from this multidisciplinary approach: *evolutionary factors drive us to seek closeness to survive.*

He proposed that the ability to seek and form strong bonds with caregivers (at the time, the focus was mothers) was crucial for an infant's survival and well-being. Bowlby argued that infant humans evolved with early behaviors designed to ensure that they were able to keep their caregivers available to them to provide the security they required to thrive.

From the beginning you can see the deep roots of influence the study of animals had on his thinking. Bowlby was especially influenced by his American colleague Harry Harlow (1905–1981), who (in)famously studied the effect of maternal separation and social isolation on baby rhesus monkeys in the 1950s. There is an interesting backstory about Harlow and his monkeys that is very much relevant to our secure relating journey. It may be hard to believe today, but prior to Harlow's research, it was widely accepted that attention and love would "spoil" a child. An unexpected observation triggered the beginning of his team's experiments, ultimately debunking this popular parenting lore.

After a tuberculosis outbreak in his lab wiped out an entire colony of monkeys, Harlow began to separate infants from their mothers to prevent another contamination. The only thing present in the young monkey's cage was a cloth on the floor of their cage for cleanliness. Whenever someone removed the cloth in order to clean the inside of the cage, the baby monkeys shrieked in protest. Without a mother present, they'd become attached to the cloth, the only softness available.

Observing their terror gave rise to Harlow's first concept, *separation anxiety.* These isolated monkeys started exhibiting unusual behavior, including rocking, staring into space, and, as mentioned, clutching the cloth lining at the bottom of their cages. His curiosity piqued, Harlow delved deeper into the nature of emotional bonds and the significance of caregiver relationships in early development.

When John Bowlby visited Harlow's Primate Laboratory at the University of Wisconsin–Madison in the late 1950s, he speculated that the unusual behaviors were likely due to the lack of motherly affection. Subsequently, Harlow initiated his well-known but highly controversial studies, deliberately isolating these infant monkeys from their mothers and peers in different experimental conditions to test the idea that affection was needed for healthy development rather than food alone.

They created two unimpressive "mothers," for the infant monkeys to choose between. Both were made with a wire body and a simple wire head to roughly resemble a monkey, one had a cloth draped on it and no milk, while the other had no cloth, but was equipped with a milk bottle. These studies determined that the baby monkeys consistently preferred a substitute cloth "mother" (providing soft-contact comfort but no food) over a substitute wire "mother" (providing milk but no comfort). It became evident that these young monkeys needed more than just basic physical care: without contact comfort, they became withdrawn, stayed socially isolated, and stared into space. Some even resorted to self-mutilation. Fortunately, this painful story didn't end there.

Harlow was eventually also interested in finding a cure for the monkeys' "depression" caused by being deprived of maternal affection. In the face of enormous skepticism from the scientific community, for decades he tried to reverse early damage and rehabilitate them. Eventually, his team stumbled upon an effective treatment: group therapy!

The "therapy group" consisted of several younger monkeys (the "therapists") who had been raised in normal conditions with their mothers and spent a few hours a week trying to engage the previously isolated monkeys (the "patients"). Smaller, less threatening monkey therapists were necessary, since same-age peers would act aggressively toward the socially awkward patients.

As expected, the formerly isolated monkey patients initially rejected their young therapists' efforts to engage them in social interactions. But the young monkeys kept at it, touching, grooming, vocalizing, mimicking, sharing objects, and playing. Their persistence eventually paid off. With enough exposure, the patients began to respond.

For instance, when the young monkeys held on to them, the formerly isolated monkeys gradually began to return the embrace. After six months of this primate group therapy, the psychologically damaged monkeys' social behavior had become indistinguishable from that of the rhesus monkeys who'd never been isolated from their mothers. As if that wasn't exciting enough, they also found that if you allowed young monkeys who didn't even have cloth or wire "mothers" to socialize with their peers as infants, they did better than those who had a cloth mother but were denied social interaction. Said another way, those that had no mothers at all—not even cloth ones—but got to play with friends did better than those with a cloth "mother" and no friends. This confirms a takeaway we are hoping for from this book—*safe, real relationships are life-changing and heal*!

The upshot here was that both friends and a mother's love were important to healthy development. The news that primate maternal deprivation was potentially curable surprised and delighted Harlow and his colleagues. The hope of recovery after what was thought to be persistent psychological damage foreshadows the story of human attachment over time.

Dr. Bowlby used these findings to forge ahead with his then radical ideas promoting attachment as an innate behavioral system shaped by early experiences of care. He published several seminal books that form the basis of attachment theory, but the key turning point for the theory was Bowlby's association with Mary Ainsworth (1913–1999).

A talented psychologist originally from Ohio, Ainsworth's first published work was her dissertation entitled "An Evaluation of Adjustment Based on the Concept of Security" written in 1939 under the supervision of William E. Blatz (1895–1964). Well before Bowlby, Blatz postulated the theory of security as the primary goal of the human being. He thought of *security not simply as safety, which is subject to disruption, but as a cultivated state of mind nurtured through early relationships*. Security for him grew out of trust in one's ability to deal with the future and was characterized by serenity and a willingness to accept the consequences of one's decisions. Blatz's security theory can be considered the precursor to the now well-known attachment theory.

While living in London in the early 1950s, Dr. Ainsworth began working at the Tavistock Clinic under Dr. John Bowlby to research the effects of early separation on personality development. Trained as a careful observer and empirical researcher (using data versus just theory), her scientific work put attachment on the map forever. As a female academic at that time, she was subject to being overlooked, underpaid, and undervalued. However, she went from student to treasured colleague of Dr. Bowlby, and attachment theory is sometimes referred to now as the Bowlby-Ainsworth theory of attachment.

Her influence began with what became the first attachment study in 1954 while she was at the East African Institute for Social Research in Kampala, Uganda. As part of her work on the study of child development and culture, she carefully observed infants' comings and goings from their mothers and noticed a pattern of responses in how these babies' sought closeness and physical comfort. During this time she stayed in correspondence with Bowlby to develop their ideas about what she was directly observing.

After returning to the United States, she continued her research at Johns Hopkins University in Baltimore and devised the field's standard for evaluating attachment patterns in children: a laboratory research protocol known as the "Strange Situation" (SS). In this method, an infant, accompanied by his or her mother and a stranger, would be observed closely through a one-way mirror while playing in a laboratory room. The mother was instructed to leave the room briefly, triggering the child's separation stress response. A few minutes later she returned to the playroom. The researchers assessed the child's attachment behavior in response to the mother's absence and subsequent return

In this controlled playroom setting, Ainsworth and her colleagues described attachment in terms of its "quality." Contrary to the long-standing views of behaviorists and pediatricians, who focused on the intensity of the baby's response during the brief period of separation (for example, whether he or she cried and how much), Ainsworth focused on the quality of the interaction between the mother and child. Specifically, how the infant greeted the mother upon her return to the room and how the child and mother reestablished contact together.

Developmental Attachment Classifications

Dr. Ainsworth's seminal work led to establishing a framework of attachment patterns. After years of extensive research by international research teams, four primary behavioral attachment patterns have been identified in infants: (1) secure, (2) insecure avoidant, (3) insecure resistant, also called insecure ambivalent, and (4) disorganized. (Terms in attachment are highly varied, but our point here is not to present a full documentation of attachment history but to simplify it and pull out the most clinically relevant points for healing individuals everywhere.)

Toddlers classified as *secure* displayed clear signs of trust in their caregivers, demonstrating a belief that their caregivers would be emotionally and physically available when needed. In contrast, others exhibited signs of not fully trusting their caregivers to be physically or emotionally available when needed, leading them to develop different coping strategies to manage distress during challenging situations. These categories were deemed insecure.

One group, described as having insecure *avoidant attachment* patterns, appeared outwardly calm when their parent left the room, continued playing with their toys, and seemed quite independent and collected.* When their mother returned after separation, these toddlers showed little interest in reuniting, seeming not to notice the parent, and continued playing intently with their toys. Even though their bodies were experiencing distress, they avoided any nurturance and comfort and relied on themselves and their toys to regulate.

Another group, identified as insecure *ambivalent*, certainly noticed when their parent left and became upset similar to the secure children. However, unlike secure kids, when the parent returned, they had trouble letting themselves be comforted. They would go to their parent to be picked up, but then push away from them while still crying, for example. This mixed reaction, wanting comfort but not being able to take it in, gave rise to the label ambivalent. They resisted the physical and emotional comfort offered and had trouble returning to the playful state they were in before the insult of their mother leaving.

As research progressed, another category was added for the kids that did not fit the more organized patterns of the avoidant group or those

---

* Initially there was an assumption that these were the secure kids because they didn't get rattled and seemed to feel confident even in the mother's absence. Turns out, future research revealed that these infants, while outwardly appearing cool and calm, were actually experiencing high physiological signs of stress. The observers just couldn't see it yet.

ambivalent about closeness. Their behavior appeared somewhat chaotic, and no organized pattern could be identified. This group was called *disorganized* and came to be an important clinical distinction that we will discuss in depth in chapter 10.

Ainsworth's work, combined with studies by other researchers, would further confirm and fully establish that a baby's attachment pattern is linked to their parents' behavior during the first year of life. It's important to note that these labels are describing the pattern of interaction between the parent and the child; they are not pinning labels on these children. This is one common misconception—labeling a child insecure instead of thinking of the relationship between the pair as insecure. The behaviors the kids chose (distancing or not being able to be comforted) were healthy adaptations to their early experience, as you'll see as we go.

The basic premise of these four attachment patterns has persisted and been incorporated into scholarship and theory as canon, shaping future research. Considerable evidence continues to emerge, showing that these early attachment patterns persist in influencing later adult behavior. While some of the original ideas have been revised with later research, many of the original concepts have continued to stand the test of time and are integral to ongoing research and ideas of human development today.

Second Generation

Developmental Attachment

The next burst of essential developmental attachment research looked to extend Bowlby's and Ainsworth's studies of attachment in children by examining Bowlby's belief that attachment is a lifelong process and how it carries forward in adults. This cohort of work includes the concepts of *internal working models, narrative coherence, and attachment across the life span.*

Internal Working Models (IWMs)

Building on what we learned in chapter 2, our young nervous system quickly forms neural patterns of expectations of the world that emerge later as observable behavioral attachment patterns. These patterns of behavior are exactly what the Strange Situation measures. Through this early infant and toddler period, a child's brain and nervous system has learned what signs from their body, and what signs from their environment, especially their caregiver, predict comfort and safety or threat and rejection. Children at this age aren't thinking about how to react; they are just responding based on what they've learned implicitly about keeping their caregiver available. Conscious, reflective thinking about this learning doesn't come online until about age four. The thoughts accompanying the attachment behavioral patterns are called internal working models.

IWMs include conscious articulations of our ideas about the world and embodied assumptions of trust. They become a template based on our early experiences—an archetype of relationships that guides how we understand ourselves and others. These emotionally laden, dynamic ideas come together to create a stable set of beliefs about our early attachment experiences.

So, the idea is we start with basic ideas about ourselves and our parents and caregivers and then create a guiding map that generalizes to what we expect from ourselves and others going forward. This map helps us anticipate what feels threatening. Are people basically safe or scary? Can you count on others? Can you trust yourself? Are you worthy? As you can imagine, these kinds of powerful, deeply held beliefs set up a trajectory going into school, creating friendships, and, of course, in developing adult love relationships as well.

The good news about internal working models is that compared with that early limbic learning stored below conscious awareness from birth to two years old, IWMs include conscious thoughts that are accessible in words. This accessibility makes them easier candidates for change.

However, not all of the thoughts are conscious because so much of the patterning happened before language-based autobiographical explicit memory was wired up and working for us. So, researchers had two big problems: How do you uncover the powerful guiding beliefs and assumptions about relationships stored outside of awareness or that were laid down before babies had words to describe them? An additional problem is that we can't see the attachment system (the organized system of thoughts and behavior associated with attachment patterns) until it's activated—that is, under threat conditions. When safe, we all look pretty good! Researchers had to develop assessments that sneak up on the person's unconscious to discover how their mind represents attachment relationships at the deepest level.

Working directly with Mary Ainsworth, several of her students extended the research on attachment theory by finding ways to measure attachment representations in later childhood and adults. Mary Main, Carol George, and Patricia Crittenden are key developmental attachment superstars who developed these breakthrough assessments.

Main (1943–2023), a preeminent attachment researcher and psychologist, led the research on what has become the gold standard of adult attachment assessment: the Adult Attachment Interview (AAI). The AAI asks questions such as "Tell me about your childhood relationship with your [primary caregiver]. How did [he/she/they] respond to your emotional needs, and how did you feel about that response?" While these may seem like simple, direct questions about your family history, the follow-up prompts are designed to be gently probing and thus subtly stressful, activating your stress response system to get a better picture of how you cope and revealing your IWM. Remember, everyone looks good when they feel safe and secure; it's only under relational stress that our attachment strategies emerge.

For those interested in clinical application of attachment research, we turn to George and Crittenden. Carol George's dissertation led to groundbreaking work with the AAI, and she went on to develop the Adult Attachment Projective Picture System (AAP) together with Malcolm West. The AAP is a more accessible measure of early attachment representations (IWM) because it doesn't rely on an in-depth professionally administered interview, during which people may distort or modify their narrative to keep certain aspects of their distress deflected from their own awareness. The AAP does not focus on autobiographical narratives. Instead, individuals are asked to respond and create stories about simple line drawings that depict attachment scenes. It was designed to uncover walled-off aspects of attachment-related narratives and reflect a person's internal working models of attachment relationships. Unlike the AAI, the AAP can also code more broadly for trauma and can statistically identify shame, which are both useful for clinical purposes. For more on the important underpinnings of attachment assessment, you can find two in-depth interviews with Dr. George, a psychologist, on our podcast.* We also recommend her most recent book, *Working with Attachment Trauma* (2023).

Psychologist Patricia Crittenden, who studied under Mary Ainsworth, took a slightly different view and incorporated more representational attachment patterns that add more dimensions to adult attachment. Her model, the Dynamic-Maturational Model (DMM) of Attachment, is complex but especially valuable for clinicians and those working with families. Crittenden's model stresses the role of adaptation and how individuals dynamically adjust and navigate their particular environment.†

Narrative Coherence

One of the most important and fascinating findings from AAI research was the realization that it's not what you say but how you say it—your *narrative coherence*—that reveals the most about your unconscious adult attachment patterns. Patterns in speech are noted with an eye toward narrative coherence—the degree to which your stories about your experiences and significant relationships makes sense as a whole.

It's not woo-woo.

How we speak about relationships exposes the organization and neural coherence of our underlying thinking processes, beliefs, and assumptions, which points to our basic neurological wiring. This makes sense if you think about early biological stress response learning.

Securely attached adults likely experienced relational learning free of highly charged physiological stress experiences, or if it was there, it was resolved rather quickly. Their protective system is more relaxed. This early learning is evident in their ability to be forthcoming in answers to attachment-related questions, responding with relevant, detailed answers

---

* See episodes 163 and 210, https://therapistuncensored.com.

† https://therapistuncensored.com/tu96; https://therapistuncensored.com/tu97.

that they can back up, if prompted, with believable examples. This means they can think and feel simultaneously and don't tend to distort the story; in other words, they don't exaggerate or disavow information.

Those categorized as secure tend to speak freely about their family history and can reflect on both positive and negative aspects of their experiences. Importantly, they can maintain concise and coherent focus on themselves and the interviewer. They can also develop new insights into their experiences while talking about them. Thus, the secure adult is free to explore the past in light of the present. Their nervous system can remain in an open, non-threatened experience, which promotes a non-defensive discussion and exploration.

You might begin to imagine the cooperative interplay of the amygdala (feelings), hippocampus (memory), and prefrontal cortex (CEO) working together to relay an explicit autobiographical story. An exciting takeaway here is that coherent life stories stem from secure attachment, but they are also a path to getting there!

When questions about parental relationships are posed in the AAI to those with higher attachment anxiety (leaning red on the spectrum), these individuals tend to respond with more wordy and somewhat meandering narratives. They bring in unnecessary detail and can get lost in their story or their feelings about the relationship they are discussing. They tend to speak in essays, not paragraphs, and their stories wander. Rather than staying connected to the listener and themselves, they get lost in their own experience and can lose track of the listener. In fact, their words may unconsciously act as a bridge to *hold on* to the listener.

As you'll learn more in part II, those that learned to remain more vigilant to keep their important people close tend to experience anxiety and stress when discussing relational events. This stress creates more intensity neurologically, so their words and stories are delivered with more vibrant emotional color. You might liken this to the story of Goldilocks— remember how she tries each of the bears' beds looking for one that is a good fit? Think of this story style or narrative as the bear's bed is too soft and a little mushy.

The narratives of those who learned avoidance and emotionally distancing strategies—those that trend toward the dismissing, blue side of the spectrum—tend to show limited vulnerability and emotional expression. Their narratives are short and unconsciously conceal more than they reveal. For example, "My childhood was happy," in an interview about relationships, with no elaboration or evidence to support it, conveys the speaker's avoidance of the topic. Subliminally, the message is "Move along, there is nothing to see here." Some give external details (Just the facts, ma'am) that conveniently omit emotional details or reactions.

They are not necessarily trying to be deceptive, that is just how they think. They've learned to avoid talking about or taking in emotional and relational information, so they may not get the point of the question. They are "fine," they insist. (But remember what we said earlier about what fine means? It is a non-answer.)

These narrative styles of communication show up in our everyday relating especially when we are stressed and activated. As we will discuss more in later chapters, these differences are often a point of conflict in relationships. For instance, those who lean blue often speak in scripts and bullet points when it comes to emotional or personal disclosure, leaving their partner wanting more. Their speech patterns tend to subtly close up the conversation, conceal potential vulnerability, be short, and contain elements that signal a lack of interest in exploring attachment related experiences.

For some of us who lean blue, we share our thoughts easily and freely about topics we are interested in and know a lot about but have more trouble participating when the subject leaves this familiar territory. This is not the same thing as narcissism, which can look similar, but can have some overlap. Those who lean hard into the dark-blue zone may make the person asking the questions feel intrusive or dumb for asking. From Goldilocks's perspective, think of it as the bed that is too hard.

According to attachment assessment expert Dr. Carol George, those characterized as unresolved (tie-dye for us) were often raised with the experience of life- or relationship-threatening danger without parental protection or had significant unprocessed loss, emotional neglect, or trauma. Historically the categorization of *disorganized* referred specifically to attachment patterns in infancy. Today Dr. George suggests the term *dysregulated* for adults whose narrative style reveals a less organized attachment strategy because dysregulation is such a strong feature for these survivors.

They often exhibit common signs of trauma during interviews. For example, as they share a detail, they may unexpectedly become flooded by emotion. They often have trouble making sense of their experiences—sometimes adhering to a story that they are responsible for the actions of those who abused them and are actually responsible for their trauma. Understandably, this emotional dysregulation causes them to have difficulty making sense of their early experiences. Clinically, their narratives are often confusing, with themes of danger and fear.

Getting back to the Goldilocks metaphor, they are wily and won't reliably choose any particular bed. Why be pinned down to one predictable space when you aren't sure it's safe to let your guard down and sleep?

Finally, as we mentioned, those with a secure relational pattern (green attachment maps) have a style of speech that integrates thinking and feeling and maintains the integrity of the story or the interview. They generally stay connected to themselves, can track their listener, and elaborate on answers while staying on topic. They don't get lost or shut things down, and their speech patterns feel natural and comfortable. They have the "just right" cozy bed you can relax into.

Coherent Life Narrative

Having a coherent life narrative—the "just right" bed—suggests a secure attachment base because it indicates that an individual has come to understand how past experiences shape their present relationships and assumptions. An incoherent narrative means that a person may have difficulties introspecting or may have internal emotional conflicts that have not yet been navigated through.

Before you begin diagnosing yourself or your friends, let's be clear. Listening to someone's style of speech in casual settings is not enough to know for sure about the impact of their early life story. The actual attachment assessments are complex, carefully coded, and must be administered by trained professionals. However, this important finding on narrative coherence is so strong and consistent that tuning in to how someone speaks versus what they say can certainly provide strong clues as to whether or not they have an integrated sense of themselves and their life story. Also, developing a more coherent narrative—being willing to explore and make sense of your relational leanings—is a path toward shifting your internal working model and moving toward the more green zone, secure relating. Even learning to shift small aspects of your own narrative style can have significant benefits in the way you relate to yourself and others.

Ann relates to getting wordy when she is anxious about setting a limit or saying no to something that is important to someone else. For example, when not in the solid green zone, she can overexplain and take longer than necessary to say what she means. Underneath, she's trying to manage the other person's imagined disappointment by getting them to understand the reasonableness of her point before she ever makes it. When it came to the children, by unintentionally taking a subtle apologetic tone, it reduced her authority and invited the very resistance she was trying to avoid.

She has since adopted the practice of starting with where she wants to end, then backing up and filling in details as needed. It really works! She is much better today at knowing what she wants to convey first and then conveying it without an implicit apology, which just enhances her natural graceful authority. This tone signals safety to her listener, which invites interest, care, and cooperation—and who wouldn't want more of that? This is a great example of how listening to your own narrative style can help you recognize a pattern that may have remained otherwise unconscious. By intentionally practicing a change in your style of speech, you can shift your internal experience and grow security in those relationships that matter so much.

Attachment Through the Life Cycle

By the 1970s, researchers delved into questions about how our past experiences impact our development and when and how we can change. The Minnesota Longitudinal Study of Risk and Adaptation, led by Alan Sroufe and Byron Egeland, is a primary pillar in the second wave of attachment research. It is an impressive long-term study that has been active since 1975 and continues today. It began with a large group of mothers, many of whom faced poverty, and has followed their kids through school age, relationships, and now having their own families and children.

It provided the first longitudinal empirical evidence of how early attachment relationships have implications for adulthood. The findings fine-tuned some important points in the theory but confirmed that attachment plays a crucial role in organizing physiological and emotional regulation. Basically, it was confirmed that children with insecure attachment patterns were observed to have difficulties regulating their emotions, and these patterns tended to persist into adulthood.

We can see this process in action when we consider Derek as the child version of DJ, whom we met going out to dinner with his wife, Mia. Since baby Derek had to deactivate his attachment system to keep his mother close, he didn't get the natural opportunities to have a range of emotional experiences, learn what all the squishy feelings meant, learn how to talk about them, and gain skills to respond to emotional bids from others. This meant as he moved forward into school, he was rewarded for unconsciously ignoring his needs and developing a pseudo-independent self-identity. Fast-forward, these patterns continue, and he avoids emotionality because it's baffling and uncomfortable. You can see how this shows up in his marriage now, for example, with DJ wanting to focus on his work and his identity as a provider over more intimate family engagement.

However, the example above is Derek with minimal intervention and many social and cultural influences that also impacted his development: teachers who may have noticed him for his achievements but missed other, natural insecurities; peers who teased him if he showed signs of being soft; little extended family support to crack his independent facade, as well as being a cis male (cis means his gender expression matches his gender at birth) living in a culture that supports machismo and favors rationality. There were many points of intervention for baby Derek to have developed more comfortability with his emotions and value relying on others. Adult DJ now has many growth opportunities to expand his secure base as well.

So, yes, attachment matters, but Sroufe and his colleagues also discovered that early attachment relationships can be less deterministic than first thought. Just as Harlow's monkey group therapy demonstrated, many important variables affect us along the way, including the impact of peers, school, teachers, siblings, having children ourselves, and adult love relationships. These additional factors are subsumed in the impact of culture and context that is described in the context umbrella.

That infant attachment insecurity does not always continue into adulthood is great news for those of us interested in how humans grow and change. The quality of these combined relationships and the extended network of attachments is said to be a better predictor of attachment through the life span than the early relationship with the mother alone. This also tracks with many studies that show the importance of peer relationships on social and emotional development. All this means is that it's not over till it's over, every safe relationship matters, and you have no reason to give up now.

Ultimately, Sroufe concluded that early experience could be conceptualized in terms of creating vulnerabilities and strengths rather than directly producing particular outcomes. For those interested in much more detail from the culmination of findings from more than forty years of attachment research, you can find two in-depth interviews with Dr. Sroufe on our podcast. In addition, his excellent book *A Compelling Idea, How We Become the Persons We Are* (2021) contains a summary of this long-term study of attachment across the life cycle and is highly recommended for our neuronerd readers.

Third Generation

Adult Attachment Styles

Many people think of the popular adult attachment styles you see on the internet as the same as the infant attachment styles described above. This is a common misconception.

Let us explain—in the 1990s another branch of attachment research emerged and continues today. A group of social psychologists (a subfield of psychology with a special emphasis on how we are impacted in the presence of others) zeroed in on adults' beliefs about and their comfort in getting close to others, especially romantic relationships. This differs conceptually from the developmental branch which studied infant-caregiver patterns and nonverbal, lower limbic models of closeness. Remember that the developmental branch had to use projective assessment measures such as the Adult Attachment Interview (AAI) and the Adult Attachment Projective Picture System (AAP), or direct observation of infants such as in the Strange Situation protocol, precisely because internal working models of attachment are largely unconscious.

The social psychology approach to attachment is measuring something entirely different—higher cortical conscious thinking about how comfortable you perceive yourself to be seeking closeness and how you value yourself and others. They use self-report paper and pencil instruments (or these days, online measures). The argument is that since the early learning that forms the basis of one's comfort or discomfort with

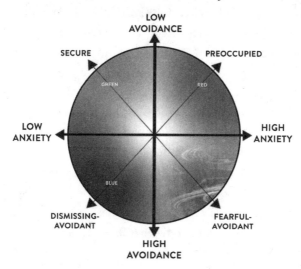

Figure 7: Adult Attachment Styles (adapted from Brennan, Clark, and Shaver, 1998)

closeness is not accessible directly, self-report measures are used. However, direct questions about beliefs and self-assessment are not measuring the same concepts as developmental research measures.

One highly referenced study by psychologists Cindy Hazan and Phillip Shaver used the original infant attachment categories and adapted them to what came to be known as adult attachment styles: secure, anxious-preoccupied, and dismissive-avoidant. Later, psychologist Kim Bartholomew added to the other adult attachment styles the fearful-avoidant category, which included individuals who were less skilled at cutting off their feelings than dismissing them but whom also avoided intimacy.

On previous page, in Figure 7, you'll find our adaptation of the adult attachment styles referenced by Kelly Brennan, Catherine Clark, and Phillip Shaver.

Most contemporary researchers agree that developmental attachment patterns and adult attachment styles are only moderately correlated; this means the dismissing attachment pattern in infancy is not the same thing as dismissing-avoidant adult attachment style. This makes sense because each branch is studying two related but different things, but it is a very common misconception. It also means that you can take the Experiences in Close Relationships-Revised Questionnaire (ECR-R) and score secure, but that is not the same thing as having a secure developmental attachment history.

There are many researchers and iterations of study in this branch, but for our need-to-know and apply-to-real-life purposes, the notable finding is that adult attachment styles came down to two dimensions: anxiety and avoidance.* Those who score high on avoidance minimize the attachment system and associated emotions while focusing on their own self-reliance. This causes trouble with intimacy and the ability to form close, supportive relationships. As they have generally deactivated their own awareness of their attachment needs, they display limited attachment-related anxiety. In contrast, those who show high attachment anxiety tend to maximize the attachment system, and their emo-

---

*   Those dimensions used to be positive-negative sense of self versus positive-negative sense of others. However, people with high avoidance and low anxiety often don't feel great about themselves, so the anxiety-avoidance dimensions are preferred.

tions can reflect preoccupation, and fear of abandonment and rejection. Their desire and reliance on others create active focus on the relationships, and they generally score low on avoidance. This also causes trouble in relationships and intimacy.

Those with insecure attachment—either the avoidant or ambivalent styles—do not feel they have a reliable partner (attachment figure), and both styles have mixed feelings about the safety of closeness. How they manage these mixed feelings shows up in their different coping strategies. Those with more fearful styles of relating tend to have a combination of both high anxiety (they want closeness, but don't trust that it will happen) and high avoidance (as they lack trust that it is possible, they are afraid of it). Those who fall in the adult secure style category show low attachment anxiety (as they trust others will be there) and low attachment avoidance (as they seek out and value the connection with others).

Today the most widely used self-report measure for adult attachment is the Experiences in Close Relationships (ECR) scale. It is free and accessible online and is a reliable measure of your adult-conscious thoughts about comfort with intimacy and closeness. Interestingly, you can take it thinking of your parents, partner(s), ex-wife, and boss, and the results will likely vary for each person. It measures explicit memory and shows that attachment relationships change over our lifetime of experiences and differ depending on the felt safety in particular relationships. However, a deeper-held, limbic-level attachment map that appears to be sturdier over time and gets expressed unconsciously during relational stress has also held up in the research. This means that while attachment styles may shift, those early years looked at in the developmental attachment literature are still in deep limbic learning, making them harder to change and more liable to reemerge in times of stress.

Attachment Research Today

These days, attachment research includes a wide range of measures. Relational neuroscience has validated the power of early experience on development and further expanded original concepts such as internal working models (IWMs). Researchers continue to study biomarkers, such as variations in heart rate, cortisol levels, skin conductivity, and micro-expressions, to give insight into how adult attachment patterns and styles relate to physiological functioning. Imaging procedures verify which parts of the brain are active in various relational functions and validate the idea of unconscious attachment models. And the genetic and epigenetic components of attachment behaviors and neural functioning are being examined as we speak.

Pulling It All Together

As you can see, a beautiful intergenerational story unfolds when we take a high-level look at attachment over time. It has different branches, with the accompanying normal family feuds and loyal alliances. The concept has evolved and stood the test of time. It didn't turn out exactly as the theory's parents, John Bowlby and Mary Ainsworth, first imagined; but in some ways it is even better. They were mostly correct in their original hypothesis that attachment is a powerful predictor of many human development outcomes. Secure attachment, in particular, imbues you with sturdy, long-lasting emotional and relational health. Insecure patterns in childhood are less predictive than expected, and it's not automatic that insecure parents raise insecure babies—all of which means there is hope for change. This is why this body of work continues to be so influential and why this book is all about increasing your capacity to relate from your most secure state of mind.

Here are a few other takeaways to make navigating the attachment world less confusing. When researchers say attachment "patterns," they typically refer to that first- and second-generation developmental attachment research. For adults, this will typically involve assessments such as the AAI, AAP, or other, more in-depth assessment measures that help illuminate your mostly unconscious internal working model.

Attachment "styles" typically refer to the social psychology adult attachment styles research discussed above as the third generation. With the ease of assessment via self-reporting, research from this area is exploding and helping to refine and specify personality concepts. They use dimensional measures, which help move from discrete categories to capture degrees of security and create a more complex representation of the whole person. This is important as the degree of security or insecurity matters a lot, and small changes can be huge for an individual person!

Ultimately, we see these branches as complementary. They belong to the same family tree, and all point to the same important message: relationships deeply matter and impact us throughout our lifetime. As Dr. Sroufe said, early experience sets up a trajectory by setting up vulnerabilities and strengths, but this trajectory can be impacted throughout the life span. Parents are important, but so are all the ever-expanding relationships that come after them. Also, the most effective way to change painful early relational learning is—you guessed it!—more secure relational experiences now.

5

Moving Attachment Maps

How we feel about ourselves and rely on others is determined largely by an interplay of *states* (in-the-moment nervous system activation) and more embedded *traits* (attachment maps, which include both developmental patterns and adult, more conscious strategies).

As a reminder, states are temporary moods similar to the weather, which can change abruptly from stormy to cloudy to clear, ebbing and flowing even over the course of an afternoon. The spectrum in MARS represents state activation, which is why it can be so useful to use it to recognize where you are and turn your focus to scooting back toward the green zone rather quickly.

Attachment patterns, on the other hand, tend to be more stable over time and function more like traits. In MARS, we refer to these more persistent patterns as **attachment maps**. While emotions come and go, attachment maps stick around and influence life choices by guiding your interpersonal responses over time. Figure 8 shows how these maps are represented in the MARS framework.

Figure 8: Attachment Map

Most simply, attachment maps include biology, relational experiences and context. Your personal attachment map integrates your internal working model (IWM) and your lifetime of experiences, including default beliefs such as your sense of belonging, worthiness, lovability, and whether you can trust others to be there for you. It also impacts your capacity to be emotionally available for others. The cultural norms from your personal history and current context are also embedded deeply in your attachment map. It serves as a guide to understanding yourself, and it influences what you expect from others. It is both embodied and cognitive—involving both deep limbic early learning that develops into more conscious understanding: thoughts such as "Daddy loves me," or "Mommies are scary," or "Boys don't cry." These maps help us form personal policies about life, such as *Keep your business to yourself*, or *If they wanted me to know, they'd tell me.*

They influence whether or not you tend to make eye contact, how expressive your face is, and whether or not you notice and how strongly you respond to others' nonverbal cues. They influence whether you reach out and hold your partner's hand while watching TV, whether you will let yourself recognize and admit that you need help—and when you do, whether you pick up the phone and call or text somebody, or secretly wish a certain person would reach out to you.

How Attachment Maps Form

As we add layers of understanding to the spectrum, things will begin to feel familiar because we build on earlier ideas to add nuance and flesh them out. The familiarity is good; it means you are with us.

Let's meet Jacki, a five-year-old with a smile that makes people want to say things like "She's going to be a heartbreaker." Jacki has been raised by her grandma Mimi since she was nine months old, when her mom left "to get her life together" and never returned.

Mimi smokes hand-rolled cigarettes, sips Johnny Walker from a teacup, and can make you snort-laugh so hard your belly hurts. But her charm is fickle and can turn unexpectedly. She and Jacki love baking together, but when Jacki spills flour or makes a mess, it's hard to predict how Mimi will respond. She might laugh it off or she might ice Jacki out, stalking off with the dreaded "You do it!" When that happens, Jacki is left alone to deal with the mess but, even worse, to soak in her shame. Mimi's sudden absences leave Jacki scared of doing things wrong, and she didn't know it at the time, but she would eventually realize that Mimi blames her for her mother abandoning them both.

This little girl has learned to track Mimi's ups and downs, observing the subtle signs and staying close by her grandma's side when she can. Jacki knows she's loved but can't settle emotionally because of Mimi's mercurial moods. She works hard to be the light in Mimi's eye and has learned to smile, dance, and be adored. Unlike Derek, Jacki has not given up hope that someone will be there for her when she's emotional or in need. She is maximizing the importance of attachment, not minimizing it.

Mimi's inconsistency leaves Jacki trapped in a hope-disappointment cycle, and she carries this pattern with her throughout her development. As an adult, when Jacki does feel cared for, she often has fear running in the background that the care will go away. This leads her to hold on tightly to important relationships, a bit too tight. Mimi's inconsistency kept Jacki's little amygdala on mild alert at most times and set up a pattern of hypervigilance to relational attention. Jacki developed the belief that she's okay as long as she's connected to others, and that to stay in contact with Mimi, she needed to track her closely.

She doesn't remember her mom consciously, but, sadly, both her mother and grandmother have imparted the hard truth that you can love someone and depend on them—and yet they can leave you suddenly, without explanation. Jacki had come to encode these lessons so deeply, from head to toe, that her body perceives danger when she lets down her guard.

These experiences are part of the core of her attachment map, which has internalized her young attachment relationship with Mimi and later to other important people in her life. It's the biological start and early learning that get integrated into her working model of self, and this layer of learning sets a pattern in the little girl's interpretation of events. Without new, more secure relational experiences, Jacki could continue on a path where her body believes she needs to cling to those close to her, and she'll have trouble trusting that someone will consistently be there if she needs them.

As a result, her body's solution was to up-regulate in hard moments—to stay alert and look for signs of impending loss or rejection. This becomes a symptom in her adult life, but we like to think of symptoms as solutions at one time. She yearns for closeness, which is good and will help bring people in as she grows up. But she's not quite able to trust that the person will be there for her, so her nervous system seeks and holds on, focuses outward to get comfort, and highlights emotional expression. This pattern and understanding of the world shapes Jacki's red-leaning attachment map.

In the MARS model, we thumbtack the maps to the spectrum (see Figure 9) to remind us that while these learnings are stable compared with the more fluid movement of emotional activation along the spectrum, they are not permanently fixed and can definitely move as you grow and evolve. Figure 9 below shows maps thumbtacked on the spectrum.

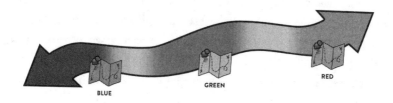

Figure 9: Maps pinned to the spectrum

Little Jacki has a lifetime of relationships ahead of her to help her change course—she could have secure experiences with other family members, extended kin, friends, teachers, coaches, mentors, employers, her community, or lovers, and even having children (!) can help us heal our attachment injuries.* Healing can come in surprising ways. You may enjoy the heartwarming story of a clinical case with a goose named Feli, by Dan Stern.†

Over time Jacki will accumulate ongoing relational experiences that will add to her sense of security and presence in the world. She might also seek professional help to begin to "right-size" her reactions in moments of activation.

Information Distortion:
Your Polarized Sunglasses

These attachment maps do a number on us. They literally impact how we take in information from the world, and they can cause us to distort incoming information in specific ways based on which direction on the spectrum our map leans. This is critical because most certainly your perceptions and expectations impact your immediate experience of events. Think about when you are angry and upset with someone; you are biased to feel justified and to think that your feelings and emotions are correct. In the morning, the fight always looks different because we are likely on a different place on the spectrum, well rested, more flexible, more open (green zone) and, in truth, can now see things more accurately.

We liken it to wearing a pair of sunglasses, as you can see in Figure 10 on the next page.

In the green zone, your shades are cool and clear, they don't amplify or minimize anything, and you see yourself and others mostly accurately. You look pretty darn good in them, and they don't interfere with anything. As you shift right, your perceptions maximize relational information, such as intensely focusing on what was said (or not said),

---

* Healing through parenting may raise eyebrows, but remember the healing power of the younger therapist-monkeys from chapter 4? Parenting brings a window to reexamine your own early experience; the feelings of love you have for them can help you understand what was missing from your early experience and their need of you and the so-sweet cuddling can open up even armored hearts.
† http://thebowlbycentre.org.uk/wp-content/uploads/2014/10/Editorial-V1-N1.pdf.

Figure 10: Sunglasses—Information Processing Distortions

facial expressions, or others' shifts in moods. This intense focus will generally have a negative tilt toward disappointment and signs of rejection. As you move further and further out on the spectrum, think of large, polarized, red-tinted sunglasses. With these on, the emotional world is a bit magnified.

When you shift left, toward blue, you unconsciously begin to minimize relational information. You miss details and overlook the importance of social communications but think that what you see is how it is. Imagine these as thick, dark aviators that both block information coming in and hide your emotional expression as well.

Our sunglasses affect both in-the-moment emotional activation and ongoing expectations—both our states and traits. If activated red in the moment, your experience of a stressful relational exchange will be slightly exaggerated compared with when you are in the green zone, reinforcing the dangers encoded in your system urging you to act fast and attend to both the threat and the intense emotional activation. These perceptions drive action, so for example you may clock if your message is left unread or not, or how long it takes for them to text back. Sometimes this is important relational information, but more often than not, others aren't tracking things in this level of detail. When wearing red glasses, things are interpreted differently than in in the green zone.

Our need for a little extra reassurance is due to the neural distortion and this is represented by your red vivid sunglasses! Of course, this works in reverse, too: if activated toward the blue, we are literally distorting what is happening by shrugging it off—"It's no big deal"—and we forget quickly, leaving the other person further away emotionally and us blissfully unaware or actively disconnected from our care.

Keep these sunglasses in mind as you hone your ability to observe your reactions and identify your activation in various situations. Recognizing when someone close to you is activated and distorting their perception can be especially helpful. You might think, *Oh, be careful, he's got his red sunglasses on so those tears aren't fake; he's feeling things big right now and needs a little kindness* (rather than arguing about whether his feelings are justified or not).

This decoding of what is automatic helps you fire up your prefrontal cortex and gain a clearer look at any specific situation—taking off the sunglasses or at least turning the color down, so to speak.

Attachment IWMs Versus Maps

In the MARS model, attachment maps include IWMs but also incorporate other elements embedded in our models of self and others. This can include gender scripts (social expectations that dictate behavioral roles based on gender), cultural identity, and recognition of positions of power in society, all of which contribute to shaping our attachment patterns and relationships throughout life.

For example, having a body that looks or works differently (which is often misinterpreted as "less desirable") than others, or gender proclivities that threaten the status quo, impacts how others engage with us, our sense of safety and thus our developing nervous system. A Black man in a white society will likely have ingrained conscious and nonconscious expectations of others—vigilance—that has little to do with his relationship with early caregivers. He may be secure or not, but his map will likely have incorporated reality-based awareness of others being afraid or suspicious of him, and that others in authority are potentially dangerous. He is not preoccupied with attachment, yet these expectations of self and others are still embedded deeply in his attachment map and impact how he responds interpersonally.

All of the reality-based scripts and dangers and inequities we have encoded deep in our nervous system are recognized in the MARS map so that we can take out the judgment of right or wrong, pathological or otherwise. The biology of your cumulative experience has shaped your expectations of yourself and the world today.

Deion's Attachment Map

To see how different attachment maps might affect how we engage in our everyday life, let's consider Deion, a third-grader who cares about school but happened to forget his homework today. Depending on Deion's attachment map, he will react differently to this common situation.

If Deion believes he's basically a good kid and that people will generally be there for him (greenish, secure map), he might recognize his mistake and ask the teacher if he can bring in his homework the next day. Or perhaps he would call his parents and ask them to please drop it off at school. He might decide to redo the assignment during lunch because he has a sense of agency and can lean on others and rely on himself.

However, if Deion's early experiences taught him to doubt himself and to lean too heavily on others in order to feel okay (reddish, preoccupied map), it's a different story. He might feel overwhelmed by worry that handing in the homework late will ding his grade. He might get angry at himself for the "dumb mistake" and lean on the teacher for solutions and comfort. He might also externalize the problem and blame someone else—the teacher for not being clear or his dad for not reminding him to pack the assignment in his schoolbag.

With that red-leaning working map of the world, Deion is more likely to focus on stressful events and regard most things as high stakes—in this case, that it's a big deal he forgot his homework. Rather than negotiate a fair solution, he's more likely to use emotion and passivity to get through the challenge because, to him, assertiveness is dangerous. (Remember, we are not judging Deion; he's just a goofy third-grade kiddo. We're merely describing the narrative that shapes what he expects from the world based on his early experiences and environment. Making sense of this will only help Deion.)

Finally, if Deion internalized the importance of self-sufficiency like Derek did (bluish, dismissing map), it might not even occur to him to ask for help with the forgotten homework. He might decide that the homework was stupid, and, oh well, he'll turn it in tomorrow. Or he might decide that he doesn't like the class anyway. Here Deion's underlying narrative is that his thoughts are valid, and emotions are weak—he'll think his way out of this problem.

His aloofness might get read as not caring and, if so, could impact how his teacher and his peers respond to him. For example, if Deion has learned to mute his emotions, he might not receive his classmates' bright welcome when he arrives at school because he doesn't beam back at them in greeting. His classmates may even be a bit intimidated to approach him. It's extremely easy to misread those who unintentionally mask expressions, and teachers are stretched so thin that it's a challenge to counteract what *their* own attachment maps evoke.

This is how attachment maps can become a self-fulfilling prophecy, but also why it's so important to understand them: together we can counteract these powerful forces that shape Deion's—and all of our—development.

Attachment Maps in Adulthood

Attachment maps are carried with us over time and can influence relationships throughout our lives. Let's return to Jacki's story to see how attachment maps play out in adulthood.

We met little Jacki when she was young and being raised by Mimi. However, Jacki is now twenty-eight and has just been out with friends. As you read her story, keep track of your reactions to Jacki and her buddies because, like with DJ and Mia, we'll return to Jacki later in the book. Investing a little energy in understanding her (and how you react to her) will be helpful as we go.

Jacki—Queen's Night Out

Jacki sits in her car on the side of her neighborhood street, seething. On her drive home she had been mentally crafting an important text message to her friends, with whom she had just had "happy" hour. As her thoughts flowed through her, she pulled over to the side of the road so she could capture her words. She did not want to forget anything.

Her thumbs fly across the phone's screen as she types out the message.

Images of her friend Grace's cool demeanor during their good-bye and the overly polite hug flash through her mind, causing her stomach to roil. She lists the slights, feeling a sense of relief as she goes. On a roll, Jacki adds some points she's been holding back, and the length of the text message grows in proportion. It feels cathartic to finally express herself fully.

She momentarily considers a tiny thought, warning her to slow down— she could regret this, after all—but quickly discards the idea. Nope, it's better to fight and be real than to be walked on like she was tonight.

With a quick inhale, she hits Send.

Okay, which nervous system circuit is in charge right now inside of Jacki, protection or connection? And which direction on the spectrum do you think she's tilting in her activation? Blue or red? How do you know?

Her heart is pounding, she feels a sense of urgency, is being verbose and reactive in her text, acting on impulse, and feeling rejected and mistreated. All of these are signs of being emotionally up-regulated, maximizing focus and losing track of her listener (those receiving the group (!) text). We already know from earlier in this chapter that young Jacki has tremendous loss and uncertainty in her childhood, it is likely clear by now that she dysregulated and shifted pretty far red in activation in the moment.

Let's see what happened to fire up her protective defense department.

Two Hours Before Text Deployment

Jacki sits in the parking lot of Julio's Tex-Mex restaurant, the group's go-to for Mexican margaritas. She is regarding herself critically in the rearview mirror and adjusts her thick hair behind her ears as naturally as possible, and then plucks a wild, curly stray from her scalp.

This is the first time in a few months that her group of friends has gotten together. The die-hards used to meet here for dinner and drinks every Friday night, but the group has been slow to reconvene after the resurgence of the Covid pandemic confused everyone's strategies as to what was safe or not to socialize.

Jacki is pleased that the guys—Pete, Atlas, and Dre—will be there tonight. They are buffers and help things go more smoothly between her and Grace. Pete named the gathering Queen's Night Out as a fitting compliment to them all.

As Jacki approaches the table, she's met with enthusiastic hugs and warm smiles; everyone seems happy to see her. Dre arrives behind her and touches her waist as he moves by. Jacki loves Dre, the peacemaker. The table of old friends is loud with excited chatter. Atlas and Pete are back together, apparently. Denise has been home with her one-year-old, and she's complaining about her partner, whom they all know she adores.

"It's a miracle I haven't committed infanticide!" Denise announces, and Jacki can tell she either drank before she came or has been here awhile, because she's at least second-drink loud. Grace, the group alpha, is in her element and is commanding the center of attention. She is radiant, filling the air with vivacious energy and relishing the attention. Finally, there's Chelle, sitting as she always does, present and content, with no pressure to perform. She somehow feels part of the group without exerting any apparent effort. There's nothing not to like, yet Jacki sometimes resents her self-confidence.

As the night proceeds, Jacki can't catch her groove or find her way into the animated conversation. She laughs easily so that no one would know how hard she's working to appear relaxed. Jacki's stomach begins to churn, and the carbonated feeling of performance anxiety bubbles up. She realizes she hasn't talked enough and that soon her silence will mean something. She should say something interesting about herself or she worries she will appear awkward. She can feel herself begin to spiral.

What can I say? I don't have anything going on. At all. My life is so dull.

She feels increasingly alarmed as she realizes she can't think of a single thing cool enough to add to the conversation.

Warding off the attention she longs for, Jacki amps up Grace's monologue by being extra responsive and complimentary to her. She asks questions and then cringes inside whenever Denise describes unwelcome details of diaper changing and baby bowel habits.

She's sure people can sense her self-consciousness, so Jacki excuses herself to go to the restroom.

Chill out, Jacki! she thinks, exhaling slowly to steady her nerves and quell the swarm of negative thoughts. It's been a while since she has felt so stirred up.

Dr. Horowitz, her therapist, has encouraged Jacki to use some simple techniques whenever self-defeating thoughts arise. He calls the thoughts ANTs, automatic negative thoughts, and when she is stressed, they attack. She's found deep breathing helpful to slow down and recenter herself in the moment, so she takes long huffs of air into her lungs. After imagining herself truly engaged in conversation with her friends, she walks back to the table, just in time to see Denise glance up at her and abruptly change the subject.

Denise tosses out a question, "So, when are y'all going back into the office, Pete?"

But it's too late; Jacki felt it. They'd been talking about her. She hovers over the table.

"What?" she manages to ask, but her voice comes out strained and clipped.

"What, what?" Atlas responds, smiling, keeping things light.

"Did I interrupt something?" Jacki asks as she sits down, realizing that the question came out more accusatory than intended. She notices side-glances among the others, which fires up her shark music.

Dre inhales. "Hey, J. It's no big deal. My boss gave me a couple of extra tickets for a concert at the last minute, so I grabbed Grace to come with me."

"Yeah, thanks again, sweetheart," Grace chimes in. "When he texted, Denise and I were talking, and, you know, Denise really needed a break from the baby, so she and I jumped at the chance. You know she has been super stressed—it was last minute, and, really, it was no big deal."

"Sure. Of course," Jacki says, forcing a smile.

Dre could have probably gotten as many tickets as he wanted, she thinks. Everyone at the table gets quiet. Too quiet. No one quite understands what's wrong, but they are all uncomfortable.

"Awwwkwardddd?" Atlas sings, both a statement and a question.

"I don't know why it just got weird," Dre continues after a few beats. "Honestly, I think I was feeling bad because I didn't want you to feel left out. It's no big deal." He then checks his phone as if that were the natural thing to do next.

"Yeah, okay, it's all good," Jacki says, trying to feel relieved. "What concert was it, anyway?" she asks casually.

Grace looks down when Dre answers. "It was Bob Graves and the Resentments. Good show!"

Jacki's cheeks go hot as she stares incredulously at Grace. Bob Graves was *her* favorite artist; she'd introduced Grace to him last year. How could Grace have invited Denise and not even think of asking her? Unfortunately, Jacki's exasperated expression must have given her away because Pete intervenes.

"Whoa, Dorothy. They just went to a concert. It's no big deal, don't let it bother you for one second," Pete says the second part decisively but through a bright smile, pretending to fan Jacki with his napkin. He then mouths the words, "I love you," as the relief of conversation resumes around them.

Good try, but it doesn't work this time. Using humor usually helps when Jacki is fired up—being light but saying the truth, setting boundaries but playfully, and providing reassurances. But this time it didn't land right.

No way this was an accident, she thinks to herself. Her thoughts are spinning now, but she knows enough not to trust herself to speak. She tries to set it aside for later and move on.

Jacki is able to feign pleasantness for the rest of the evening, though her body never relaxes.

After finishing their drinks, everyone begins getting up and saying their good-byes. As Jacki makes her way to Grace, she can feel her heart beating in her neck. Her eyes reach for Grace's. Instead of making eye contact, Grace quickly hugs her.

"See you around, love," Grace says sweetly before moving away to embrace the next person.

Jacki is stricken—she feels slapped in the face. Grace knows precisely how Jacki would feel about being left out, but to go to *that* concert and not say anything to her? As she walks quickly to her car, she's reeling. What has happened to their friendship? They used to talk all the time; now she can't think of when Grace last called her.

The hug felt wrong, too. It was . . . polite. Polite!?

As Jacki drives away, she can feel the rage building. She can't stop replaying the injustices of the night. Grace had been fake, aloof . . . and polite? To her, her supposed best friend? Ugh.

Her mind fixates on Grace's parting words as she drives a bit too fast. *What the hell? "See you around?" That is so cold.* Everyone else said how wonderful it was to get together and how much they enjoyed the night. No one came to her side, and everyone expected her to ignore the slight. Dre didn't even think to include her and then basically told her that her feelings were off, "it was no big deal!" If they were so off, why did everyone talk about it when she was away from the table?

And why would Grace call her *love*? That was so weird. That's what you say to a child.

And so it goes until—well, you already know what happened next: Jacki kept replaying the evening in her mind, becoming so dysregulated that she pulled over and fired off that long, accusatory text. The one she knew deep down she shouldn't send. Cringe. And she sent it to the whole gang as a group text so that they would all know how upset she was! Double cringe!

Making Sense of It All

Do you have a beautiful human in your life with struggles similar to Jacki's? If so, give her or him some extra love. Have you had moments like this? It is hard when our defenses hang out there a little and are visible to others! Some of us can hide our stuff more easily, but not Jacki. Remember, it's not her; it's her amygdala.

Also how did you respond to her? Did you relate to her? Recoil?

Let's light up our hippocampus and higher brain to imagine for a moment what was happening in Jacki's brain and body. When she entered Julio's, she had access to her bright, thinking mind and was in touch with all the work she was doing in therapy. But then she encountered two particularly loaded experiences. First, long absences are hard for those who lean red. Separations and reunions are tough for someone uncertain of themselves already, and, to make matters worse, this was a public reunion. Second, group gatherings can be especially vulnerable when we are highly in tune with others' reactions. When we are with only one person, we can more easily track and try to manage how we are being perceived (another common coping strategy for those who activate red). With multiple people, our nervous system can feel much more on overload.

Even though Jacki tried her best, her default story ultimately took over: people will disappoint and reject her. She is on the outside of things and is stupid for trying and trusting. She needed to let everyone know she was no idiot; she could see how they really felt about her. The aggression went as it often does, from self-attack to externalizing blame—reinforcing Jacki's internal working map that began when she was a little girl abandoned by her mother and kept perpetually on guard by Grandma Mimi's inconsistent affection. This cycle of self-attack, external blame, and back again might make it seem like Jacki is simply torturing herself, but it's actually an attempt to have a new experience.

The more challenging part here is that we can't readily see our inner story—it's too ingrained.

Jacki knows she's reactive but can't control that her limbic system scans for being left out and signs of interpersonal danger. Worse, she slips into believing that the solution to her threat is outside of herself and in the other person. In this case, Grace holds the key to Jacki's well-being, which only makes her more preoccupied. Jacki loses her capacity to manage big feelings such as letdown and rejection. Instead, the letdown likely triggers unconscious pain she has stored from her early losses as a child. Her defense system kicks in to block these implicit feelings, and her anger serves to protect her. She experienced her friends' actions as a personal attack and high betrayal.

Keep in mind: if Jacki's amygdala pings too loudly, her hippocampus and higher cortex start to sputter, slow down, or go offline altogether. This means rather than having fresh experiences that can update her old narrative, she perceives the event playing out according to the old script, practically line by line. This means the history gets enacted yet again, further reinforcing the old story. If we don't work through painful things that happened to us, we will often repeat them, a phenomenon called enactments. Unfortunately, in this case, you can see that Jacki is squeezing her friends so tightly that her attempt to maintain closeness is backfiring.

Her limbic system doesn't realize she's already safe; they are right there, and there is no actual danger.

So, we agree that Jacki's map tilts red, right? Now let's look at degree: Where would you tack her map on the spectrum? Think about Jacki's state before the evening started, how her body seemed slightly primed, her preoccupation and underlying doubt about her place in the group, and how she tended to slightly amplify information toward rejection. Also, consider how hard she's working in therapy and her attachment to Dr. Horowitz.

The place you mentally thumbtack her map doesn't need to be exact; this isn't an assessment, of course. We just want you to get used to the idea of gradients and dimension, so that you can become more discerning as you learn to process the details of these ideas. This conceptual framework is designed to help us get perspective on our patterns, not turn them into another label or identity.

To us, it seems likely that Jacki's map falls fairly far toward the right on the continuum. Given what we already know of her history (the story of Little Jacki and Mimi), she's experienced early maternal loss and a consistent primary attachment to a grandmother who was loving but unpredictable, and having a high activation at this social get-together suggests a pretty solid red map.* Her close attachment to her therapist and her active use of the security she feels from their relationship to try to settle herself are signs of more security, so she's surely not the darkest red. Her early experience of loss and trauma may show up in unresolved pockets (tie-dye), and her therapy has helped her in this process. We will discuss tie-dye in more detail in the following chapter, but it's an interesting example of how you can be primarily red or blue or green and yet fall into pockets of dysregulation from unresolved trauma.

There are positive signs for Jacki's future: she's working on identifying the young scripts that set up her early working model, turning off

---

* MARS is specifically designed *not* to label anyone or be diagnostic; it's more dynamic and from the hip. Don't get caught up in the details of where Jacki or you or your partner may fall on the map; the point is to incorporate the idea that there *is* a defensive spectrum operating just outside our awareness and to empower you to recognize and outsmart it.

biological autopilot, and managing emotional reactions more intention-ally. She doesn't *want* to cause disconnections in her relationships. In fact, she's working very hard on herself and has successfully attached to her therapist and trusts their work together. She knows that when she gets triggered, she takes things more personally than she should and that her negative self-talk is part of the problem.

To create change, you need to understand your personal baseline of "normal" and figure out what sunglasses you may be wearing that cause you to shift interpretations of events. Your instinctive reactions to the characters in this book will provide clear clues into your own tendencies. Periodically running quick X-rays of your internal world—trying to discern any physical sensations, patterns of thoughts, favorite feelings, go-to attitudes, or default moods in any given moment—can be a helpful start.

Jacki's story is a testament to the power of attachment maps. It shows how they influence adult relationships even when you're working to ad-dress patterns, as Jacki does with her therapist. They are deeply embed-ded, so updating them will take work and require opening up to new relational experiences.

What about you?

It's time to think about your own story and patterns. In your mind, lightly "pin" your map to the spectrum. Figure 11 provides just a few of the more common characteristics that emerge for each working map. Some of us may live more predominantly in one color or another or may recognize where we quickly land when we begin to feel defensively activated.

If you spend much time in a more up-regulating, self-protective red state, this does not mean you never engage in secure relating. It means that you *trend* in the red direction most often when you are activated, such as when your protection circuit is firing. Remember, Jacki doesn't live in the red; she was activated by the stress of being in a large group of people who hadn't seen one another in quite some time. The day after the incident at work Jacki will be functioning quite competently and her coworkers may never expect that she could be so reactively volatile.

What Shade is Your Map?

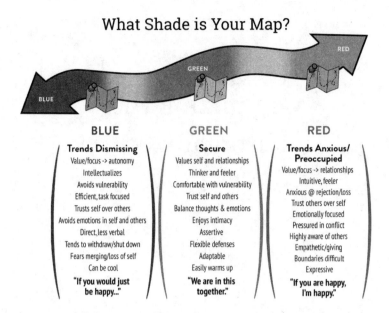

BLUE	GREEN	RED
Trends Dismissing	**Secure**	**Trends Anxious/ Preoccupied**
Value/focus -> autonomy	Values self and relationships	Value/focus -> relationships
Intellectualizes	Thinker and feeler	Intuitive, feeler
Avoids vulnerability	Comfortable with vulnerability	Anxious @ rejection/loss
Efficient, task focused	Trust self and others	Trust others over self
Trusts self over others	Balance thoughts & emotions	Emotionally focused
Avoids emotions in self and others	Enjoys intimacy	Pressured in conflict
Direct, less verbal	Assertive	Highly aware of others
Tends to withdraw/shut down	Flexible defenses	Empathetic/giving
Fears merging/loss of self	Adaptable	Boundaries difficult
Can be cool	Easily warms up	Expressive
"If you would just be happy..."	**"We are in this together."**	**"If you are happy, I'm happy."**

Figure 11: What Shade Is Your Map?

Here is the fun part:

Now think of those closest to you. You've probably already been doing this, but if not, guess where their maps might be pinned on the spectrum. Once you've made your best guess, invite them to read this chapter and then ask them where they think they fall on the map! It's a great conversation starter. We will dive deeper into each map in later chapters so that you can continue to build on these insights as we go.

Security is love and trust embodied. Insecure relating is fear internalized. Healing requires the former, taking in and accepting the love you deserve. Remember, if this is hard for you, there is no moral judgment toward you or any of the people you've been meeting in this book. DJ is not better than Mia, who is not better than Jacki. They are all people doing their best with the emotional skills they have at their disposal. The fact that your internal working map has such a strong effect on your everyday relationships—even to a degree that you might wish it didn't—doesn't make you weak, or unevolved, or out of touch. It simply makes you human.

6

Organizing the Disorganized

Tie-Dye

When our bodies feel threatened and our activation spikes, it can feel pretty chaotic. No one likes to feel as if they are grasping for control or that their body—or the world around them—is in disarray. Managing emotions during confusion and chaos is challenging for all of us, but confusion can sometimes also be a survival tactic. When we are in a dangerous environment with no sense of escape, we may have no choice but to get scrambled. And, strangely, being unclear internally can sometimes help us block out overwhelming danger and threats that we are unable to face at the time.

By working to increase secure relating, we're looking to develop the ability to maintain a modicum of emotional regulation when our body's intuitive response is to erect our defenses and get activated. This is *especially* hard when your history has caused such upheaval that your responses to activation are confusing and messy. As the name indicates, disorganized attachment patterns don't follow organized coping strategies, so your activation and defense patterns will be much harder to predict. The defensive patterns get mixed up, like tie-dye colors rather than one clear pattern.

In Figure 12, we represent this experience of disorganized dysregulation as a tie-dye puddle lying under the more predictable spectrum.

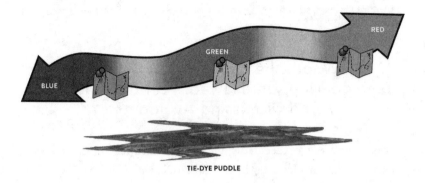

TIE-DYE PUDDLE

Figure 12: The Tie-Dye Puddle

There is a lot to sort out as this is by far the most confusing area of attachment. Let's clarify a few of the biggest misunderstandings with the caveat being that this is an evolving area, and it is very difficult to translate disparate research findings to clinical relevance, so some slack here is requested.

First, tie-dye is not an organized coping strategy, which means it doesn't work like stable attachment maps. You can have a blue, green, or red map but tend to drop into disoriented tie-dye puddles when triggered, or you can spend a whole lot of time in disorganized states. An important goal of treatment is to increase the time you spend on the spectrum in a predictable coherent mental space, even if that state of mind is reliably dismissing or preoccupied, and decrease the time and intensity of paddling around in that dysregulated puddle.

The next clarifying point is about terminology, all of which is discussed in more detail in chapter 4. The original language for infants was disorganized or disoriented attachment. For adults it has historically been coded as *unresolved attachment*, meaning there was trauma that had not been processed (unresolved) and still impacts them today. Dr. Carol George suggests using the term they've adopted in AAP assessments, *dysregulated attachment*, because the primary feature of this category is *dysregulation.**

---

* Personal communication with Sue Marriott, July 23, 2023.

The phrase *fearful-avoidant attachment* has caught on related to adult attachment styles, and that category is a close sibling to dismissing avoidant.

What's the Difference Between Disorganized, Unresolved, Fearful-Avoidant, and Dismissing-Avoidant?

Great question! We are decidedly and intentionally leaving the confines of academic research and fleshing it out based on our current understanding and clinical experience. The fine points may be debatable from a research perspective, but for us the idea is to get the gist to promote the most secure coping styles possible.

And remember, the idea isn't to put anyone in one bucket—ever—but to make sense of the various ways tie-dye dysregulation can show up.

Disorganized attachment—We think of this group as having the most severe histories of loss, abuse, and neglect and being associated with disorientation and dissociation. The pain, loss, and fear are so confusing and unprocessed it is very difficult to find words to even name it, much less process through it. Key markers of disorganized attachment are frequent flooding, emotional dysregulation, and dissociation. A group of neuroscientists reviewed the studies of the neurobiology of disorganized attachment in a paper published in February 2023. They showed findings of both neurodevelopment (the stress response system, specifically cortisol and oxytocin) and physical differences in brain anatomy, most notably, the hippocampus.

Unresolved/Dysregulated attachment—We think of this clinically as having pockets of trauma. You may be doing fine but when stimulated into the unprocessed pain or fear stored carefully away in your limbic system, you can drop into a disorganized/dysregulated pocket. The trauma stored is often associated with early attachment figures and issues, and this is different than straight post-traumatic stress disorder (PTSD). Those with unresolved attachment may have PTSD, but having PTSD doesn't mean you have unresolved attachment. We generally dysregulate temporarily. Working on mapping this and compassionately understanding our history is helpful. Someone unresolved could have their attachment map pinned anywhere on the spectrum, including secure—it would just come with a shade of tie-dye.

Fearful-avoidant attachment—Our take on this description (remember it is a different branch of science than developmental attachment) is that it presents as a paradoxical mix of desire for emotional closeness and fear of it. You want intimacy but are deeply afraid of vulnerability and getting hurt, so you may avoid it altogether or engage in push-pull dynamics. You have trust issues and emotional turmoil because emotional states can fluctuate dramatically, swinging between extreme longing for connection and the need for independence and avoiding closeness. Dropping into the puddle is less visible and perhaps less common than in straight disorganized or disoriented attachment. Your attachment map likely leans blue with a tint of tie-dye through it.

Dismissive-avoidant attachment (dark blue)—This manifests as emotional detachment and self-sufficiency. We cover this exclusively and in depth in chapter 8. These individuals downplay the importance of emotional intimacy in relationships, relying heavily on self-reliance. Their map is definitely blue, but it can vary by degrees, with the darker shades more rigid, making it harder to penetrate their defenses. In some ways, a dark blue map is harder to change than those listed above because distress that motivates doing hard things such as opening up to connection and dismantling basic stories about your identity and the world is minimal or absent. Why bother?

In summary, clinically we think of disorganized/dysregulated grouping as characterized by frequent flooding, disorientation, and dysregulation; unresolved attachment as rooted in unprocessed trauma or loss; fearful-avoidant attachment as involving high relational ambivalence and emotional turmoil; and dismissing-avoidant attachment as emphasizing emotional detachment and relatively rigid self-reliance.*

---

* Sending appreciation to the researchers out there who know the fine details too vast and complex to be presented in this format.

Disorganized/Dysregulated Attachment

We should return to this primary attachment description for developmental attachment because it has the most consequential findings to date.

Kids who meet the categorization for disorganized attachment were likely exposed to severe stress and feelings of danger that overwhelmed their nervous system. Often the home lives of these children were not reliably attuned or stable enough for them to relax and develop more organized and predictable ways for managing all that was happening to them. Perhaps they grew up in a household racked by domestic violence or lived among extreme poverty in an unsafe neighborhood with under-resourced parents. Of course, experiencing direct physical and/or sexual abuse, serious emotional neglect, or the death of a parent also increases the risk of disorganized and unresolved patterns. Frequently, one or more parents of kids identified as having disorganized attachment suffered from substance abuse, depression, or their own unprocessed loss or trauma. The bottom line is these children are survivors who used whichever strategy worked at the moment. Symptoms in adulthood point to the solutions they found to adapt as a child, which required various coping strategies. This doesn't mean they were necessarily confused, it means that is what worked at the time!

No matter the cause, children raised in emotionally unsafe or physically dangerous conditions are understandably at higher risk for anxiety, depression, aggressive behavior, and self-harm as they age. Because they had to focus primarily on merely surviving while growing up, they never got the chance to develop a stable sense of self or learn needed skills to express and manage their emotions. To cope, many young child-parent pairs often end up in role-reversal relationships, with the child taking responsibility for the parent's welfare as a way to get their needs met as well as to exert a desperately needed sense of control and mastery.

As these kids transition into young adulthood, they often have trouble in their close relationships. Without intervention or support, these young souls have an increased chance of developing serious mental health concerns such as personality struggles (enduring patterns of distress and impairment) and dissociative difficulties (disconnections of memories, thoughts, feeling—even one's identity and sense of self). As parents themselves, many are loving, devoted caregivers who work hard to give their children a better path, but with such a painful early history, the parenting journey often requires a heavier lift. Parenting is deeply influenced by our unconscious stories and early coping strategies, so those with disorganized/dysregulated attachment in childhood are at increased risk of passing on the pain they experienced to their kids. The more these mothers and fathers work at addressing their troubled histories, the more likely they are to break the patterns of danger and risk that plagued them while growing up.

It's Not What Happened to Us, It's What We Do with It

If you're a parent and are worried about your child *or* your parenting skills, we hear you! Even if you think *you* may "be disorganized" or have unresolved trauma, you are not doomed to repeat the past. Many of our most difficult struggles also help us build resilience and insight, especially when we are open to exploring their impact. The fact that you're holding this book in your hands demonstrates that you're interested in healing your hurt heart. You are already practicing mindfulness and self-compassion, and these are two huge parenting wins.

Being reflective about your parenting is excellent; beating yourself up doesn't help anyone and depletes resources you need and deserve. So, take it easy on yourself. Both Ann and Sue have parented for years before fully understanding the impact of the trauma they still carried. Many of us have pockets of unresolved trauma that can creep in when our systems get overwhelmed. Don't be afraid to explore how your painful history is impacting your ongoing relationships; it's *not* looking at it that is much more likely to cause further pain.

And remember this—those of us who started off rough but grew security by working on it can have more capacity for reflection than those who are securely attached naturally. We've worked hard on it, and that work does pay off—for us, our children and their children. We even like to think we are working this hard for those who came before us that were also harmed by people or systems and didn't have the opportunity to understand their pain.

So, don't get discouraged! You are worth it and deserve the rewards that earning security and close relationships bring.

Trauma

Unfortunately, the word *trauma* has become trivialized in popular culture to the point where Hollywood's reliance on a character's experience of trauma has become a plot trope and being in therapy and "working on your trauma" has been included in online dating search criteria. We hear from teenagers that a young breakup or even a bad haircut was "totally traumatic." So, first, let's get clear about what it actually is—and isn't—from a therapist's perspective.

The bottom line is that it's not the event that defines trauma; it's the *experience of the event.* Two people can experience the exact same event yet respond to it very differently. Renowned trauma therapists Bessel van der Kolk, Peter Levine and Paul Conti, for example, see trauma as the imprint of an experience of overwhelming pain, horror, or fear that lives inside you. You remember it not through normal recall, but as a physical reaction in the present.

Think of a balance scale with a pivot point in the middle and two cups on either side. When the incoming shock of an experience outweighs your resources to cope, it tips the scale and impacts your brain and body. The coping resources you have come from inside you (your age, maturity, resilience, emotional regulation skills) or from your environment (a protective person stepping in, adequate support immediately following the event, community pulling together). Said most simply, if the bad outweighs the buffer, the anguish lodges in your body to be understood and processed later (when you do have the resources to cope).

Developmental trauma is associated with attachment disruptions. It occurs when there are many seemingly small incidences, often involving caretakers, that accumulated. Neglect is an overlooked part of developmental trauma and especially damaging because it's the *absence* of something that harmed you, so how do you wrap your young mind around that? These small injuries tipped the cup and overwhelmed the child so that the pain and confusion were partially tucked away in deep limbic implicit memory instead of the normal, hippocampal explicit memory. Since there are often no words with developmental trauma and no explicit narrative understanding available, you sometimes feel like what is wrong is "just you," not what happened to you. Our protective system helps us survive by packing it up and hiding the memory out of plain sight, but that means we continue to carry that loaded suitcase forward and don't know it.

A few more important things about this kind of suffering that set us up to deeply understand unresolved trauma as a factor in adult attachment strategies. Trauma is, to the nervous system, what a concussion is to the brain. A single concussion predisposes the brain to another one. Similarly, once your nervous system has experienced trauma, you're more likely to have trouble processing the next overwhelming event, increasing your chance of developing ongoing symptoms.

An example might help here.

Let's say that you have a parent grappling with serious alcoholism. Maybe that parent didn't "hurt" you directly, but the unpredictability and the lack of recognition of your needs undoubtedly impacted your sense of self. If you later experience sexual abuse or relational violence, those unprocessed memories can become stacked. Now, suppose that in addition to all that, you are gender fluid in a society that is targeting those who stray from gender scripts, so your neuroceptive sonar is playing shark music in the background every time you hear about new laws being put forward to deny autonomy to people like you. You may hardly notice and think you'll simply shrug it off, just as you shrug off so many other microaggressions (subtle signs of bias or outright discrimination that convey hostility, rejection, or disrespect). You ignore sarcastic and demeaning comments and eye roll those who you see subtly pull away, but it adds up.

As a struggling adult, you don't understand how much pain your body is holding because you believe that nothing horrible has ever "happened" to you. Instead, you attribute the problem to yourself, reinforcing negative messages encoded in your attachment map. This is why understanding our nervous system and updating our narratives about ourselves and the sometimes-threatening world we live in is vital in helping you reconnect with your best humanity.

Unresolved Trauma—How to Spot It

How might a pocket of trauma appear in everyday life?

Fortunately, most people who experience tragedy or loss recover naturally, but if you have symptoms today where the past intrudes into the present, you should pay attention. As discussed, simple triggers are small examples of something from our past infiltrating the present. So is avoiding reminders of that event completely. Chronically losing yourself as you compulsively caretake others is a common example of a by-product of unprocessed trauma.

Specifically, trauma can also show up as intrusive thoughts, physical startle reactions, or unexplained hatred of something benign that reminds your amygdala of a threatening experience. It can also come in more subtle forms, such as frequent unexplained headaches, digestive complaints, and many other poorly understood chronic physical conditions.

The bind between wanting closeness but being too afraid to allow it (because at one point that vulnerability was actually dangerous) begins to get at the double bind of unprocessed trauma. Your amygdala "remembers" the danger of your longing even though your PFC does not.

Beth and Carmen, whom you are about to meet, are an example of a relationship in which one partner deals with a history of unprocessed trauma still lodged in her nervous system, leading to confusing tie-dye patterns. Once again, as you read, notice your thoughts and feelings. It takes a lot of practice to make sense of all the incredible data streaming from inside your body and mind at any given moment. We are using your ongoing awareness—and your curiosity about your thoughts, feelings, sensations, and urges—to further develop your most important relational instrument: your sense of self.

Beth and Carmen

Carmen can sense something wrong before she's even fully awake. However, it's the low ghostly sound that gives her body a full shot of adrenaline and pops her eyes open. It's all too familiar, but this time the guttural noises sound otherworldly, like grunts from a wounded animal rather than the love of her life sleeping beside her. She rolls toward Beth to try to rouse her, but she knows better than to startle her.

"Hey, babe, it's me. It's okay . . ."

Carmen places her hand firmly on Beth's strong chest and presses down while moving it back and forth, rocking her gently. She's learned a delicate balance: waking her up just enough to disrupt the nightmare but not enough to wake her up fully. Here's hoping.

"Beth, it's me, babe. You're dreaming. It's okay." Carmen keeps steady pressure on Beth's chest, trying to activate that calm spot that will slow her racing heart.

Beth quiets, and Carmen eventually begins to relax and her eyes grow heavy, but she keeps her hand on Beth's chest to keep the connection. The next thing she knows, Beth pushes her hand off and flails, trying to get out from under the sheets. Snarling at the covers that entrap her, she has flown into a panic.

"Beth!" Carmen says sharply. "Wake up!"

This dream is a bad one, Carmen can tell. She has to get Beth up.

"Hey, hey, hey," Carmen coos, "I've got you." She tries to help Beth throw off the covers but Beth resists letting her help, the visuals from inside her nightmare still flashing before her.

Carmen is too nice for all this—she's a Tinker Bell, not a Hulk—she will never understand the intensity of what emerges in Beth's body, a felt *knowing,* a dream thought.

Now nearly awake, Beth finally frees one leg from under the covers. The cool air on her bare foot brings some measure of relief. Somewhere in her mind, she knows she's overreacting. It was just a dream, but still, she has to get out from under the damn covers she feels are binding her.

"Get *off* me!" she says aloud as she kicks the sheets away. Beth knows only that she wants to escape, and kicking the covers off feels good—so she keeps at it. With a decisive final flick, the remaining cover flops listlessly to the floor.

"Hey, babe, open your eyes, look at me. It's just a dream, I'm right here." Carmen's voice is firm now. She's trying to take charge because she isn't sure what's worse, the nightmares or what she knows is coming next.

"I *am* awake," Beth snaps. "I just got tangled in the sheets; it's too hot in here. It's no big deal." After a pause, she adds, "Go back to sleep." And as she turns onto her side with her back to Carmen, she says, more softly now, "Sorry."

Carmen takes a deep breath to contain what she wants to say and then rolls away from Beth as directed. She's wide awake, of course, and despite the quiet between them, Carmen knows they're both staring into the dark, hearts pounding. They don't speak, but each hopes the other will come close and cuddle or fall asleep without any further interaction.

Carmen weighs whether or not to try to talk to her. She wishes Beth would let her in, scoot over, and curl into her arms, but she never does. She feels the weight of her hopelessness.

She is so tired—tired because it's two o'clock in the morning and tired of repeatedly being jolted awake in the middle of the night. She'll never admit it to Beth, of course, but the truth is Carmen doesn't know what else to do. She wishes Beth would get help but can't nag her about it again without being pushed away. She loves her, but . . . Carmen can feel apathy pulling her in. She can feel her heart hardening.

Meanwhile, Beth is intentionally managing her breath—she quietly inhales, holds it a moment and then slowly exhales to slow her racing heart.

What the hell? she thinks. *Why are these damn nightmares flaring up again? I thought I was over this! Fuck it.*

She leans over and grabs an Ambien from the nightstand. The sedative had helped a lot, bringing a halt to these terrifyingly vivid dreams. She skipped taking one last night and look what happened. Beth swallows the pill without water and calls, "Beyoncé! Come here!"

A scruffy gray-and-white terrier jumps up on request, wiggles into her arms, and cuddles up against her side, letting her snout rest on Beth's arm. Ah, this helps a lot. Beth can now take full breaths, and as she cuddles Beyoncé's warm body, her heartbeat begins to steady.

Two Months Later

Carmen is startled when she arrives home after work and finds Beth there unexpectedly. She's watching TV on the couch—Beyoncé fast asleep in her lap. Something is off here: landscapers have no sick leave, it's beautiful outside, and Beth's boss is far from understanding. Plus, she *never* watches TV.

"Oh, hey, babe, you scared me. What are you doing home so early?" Carmen asks.

Beth doesn't respond. She seems lost in thought. Carmen circles around the couch to face her. "Babe?"

Beth looks up, her lips pursed in a thin, taut line as if trying not to say something. She begins speaking about having a half day off, but Carmen sees it in her eyes. The glaze is there again. Her heart skips.

"Damn it, Beth! You're on those pills again!"

In three long strides, Carmen quickly crosses in front of her and over to the side table, where she knows she'll find the pills, and yanks open the drawer. Sure enough, a new bottle of the powerful painkiller OxyContin rattles into view.

"How long—? Who got them for you?" Carmen is sputtering. "How could you do this again!" It's not a question; she's incensed.

Carmen heads straight for the bathroom, but Beth quickly intercepts her. Surprisingly fast, she grabs Carmen's hand to prevent her from flushing the pills down the toilet. Carmen holds the bottle tightly with her left hand while pushing Beth away with her right. She's hell-bent on ridding their apartment of these criminally addictive drugs.

That's when time slows to a crawl. For the next few seconds, it's as if the two of them are in a scene from some surreal movie. Their bodies get entangled as they move against one another, a blur of pulling and grasping and twisting, but with a shove Carmen gains space between them and is on the move again.

As if in slow motion, Beth desperately grabs the back of Carmen's shirt, causing them both to lose their footings and tumble down, Carmen hitting the floor first and Beth crumpling on top of her. As they fall, they feel the bottle dislodge from Carmen's hand.

The pill bottle rattles as it rolls down the hallway on the cold tile. Beth scrambles, moving her thick body on her knees to collect it. These were goddamn expensive; no way is she letting them get flushed! After scooping up the bottle, she looks back at Carmen, who is lying flat on her back, crying in between gasps for breath. Pain blazes in her shoulder.

"I'm so sorry, babe!" Beth apologizes while she uses the wall to clamber back up to her feet before coming back for Carmen. She tries to gather herself. "You know I didn't mean to hurt you! That fall was a total accident. Oh my God, are you okay?"

She leans down and tenderly tries to help her partner stand, but Carmen doesn't take her hand. Instead, Carmen covers her face with both hands. It's as if she's trying to block out Beth's excuses.

Just like that, something between them has changed; they both feel it. A hardness. Carmen sits up on her own.

She's no longer crying. In fact, she's strangely calm. "You have to get help, Beth," she says, her voice surprisingly calm and steady. "I'm not talking about those pills. I'm talking about getting help with your issues. You are destroying yourself and us."

Beth tries to defend herself and reassure Carmen at the same time. She is talking fast and can feel fear engulfing her. This is worse than fighting. "I'll flush them myself!" Beth swears.

But it doesn't matter anymore. Carmen gets to her feet and leans against the wall in the hallway. Meanwhile, Beth makes a big show of performing the ritual they've repeated far too many times, narrating what is happening as she allegedly empties the bottle of OxyContin down the toilet, announcing the flush as she presses the handle. However, Carmen has already grabbed her phone, keys, and bag and quietly slipped out the front door.

As she closes it softly behind her, she can feel the pain in her chest and identifies this feeling as true heart break. She just doesn't have enough fight left to save them both. And she doesn't even care if Beth flushed the pills or not. She just knows she has to leave.

Making Sense of It All

As Beth fought the sheets while waking up from her nightmare, she was "in" an experience of being trapped or restricted in some way. It felt entirely real to her, as if it were literally happening at that moment, so her urgency matched the panic coursing through her. Though Beth is a loving, devoted partner and a talented self-taught landscape designer whose customers love her, her sense of herself and her history is fragmented, and those fragments come out in snippets she doesn't yet understand.

When her guard is down at night, her stored trauma comes through as nightmares. It also leaks out as persistent unexplained feelings of unworthiness even though she is deeply loved in her current relationship—which is why Carmen's love will never be enough to heal Beth's wounded heart. Beth self-sabotages her projects at work when she begins to have success, blowing deadlines as she's given more responsibility in the growing company. This keeps her underemployed compared to where her natural talent and drive would normally land her. These behaviors just don't make sense to her or her employer, which adds to underlying feelings of shame. As you saw above, these present-day disrupted reactions are a major indicator of past trauma, as is her reliance on substances* to manage the pain she's avoiding.

Our body's solution to managing terror works in the short run. Cutting off intense feelings through disassociation, drug use, confusion, or escape does work. The problem is it's a pause button—our body holds the pain, it doesn't forget, and when the opportunity arises, it escapes one way or the other.

This is how the intergenerational cycle of abuse gets transmitted. Parents who grew up experiencing abuse firsthand often commit to themselves they will be different. They know and believe that flying off the handle and striking their child verbally or physically will only cause harm. They know what to do, they know what not to do, and they are often very motivated to be a patient parent who talks through difficulties. However, the problem emerges when the fragments lodged in their body become activated and they fill with helpless rage or confusion they try to mask.

When we act in ways that defy who we want to be, always start with massive doses of self-compassion—this is necessary to have the chops for

---

* Opiates are said to mimic the feeling of "being loved." It is not a stretch to confuse the terms *OxyContin* and *oxytocin*. In addition to the predatory aspects of the opioid epidemic, it's crucial to recognize that vulnerable people seek solace for their pain and fears yet are offered a shortcut that bypasses our inherent need for human connection, warm expressions, and a sense of belonging.

the deep exploration ahead. Chronic shame never works to heal anything and doesn't stop behaviors we know we want to change. Instead, believe it or not, self-compassion is the most direct link to creating deep change.

If that sounds too woo-woo, look to Dr. Kristin Neff's research to explore further, starting with her book *Fierce Self-Compassion*. Dr. Neff is an associate professor in educational psychology at the University of Texas and co-founder of the nonprofit Center for Mindful Self-Compassion. We appreciate the accessibility of her work; you can find the science behind these techniques and free mindfulness resources on her site, self-compassion.org. Once you recognize the benefits of self-compassion and mindfulness, there are a ton of readily accessible tools available—look into free resources from UCLA's Mindful Awareness Research Center (MARC)[*] and a personal favorite, Tara Brach's free mindfulness exercises[†] are a good starting place.

If you do the work to process your trauma—usually with a therapist or other mental health professional—you are less likely to fall into an implicit pit of trauma and repeat the self-destructive patterns that you so want to change. And, if you do, you can learn to manage the big emotions just as well as someone with a more secure attachment history. However, this can take work, and a lot of courage.

A Deeper Look at Trauma Defenses

Beth typically copes with her inner pains by dismissing and avoiding vulnerability and using blue strategies on the daily. However, because of her unresolved trauma, she often falls into the unresolved tie-dye puddle.

Beth's unconscious doesn't produce terrifying dreams to torment her; they are a natural response to the implicit overwhelming danger her body has stored. It's how the brain integrates the fragmented experience, so consider symptoms as attempts to resolve it. Beth uses OxyContin to dampen her reactivity and to regulate herself, a struggle that ultimately drives Carmen away. This is a common and painful reality for many.

For Beth, turning to pills rather than to her partner continues a

---

[*]   https://www.uclahealth.org/programs/marc/about-us/sources.
[†]   https://www.tarabrach.com/guided-meditations/.

pseudo-independent facade. We can never heal trauma alone, despite how much we wish we could. There are many healers around you—just look for safe people who care, they've been the ones delivering mental health through the ages. There are also online support communities and in-person self-help support groups. For those who cannot access services directly, there is evidence that even listening to mental health–related podcasts makes a significant difference, especially for those with the lowest level of education and mental health literacy! Still, there is no escaping that ultimately you will need new, safe connections in real life to heal at the deepest level.

If intimacy with people sounds too intimidating to start with, no worries, there are other ways to build that part of ourselves and our system. Think about Beth's pup, Beyoncé! Pets really do help! That oxytocin pathway doesn't care if the eyes staring at you in adoration belong to a human being or to a scruffy gray-and-white terrier; it needs the back and forth of attachment, that feeling of another wanting to be close to you.

In the MARS framework, Beth's experience of disorganization is represented in the multicolored puddle you see *beneath* the spectrum, which represents how we feel when our organized coping strategies collapse. As you can see, we don't conceptualize disorganization as a place *on* the MARS spectrum arrow, but below it. Tie-dye is not a trait or an organized attachment map. You don't have an identity that is "unresolved attachment"; rather, you get disorganized at times. These can be rare moments or happen frequently and last for longer periods of time. It is all dependent on how much trauma you carry with you, whether or not you've received help, and how safe you are in the present.

What Does a Disorganized Pocket Feel Like?

When you're stranded in a more severe disorganized pocket, you'll likely have trouble tracking your thoughts, experience confusion about what is happening, or feel overwhelmed or overactivated. Your mind and even your body might feel like it's spinning, and you might dissociate, a word that describes a feeling of disconnection from your surroundings, emotions, or even from yourself. When in this state, you may feel frightened or overwhelmed and want to be taken care of, yet you are understandably terrified of dependency and closeness. Even in safe relationships, we may get triggered and want to push away, begin to quarrel, or test the other person, to see if they really care. These symptoms were once solutions, and they were the most adaptive solution in times of danger when no relief was in sight.

This is a tough topic. We mean this with our full hearts when we say: Even if your soul has been trampled, please work to heal and discover your worth, value, and preciousness as a human being.

Later That Day

All afternoon, Carmen's phone is blowing up. Beth is desperate, apologetic, and saying all the right things. She's off the Oxys for good, she insists, having flushed them down the toilet for the last time. It was a bad idea, she knew, but she just wanted to be able to rest. Her back really hurt; it wasn't what Carmen thought. Same song, same verse.

This time, things have changed for Carmen. About a year before, Carmen began attending meetings of Nar-Anon, a support network for families, friends, and loved ones of people addicted to narcotics. The groups were helpful, but things really improved once a fellow member agreed to be her personal sponsor, about nine months in. Carmen has come to understand that she can't love Beth into sobriety and that, frankly, the conflict between them wasn't only about the pills. She needed to see who was directly in front of her, not be in love with the memory of Beth or keep hoping for a different Beth in the future. Carmen learned to keep the focus on herself and not hide behind Beth's more obvious troubles—she had plenty to look at even if Beth wasn't in the picture. Things would never get better if Beth didn't face what she was running from, but they also wouldn't get better if Carmen didn't do the same.

This time, Carmen was ready to hold herself more firmly in her own work. Carmen stopped responding to all of Beth's texts. Instead, she types in the number to the non-profit addiction clinic Beth knows about but has so far avoided and the number to her former youth pastor, Ben. Carmen feels that Ben is the only one who might know how to help her, as they were once close, but Beth hasn't spoken to or about him in years.

After sending those numbers, Carmen powers down her phone and notices that she feels surprisingly relieved.

A Month After Carmen Blocked Beth's Calls

Ben is sitting at his desk eating lunch while catching up on some emails, when his phone buzzes. He looks at the caller ID. Blocked, it reads. He answers reluctantly.

Hearing only silence, he begins to hang up, but something stops him.

"Hello?" he says again. He can tell the line is live and the caller is still there because he faintly hears something in the background, maybe the yip of a small dog?

"Is anyone there?" Silence. It's the silence that stirs something familiar in his gut. An odd thought flashes forward.

"Beth?" he asks incredulously. He's hoped for her to reach out for so long, and this was how their calls often started.

When she disappeared ten years earlier, at the age of sixteen, he had not been surprised. He'd worked to imagine her perspective, and from her eyes, it was true that she had no choice but to leave home. Her mom had Beth when she was just sixteen, a child herself. She had a series of shady boyfriends who would stay for a bit and then rotate out soon enough. Before Beth left for good, her mom remarried, and while Beth never said it directly, Ben suspected that the stepfather was sexually abusing her. On top of that, Beth was more her mother's caretaker than the other way around, and the girl had no one else.

That's how she entered the church, on her own at fourteen. Beth was yearning for safe human contact, not spiritual enlightenment, and she trusted no one when she first arrived. Ben's role as youth pastor put working with her squarely on his shoulders, and he was up to the task. Thinking back to their first meeting, he feels a sudden surge of sadness and regret, and his eyes grow moist.

"Beth, if it's you, please . . . say something," he implores.

This time she clears her throat to speak but can't get her voice out clearly. That's enough, though; he heard her.

"Yes, it's you. Okay. That's good, don't hang up."

He's grinning and tearing up. "Okay, okay, okay . . . Have you talked to your mom? I want you to know she's okay." Ben is pacing now.

Beth is leaning against the wall in her kitchen but now slides down slowly to the floor, still cradling the phone. The mention of her mom feels like a stab to the heart; she's tried so hard not to even think of her. It is her life's greatest shame to have left her.

Oh no, I shouldn't have brought up her mom, Ben chastises himself, but then goes on.

"I want you to know that she's okay. She comes into services now and then and often stops by my office to keep in touch. She's doing well."

Silence.

Now Ben speaks slowly and calmly; he does not want to rush this. Beth's disappearance shocked them all, and Ben regretted that he couldn't protect her.

He takes a shot and says, "You did the right thing, Beth. You were in an impossible situation, you had to leave."

She'd shared enough with him that he filled in the blanks to put together the rest of the story as best he could. He saw Beth's mom as a broken woman—more of a timid child herself. She was a traveling nurse and they'd dispassionately moved many times for reasons he didn't understand until they landed in Phoenix. He'd imagined the double bind. Beth grew up with a mom she loved and felt sorry for, but couldn't trust. She couldn't rely on her mom for protection, so instead she worked to keep her mom functioning for the both of them.

This worked out okay until her new stepfather came on the scene. Ben didn't know the details but was sure he was physically or sexually abusing Beth by the hints Beth dropped but wouldn't quite say. He realized later why she couldn't say—it would destroy what little semblance of family they had.

Her "stepfather" brought her mother much-needed stability. Deeper down, Beth wasn't positive her mom would stand by her even if she did know the truth. What if her mom didn't believe her? That would just break Beth. She'd rather disappear and take care of herself than risk the devastation of betrayal from the only family she had.

If she told Ben, he'd have to call social services to protect her, but for him to turn her family in . . . Beth would have experienced it as the ultimate betrayal of her trust. So, when the young pastor asked her directly, she panicked and bolted.

Ben scrambles to focus.

"You didn't abandon anyone, Beth. You *had* to leave. It's okay, it was smart. I'm here for you. You don't have to do this alone . . ."

Beth is sitting on the kitchen floor, hugging her knees to her chest. She rocks gently back and forth while holding the phone a few inches away from her mouth so that Ben doesn't hear her crying.

Beth is listening to every word, every syllable. She pours herself into the space between the words, scanning for the truth, and she softens as he speaks.

He isn't mad at her, she begins to believe. He is being kind. Maybe, just maybe (hope can be a dangerous emotion), he understands?

Upon registering "You don't have to do this alone," the seal around her heart gently gives way.

"I'm . . . sorry," she chokes. The words catch, and she isn't sure Ben got it, but the words don't matter. The tears finally come, and her body quakes in relief. His eyes flood along with hers, and, finally, they cry together.

Her loyal terrier-mutt, Beyoncé, is on point, standing guard in the kitchen, and strangely, Beth lets herself feel hope for the first time she can remember.

***

Let's take a breath and consider what is happening in the story. What thoughts and feelings do you notice? Remember not everyone will respond to the same story similarly, so we continue to cultivate curiosity directed inward.

Did you notice how it was confusing to piece together Beth's story? That's how it is working with trauma: pain from the past can begin to come into focus, only to vanish or to get blurry and feel incomplete. That's because it *isn't* complete, it is fragmented, and the listener's experience parallels that of the person trying to put it together. It's not just that the memory itself is fragmented, but the important ongoing self-understanding that is necessary to develop a coherent sense of yourself and the world is choppy, too.

Let your thoughts catch up and notice (and honor) your feelings. Can you name an emotion or describe what your body feels like? It's funny, these will be the same instructions Beth will hear over and over when she finally consents to enter treatment for her addiction. Naming your feelings is a way to ground and "organize," which she needs desperately. By recognizing feelings and accepting them, they naturally shift; you don't have to "do" anything with them. This process is called many things in the world of clinical therapy—metacognition, mindsight, reflective function—but mindfully noticing your thoughts and feelings is just plain old self-care.

By staying in the present, resisting dissociation, and keeping your mind on track (staying out of the puddle), you can begin to take in new information and disrupt old assumptions. You can go from just surviving to growing and learning and healing.

In the moment above where she cries with Ben, Beth can finally feel her pain and share her inner anguish with someone she trusts. This is a brand-new experience of felt security that, if repeated (and repeated . . . and repeated), will absolutely shift the wiring in her lower stressed-out brain, which will change her vigilant mind, which will open her to the safety of connection and belonging that she has deserved all along.

The same is true for you. Love and understanding while you face your gremlins will physically heal your wounded brain and hurt heart.

7

When Systems
Create Insecurity

Structural Inequity: Some Straight Talk

While it may seem implausible, relating to someone from your secure state of mind increases the likelihood of the other person's social engagement, decreases misperception of threat, regulates neurobiological and behavioral stress responses, increases empathy, enhances a feeling of being part of something larger than oneself, and it directly reduces discriminatory and aggressive behavior toward those outside one's social group!

That is why the premise of this book is about building strength through connection, curiosity, and openness, rather than letting fear and unconscious self-protection control us. Holding on to your secure self is indeed a powerful tool, and it works—but boy is it slippery, especially when it comes to conversations about bias, race, gender, and discrimination. This chapter may give you a workout; let's see.

We can't rest in our own security if it doesn't extend beyond ourselves and our own epicenter because to exclude social and contextual factors in a deep discussion of secure relating would be to ignore one of its core principles—holding self *and* holding others. This inherently means to securely relate we need to unravel how the systems we live in promote and suppress the sense of security in us and those around us. To make change beyond just us, we have to play the long game. So, as we discuss having awareness and impact on the systems we live in, we want to go slow and stay curious; reflect on things we have held as certain, and challenge our own dismissing aloofness to such important matters. That is the secure relating practice.

The systems we are referring to are the ones created by those in power to hold on to that power, and they are enshrined by many local and national laws, as well as corporate policies and what are considered community "norms," designed to maintain the status quo. Maintaining status quo means preventing change, which involves reinforcing existing discrimination and continuing to perpetuate inequities that serve those in charge. Much of the support of these systems comes from the belief that power keeps us safe and change feels threatening.

We can't see our implicit bias, so why not take a test to see where you fall? Project Implicit is a nonprofit collaborative of international researchers on implicit social cognition. They work to educate the public about bias and to provide a "virtual laboratory" for collecting data and conducting research that forms the basis of our scientific knowledge about bias and disparities. Anonymously take the implicit bias test on a wide variety of subjects and get a sense of where you stand. The link to take the test is https://implicit.harvard.edu/implicit/takeatest.html.

Race and Attachment

Let's explore how race and attachment intersect by stepping into someone else's shoes by meeting Briana.[*] She is a thirty-six-old divorced mother with two school-aged children. She was raised in primarily Black and Brown neighborhoods, and, up until now, her school experience was in mixed-race institutions. She moved to Raleigh, North Carolina, with her kids about a year ago to attend graduate school at a predominantly white university.

She's academically intelligent, so she naturally excelled, but she's been having trouble motivating herself lately and missing assignments,

---

[*] Inspired by conversations with Gliceria Pérez, LCSW, and Debra Chatman-Finley, LPC. See "Navigating Racial Trauma & Identity with Gliceria Pérez and Debra Chatman-Finley, pts. 1 and 2," May 2, 2023, and May 9, 2023, *Therapist Uncensored*. Used with permission.

which is unusual for her. While she expected graduate school to be challenging, Briana didn't anticipate experiencing such high levels of stress, anxiety, and disconnectedness. As she thought about it, several unsettling interactions with her white professors and fellow students stood out, causing her to feel something she was struggling to understand. She had noticed that in class discussions, her contributions were minimized and that professors tended to overlook her. This subtle but repeated distancing stung, and she was beginning to doubt herself and her abilities, and question her decision to pursue graduate education.

Knowing that she was falling behind and afraid her grades would slip, Briana decided to seek help at the university's counseling center. There was a waiting list to get assigned to an individual counselor, but there was an immediate opening in a process group for women of color (a process group is when members explore deeper thoughts and feelings that arise within the group experience). Briana was initially reluctant to join because she didn't think being a person of color was the issue; instead, she wanted to talk about her school stress as well as her strained relationship with her boyfriend. However, when she learned the group's facilitator was a Cuban American Black woman, she was intrigued and decided to give it a try.

The impact was immediate—Briana felt the power of working with a therapist of color and of sitting with other BIPOC women in the first session. In fact, she was shocked at how moving the experience was. She'd been in therapy before with white therapists and, at the time, described the experiences as positive, but in hindsight, she realized they had never discussed the issue of race. It just never came up. The strength of this group of marginalized women engaging in candid discussions had a profound impact, magnifying the experience.

The group became a uniquely safe space where the influence of race was openly and unapologetically discussed. They enjoyed creating their own non-Eurocentric therapy norms. For example, they adopted a practice of sharing homemade food each session. Cooking and communal eating was a common expression of love for the members, and an opportunity to express some of their cultural similarities and differences. They freely hugged one another, and time boundaries were more elastic and flexible based on the group's needs.

One day, Briana had a lightbulb moment that accelerated the changes she was experiencing. She noticed that while sitting in the group space, something she was used to feeling was suddenly missing. Absent were the background feelings of her usual stress, anxiety, and disconnection; she felt safe, connected, and energized instead. What a revelation!

For as long as she could remember, Briana had assumed that the uncomfortable feeling inside was due to some inadequacy in *her*. Now she was coming to discover the truth: much of the roiling she felt internally was set off by the racial microaggressions and overt discrimination she lived through every day.

It wasn't long before Briana realized how hard she'd being trying to make herself "acceptable" to her white professors and fellow students. She had absorbed stereotypes about her race so deeply that she'd inadvertently learned to aspire to what was held up as desirable by the dominant culture. In doing so, she was rejecting those parts of herself that were rejected by the world at large and trying to be what they valued. *Who am I*, she wondered—and she set out to reclaim those important parts of herself she'd disowned. This epiphany—how she'd been inadvertently whitewashed—was all she needed to know to no longer feel so lost and timid. She was then empowered to begin "re-seasoning"* back to her spicy, non-white authentic self.

This led to Briana beginning to study race. One eye-opening thing she learned was that Black people, beginning in childhood, tended to carry higher cortisol levels than their white peers. At first, Briana couldn't wrap her mind around this; after all, she'd always had a close relationship with her warm, generous mother. But she gradually came to appreciate how the generational impact of racial violence that has plagued her community for so long has been carried forward in their DNA. This enraged her but also contributed to Briana's rediscovering herself. She now had language for the barrage of slights and subtle racism that she'd been enduring throughout her education. Overt acts of bigotry were appalling, of course, but, in a way, they were easier to fend off and not internalize than covert racism, which can be so insidious as to cause Briana and many others not perceived as white to doubt themselves so fundamentally.

---

*   Thanks to Gliceria Pérez and Debra Chatman-Finley for this term.

Briana's mother and father, like so many Black parents, emphasized her beauty and intelligence to boost her confidence. They also insisted that she focus on education as a way to buffer racial discrimination and taught her safety practices for anticipated hostility. Despite their efforts, Briana couldn't escape the constant societal messages that made her feel unimportant, overlooked, and undervalued and took such a toll on her self-esteem and sense of self-worth.

She continued this group until she graduated and credits it with opening her eyes to the now obvious signs around her and thus positively changing her life and her children's lives forever.

Invisible Wounds of Systematic Trauma

Briana's heightened awareness of the impact of racism on her sense of self points to just a few of the structural inequities and systemic barriers that are so "normal" and insidious that even this bright, articulate, secure woman didn't consciously realize the depth of how she'd been harmed. That's because we all don't truly recognize it; the subtle assumed superiority of people defined and perceived as white is so embedded it is invisible, which is why it makes white people so upset when they are accused of being "racist" (i.e., being neo-Nazis or belonging to an extreme hate group). That *is* absurd to most people. But Robin DiAngelo, in her book *What Does It Mean to Be White?*, explains that white supremacy does not refer to individual people or individual intentions. It is the political-economic social system where historical systems were erected by the people in power at the time to accumulate and hold on to wealth and power. The impact of those systems continues today so subtly that, for example, "white" is not thought of as a race but the norm, and People of Color are deviations of that norm.

It's the pervasive insidiousness of these underlying systematic inequities that has shaped Briana's relational nervous system and impacted opportunities in life right along with her relational history and early attachment experiences.

Dr. Kenneth Hardy, professor at Drexel University and president of the Eikenberg Academy for Social Justice and Clinical and Organization Consultation, has focused on racial trauma and healing. He works to name the invisible wounds of racial trauma that accumulate over time for People of Color. He describes the unrecognized impact of subjugation as including an assaulted sense of self, internalized devaluation, psychological homelessness,* complex and ambiguous grief and loss, survival orientation, and rage. Linda Thai is a somatic practitioner† trauma therapist and former child refugee that champions the experience of immigrants and whose techniques are designed to reconnect you to your history and your lost community. She amplifies Hardy's work and adds to the list above "the unconscious idealization of characteristics of those in power." Just as children can internalize the traits and values of their abusive parents, individuals and groups can internalize the messages of those in positions of power.

Again, how can your connection system purr when you are continually experiencing designed oppression and institutionalized inequities? There are institutions and policies that inherently promote uncertainty and discrimination among groups based on, for example, their religious or cultural identity, immigration status, socioeconomic status, race, ethnicity, gender, sexual orientation, age, or physical ability. Some examples include school systems with unequal educational opportunities; the persistent gender pay gap; unequal access to quality medical care; housing bias; mortgage and lending bias; and racial profiling that feeds into our criminal justice system. These are all examples of existing systems that serve to maintain oppression and protect the comfort and power of those that have it.

Let's just take the last example, the criminal justice system, but we could choose any of them.

Statistically, people of the global majority (Black and Indigenous People

---

*   Hardy's "psychological homelessness" refers to alienation from one's cultural or racial identity and the more literal experience of being displaced from one's home, or one's land. You sense you don't completely belong in your adopted land or cultural or racial group, nor do you feel you fit in within the dominant culture.
†   Somatic practitioners focus on healing through the body-mind connection, a critical part of rewiring the injured nervous system that we will review in part III.

of Color) are disproportionately stopped, searched, arrested, charged, and convicted relative to their white counterparts. Their sentences are longer and they are overrepresented in prison. Psychological factors such as the implicit bias of police, prosecutors, voters, judges, and jurors play a part, as do policies such as mandatory sentencing guidelines. Language barriers, distrust of the system, socioeconomic disadvantages, and unequal access to legal resources make people outside the dominant culture more vulnerable to discriminatory policies—and incarceration negatively impacts the individual, their family, and their community.

A study from the Center on the Developing Child at Harvard University highlights the detrimental impact of adversity and excessive stress on marginalized families. A growing body of evidence from both the biological and social sciences suggests having to contend with systemic racism and everyday discrimination fires up the stress response system. This should not be surprising to us at this point.

Since this strain is ongoing, the stress accelerator wears tremendously on the body. Black people especially but also other People of Color have more chronic health problems and shorter life spans than white people, regardless of income. The stress starts early and takes energy away from healthy exploration, school readiness, and learning about feelings and emotional regulation.

As you can see, the context umbrella has an even greater and more direct biopsychosocial impacts on our sense of self and our physical well-being than attachment alone. It's impossible to unwind them.

When Defensive Activation *Is* Security

So as you can see, for those in marginalized communities or who live in personally threatening situations, being in the red zone or blue zone may not have anything to do with attachment or unnecessary defensiveness. Your body may be accurately sensing an ongoing real threat that requires you to engage and maintain your defensive position. However it remains true that being able to turn down that chronic activation can be useful.

No one should judge how emotions are expressed or suppressed; if trust is given or withheld and whether vulnerability is displayed or down-played. When marginalized individuals consistently face unfair or harsh treatment from authority figures such as teachers and law enforcement, it is adaptive to be vigilant and be able to exert emotional control. While insecure attachment can generally lead to challenges later in life, what may appear as insecurity in BIPOC children is often a coping mechanism for self-protection.

Security for BIPOC teenagers may look different than traditionally expected. In neighborhoods where the impact of racism is prevalent, teenagers are more likely to lean blue, or have a dismissing attachment stance. This raises the question of what dismissing attachment truly signifies in that particular context. For white teenagers, dismissing attachment predicts an increase in depressive symptoms during adolescence, but its negative impact on the mental health of Black teenagers is less pronounced.

Socioeconomics and Attachment

Severe poverty, regardless of a person's race, is another rib of the context umbrella that biologically and psychologically changes us. Considering the impact chronic stress has on our bodies, it's easy to understand how poverty negatively and directly impacts parenting. Think about what happens to your parenting or personal relating abilities when you're steeped in cortisol-related daily stress.

Good parenting on one level has nothing whatsover to do with wealth. However, when our interpersonal skills suffer, robbing us of patience, bandwidth to connect, and the ability to transition to our next task, we certainly aren't our best selves. Add to that the stress of chronic worry about something as fundamental as paying the rent and affording basic necessities, and you can see how these stressors might take over any green zone ambitions and impair a person's ability to regulate.

Chronic poverty also has a cascade effect independent of your relational history. When parents must work long hours, keep multiple jobs, and don't have access to health insurance, child care, or sick leave, they are focused almost exclusively on simply surviving. With this kind of strain on the system, there are often limited reserves of sensitivity, empathy, patience, connectivity, and expressions of love and happiness.

Maintaining and passing down whatever protective strategies work is a natural side effect of living in a threatening environment. Unsurprisingly, children raised in poverty have a much higher risk of experiencing adversity in the form of neglect, abuse, domestic violence, and family instability. Each of these factors negatively impacts the child's development; the more incidents they have, the more challenges they are predicted to face. Put another way: those with higher adverse social factors show up in attachment science with lower rates of secure attachment patterns in childhood. Rather than pathologizing these kids, it is imperative that we always consider the context and biology shaping their journey.

The increased risk of insecure and dysregulated attachment patterns among children raised in poverty and from families of color is not *because of* their race or their economic status. Instead, it stems from the additional strain *imposed by the surrounding systems* that impedes healthy development of the child's protective and connection circuits.

A 2023 review of studies by the US Department of Health and Human Services—Healthy People 2030—found that both structural discrimination (housing, healthcare, schools) and individual discrimination (based on race, age, gender, sexuality, and physical ability) have measurable negative impacts on physical health and create signs of trauma. Instead of blaming individual parents or families, look at the limited access to quality education, quality childcare, healthcare disparities, racial profiling, unequal job opportunities, and housing discrimination that are not healthy, ventral vagal–friendly conditions for anyone.

Safety from the Outside In

In environments that are inherently full of stress and threat, coping strategies aimed at self-protection are on overdrive and are required for survival. A Latinx man trying to get respect at work may feel forced to be more explicitly verbally and nonverbally deferential, not because he's anxious or dismissive but because he has learned what is culturally expected to thrive in that environment and has become adept at *code-switching*,* a secure relating skill for him. This is what makes the integration of culture and context so important in any discussion about security. Focusing on this man's secure-relating ability without consideration for his real-world sense of safety and danger would be a mistake.

At times security must come from the outside in, so growing secure relating will always need to include creating more systematic protections for those in marginalized communities. Having a secure base buffers the negative biopsychological stress response of those who experience bigotry and discrimination. It's not the ultimate answer, of course; the real change needs to come from the systems, not from victims of the system—but in a world where long-term change is slow, a secure base is more than just an ability to relate well to others; it's a protection system in itself. In fact, this is exactly what Briana's group composed of women students of color provided for her.

Culture and Attachment

Families in all cultures value children and try to do their best for them, yet the expression of care and love varies wildly. In truth, there are many good paths to helping an infant become a healthy, well-functioning adult, and parents worldwide generally do what they believe is optimal for their brood.

The primary goal of parenting is to help the child best adapt to the particular environment in which they live, their specific family, at this point in time in their unique community. This gets tricky though, because defining optimal varies even from person to person, and there is as much difference within cultures and countries as across them. Just think of the different parenting values among your grandmother, your mother,

---

* Code-switching in this case refers to being able to adapt to changes in environment by shifting tone, nonverbal behaviors, and dialect to fit in. A Latinx teen going to a white school but living in a BIPOC neighborhood may code-switch in both places as a healthy adaptation to differences in culture.

and yourself. Norms of what is best for a child vary from generation to generation, even between parents within the same family, so beware of overgeneralizing when it comes to culture.

The science of attachment and what it says about culture and context has changed a lot over the decades. As mentioned, the theory itself has roots in East Africa: the foundational observations that led to the original infant attachment assessment, the Strange Situation, were from Mary Ainsworth's careful observation of Ugandan mothers and their babies. In the last two decades, there has been an explosion of exceptional cross-cultural work documenting patterns of caregiving and attachment in more than twenty-five non-Western countries.

Still, there is no escaping the truth that attachment theory has always had blind spots and inherent exclusions. How could it not? No one is free of implicit dominant culture bias: assumptions based on the idea that what seems normal to us will be normal for you. These biases exist in most social science research, which is why it's so important to include the contributions of Black and Indigenous People of Color across generations, social classes, and locations around the world. We need to include historians who have been chronicling these effects and have a deep and context-specific understanding of how to heal their communities from within. Fortunately, there are ongoing efforts in attachment research to collaborate with underrepresented communities to incorporate a more nuanced understanding of what constitutes healthy human development in non-white and non-Western populations.

In the meantime, we will summarize important cultural criticism for you below.

In an influential 2010 Behavioral and Brain Sciences paper, the authors argue that the West is the psychological cradle of the world because most researchers and research subjects in psychology fit the WEIRD acronym: Western, educated, industrialized, rich, and democratic (WEIRD). This leads to shared cultural assumptions and does not represent the vast majority of humans across the globe. Child development studies continue to be centered around Western-style parenting (i.e., families with high levels of formal education, older first parenthood, few children in the family, and a two-generation biologically related household), yet the

Western middle class represents only about 5 percent of the world's population.

It's important to get this right—the theory informs science, clinical practice, and even international policy, all of which can and does impact families directly. Making sure the theory does not get misapplied in a way that can cause harm is not just an academic exercise.

For example, as the theory was popularized, some individuals and groups used it to support policies to keep women home. They argued against daycare and jobs for mothers, suggesting that a child's attachment to their mother is compromised if she is not the primary caregiver, a misuse of the original research. In response, a very important consensus paper was published in January 2021, signed by fifty-five attachment researchers, to provide guidance for what the science does and does not say. It specifically clarified the issue in regard to using these measures in child custody and child welfare cases.

Using attachment concepts without proper assessments or believing insecure attachment is a valid indicator of insufficient care—which is not true—can have devastating effects for the child and the family in child-welfare settings. Families migrating from non-Western cultures being assessed as adequate or inadequate parents are particularly at risk for misunderstandings related to implicit culture bias when devoid of context.

Finally, the United Nations' Convention of the Rights of the Child (CRC) has adopted standards for children's rights that reflect what they believe are uniform standards for child development, but that are in fact based on Western parenting values.

Morelli et al. conclude,

A notable feature of the CRC is that children's rights have priority over parents' rights. However, this priority is unfamiliar for many communities where children are not viewed as separate individuals outside of their families, but are, instead, nested within the identity of their parents, wider kin group, or community at large. In such contexts, the notion of separating the rights of children from the family or community circle would be deeply and structurally—indeed, ethically—problematic.

Scientific knowledge based in one part of the world can unintentionally eclipse Indigenous knowledge and beliefs in another. Drawing upon and incorporating the history and trauma experienced within cultures is an important way to tap into Indigenous wisdom. Maria Yellow Horse Brave Heart's (Hunkpapa/Oglala Lakota) work has been instrumental in raising awareness of historical trauma and unresolved grief within Native American communities. She is an associate professor in the Department of Psychiatry at the University of New Mexico in the Center for Rural and Community Behavioral Health. She has worked to ensure that those working within the area of mental health for American Indian/Native Alaskan populations incorporate the damage those historical traumas have had in terms of culture, identity, and spirituality. She advocates for recognizing that assaults to a community, such as colonization, forced displacement, discrimination, and cultural suppression are passed down through generations and that mental health issues should not be attributed only to the individual suffering without also taking into account their cultural and historic context.

Using Indigenous wisdom is not just for native communities; it can be translated for children and families in many other cultures, including the West. Dr. Martin Brokenleg is a well-known educator, author, and speaker, particularly recognized for his work in the field of Native American and Indigenous resilience. The Circle of Courage is a model of positive youth development that integrates Native American philosophies of child-rearing, the heritage of early pioneers in education and youth work, and contemporary resilience research. The Circle of Courage is based in four universal growth needs of all children: belonging, mastery, independence, and generosity, but placed in context of Native American history. Youth from many cultures around the world can gain from such wisdom.

We will end this section on culture and attachment with an example of an identified culturally imbued research gap, the issue of *alloparenting*, which is cooperative primary care of children by siblings, extended family, and community members. Early attachment research focused on the caregiver-infant bond, with the mother being the major attachment figure in the life of the developing child. While research has expanded to include daycares and extended family, they are often considered exceptions, with the focus remaining on the parent-child bond specifically. Interestingly, alloparenting is a universal practice for the human species but has not been recognized adequately by those studying child development.* By the age of three, 90 percent of American children experience regular alloparenting care, and in some cultures that is the primary form of parental behavior.

Heidi Keller, a professor emeritus of psychology at the University of Osnabrück who has studied culture and attachment, suggests that the focus should shift from the individual child to the network of relationships around the child. She argues that alloparenting is the norm not the exception in childcare practices worldwide and represents a stable, nonchaotic foundation that supports the child's development within their cultural context. Primary focus on the infant is seen as a benefit of the WEIRD environment that affords a parent the time and basic security to focus primarily on her children. In other cultures, the exclusive focus on the baby could endanger them both, thus a network of caregivers—including other children—support the developing child. We can all benefit from tapping into cultural wisdom, and listening and learning from a wider, collective wisdom when it comes to raising healthy humans.

Many believe that if John Bowlby, the pioneering attachment theorist, were alive today, he would be eager to explore the influence of race, social class, culture, and context on child development. His work already recognized the significance of the environment in shaping children's lives, making the exploration of attachment within diverse cultural contexts a natural progression for him. Thus, there is a pressing need for increased focus on these critical areas to achieve a more comprehensive understanding of intergenerational trauma and the various impacts on child development that as a civil society we have the capacity to change.

Don't go guardrail to guardrail and love the theory then abandon it

---

*   It is speculated that it was a blind spot for so long because of cultural assumptions about parenting (biological parent/child focus), but also because the lab animals traditionally used did not practice alloparenting. In fact, most species do not, not even our close relatives, chimpanzees—but interestingly humans, voles, and meercats do.

based on cultural criticism. The idea isn't to throw away a trusted tested theory that has stood the test of time. The science still stands solid as described. However, this chapter brings home the point we've been making since the beginning, that the concepts need to be updated and widened to include the contemporary research and to add the culture and context element that powerfully impacts how we grow up to be the adults we are today.

In summary, there are a few things we can agree upon as accepted knowns. The biological fundamentals of human beings *having* an attachment system are universal: it is innate and can be seen in other primates and mammals such as chimpanzees, dolphins, elephants, and dogs. However, the *meaning* we apply to behaviors that come from coping patterns is certainly culturally imbued. In short, there is a universal truth regarding our innate drive for love and relationships, but wide cultural variation in its expressions.

Our Brain on Diversity

Our brains are wired to see ourselves as normal and to feel most comfortable when our thoughts and values are reflected back to us. The more different someone is, the more they register as mildly threatening. For example, hearing familiar hymns and seeing someone pray in your tradition fires your mirror neuron system and internally evokes resonance and empathy. If you are non-Islamic, hearing the Muslim call to prayer and seeing someone praying with their nose, hands, and forehead to the floor will more likely evoke discomfort (a very mild threat reaction) if that is unfamiliar. Even tiny infants already have an affinity for their own race and respond with mild threat to seeing the face of a race they are not used to seeing. Bias toward familiarity is built in to our biology. However, there is difference everywhere, and we can override that initial discomfort, and there are people everywhere working to help us with this.

So, humans naturally discriminate if you are considered "too" anything—squishy or curly or slow or hairy or tall or pale or dark or heavy or differently abled—but doing so without reflection just adds to the baseline stress pool we are trying hard to reduce. The Fat Acceptance Movement is just one example of a group of people working to raise the secure relating bar for us all. It aims to challenge the discrimination faced by individuals with larger bodies, a group of people it remains acceptable to judge. At its core, it promotes body positivity, self-acceptance, and the belief that all bodies deserve respect and dignity, regardless of shape or size. It frees us from norms that are accepted as "true," making room for those who have been pushed out (for example, debunking the ideas that BMI is everything, fat equals unhealthy, and that body size is determined solely by moral choices and can be changed with simple willpower).

Another movement we consider part of growing security is the neurodiverse community. Many within this community are actively advocating for a change in perspective. Rather than placing neurodiverse individuals at the center of the issue needing to fit with the larger world, the focus is shifting toward addressing the crucial matters of accommodation and increasing societal understanding. This approach aligns with the idea we've been discussing of looking at the system, not just the individual, which has a significant impact on promoting inclusivity and support.

Dr. Devon Price is a social psychologist, writer, and professor at Loyola University of Chicago's School of Continuing and Professional Studies who publicly identifies as autistic. He frequently publishes on topics such as neurodiversity, radical mental health, and antiproductivity. In his 2022 book, *Unmasking Autism: Discovering the New Faces of Neurodiversity*, Price said:

> *Refusing to perform neurotypically is a revolutionary act of disability justice. It is also a radical act of self-love. But in order for autistic people to be able to take their masks off and show our real, authentically disabled selves to the world, we first have to get safe enough to get reacquainted with who we really are. Developing self-trust and self-understanding is a whole journey unto itself.*

These advocacy groups are great examples of people who have historically been overlooked and ignored coming together to raise the bar and look for systematic changes, and they are indeed changing the world.

Family Systems

Following up on the idea of diversity and the wide variations of cultural norms, let's shift to the concept of *family*. The world has a wide, colorful array of family structures and living arrangements. Even in the West, *family*, in fact, includes extended family serving as primary attachment figures (alloparenting), blended families, two moms, two dads, cohabitating nonmarried couples, intentionally single moms and dads, surrogate relationships, donor families with dozens of half siblings, foster families, adoptive families, polycules, stepfamily configurations, and communal cultures. These configurations aren't weird at all when seen through a global context, but the ideas of what a family should be has been enshrined in cultural norms and laws under the guise of concern for the children.

Loving families come in many forms, and what matters, hopefully this is obvious by now, is not the definition of what a family is but the *relationships within those families*. Rather than worry about what we think a family should look like, promoting security is about supporting policies that protect caregivers and preserve families that provide attunement, care, love, and support of one another. This could not be more important from an attachment standpoint because intact families (in the true sense of the word) *are* a major source of security.

Fostering security means prioritizing and valuing caregiving and the role of caregivers. Having resources that lower a parent's sense of threat, reduce cortisol, lower the sense of scarcity, help them access resources for quality childcare, and support reducing chronic stress should be at the forefront of child-centered and attachment-based interventions. Practical support directly reduces caregiver stress and illness, and the ripple effect is powerful. Providing material support for early childhood conditions is more effective and less costly than the Whac-A-Mole of addressing the consequences of early adversity later in life.

Gender Expectations and Security

You may think it's only recently that people have adopted nontraditional gender expressions and wonder what that's all about. However, societies have recognized the existence of individuals who exist outside the binary gender concept of "man" or "woman" throughout history. The Indigenous call it Two Spirits, and in South Asia there are communities referred to as Hijra—in each case these nonconforming individuals are recognized and given special societal roles within their community. So, it is certainly true that there is an increase in the visibility and consciousness of individuals who don't fit preconceived gender scripts, but people like them have existed throughout history.

Remember, our brains are wired to see ourselves as normal and differences as threatening. This comes from the primitive part of our protective system. Secure relating is about deepening our understanding of differences so that we engage from our wiser, more evolved selves. It is also about recognizing how society biases impact you and those around you. If you are subject to harassment, discrimination, harsh judgment, loss of standing, and even violence, you will be pretty careful how you express yourself. Recently there has been more active acceptance and thus people are more open to exploring their identity in various ways, including gender expression. The problem is the socially accepted binary framework of gender exerts serious pressure to follow gendered social scripts, which not only limits self-expression but also reinforces power imbalances.

Secure societies should not be afraid to allow for self-expression and promote authenticity—what harm does it cause you? This question is important because for gender-queer* individuals, accepting and expressing their difference can be life threatening. Transgender and non-binary individuals, especially Black trans women, face increased risk of verbal and physical attacks, including murder. They are four times more likely to be a victim of violent crime than cisgender people. They often expe-

---

* There is a range of acceptable terms including transgender, non-binary, gender creative, and gender expansive.

rience heartbreaking rejection from their family and long-term friends, protective factors that would help them endure the wider rejection and harassment they face if they choose to embrace their expansive identity. Hostile political climates only add to the dangers they face.

So, unsurprisingly, gender non-binary individuals have suicidal thoughts at twice the rate of their peers, yet even one supportive context where their chosen name was used decreased suicidal thoughts by 29 percent. In a 2023 study that followed 6.5 million people for more than four years, transgender individuals had 7.7 times the rate of suicide attempts and 3.5 times the rate of suicide deaths as their peers did.

It's not that hard to improve the sense of security for those near us. Rather than assume everyone is cisgender (identifies as the gender they were assigned at birth), recognize and be curious about how others see themselves. An easy way to be respectful is to ask their pronouns and use them. If you misgender somebody (use their wrong gender or former name), don't over-apologize or make a big deal of it, just correct yourself and thank them for reminding you. Even just allowing access to gender-affirming care eases depression and reduces suicidal thoughts. When gender-diverse individuals are free to recognize and express themselves authentically, they feel safer—and by now, you know all the reasons why that is such a good thing for everyone.

Tame your amygdala! Accepting what may feel weird and different to you when it doesn't actively harm anyone is an important step. Working to recognize and cope with your discomfort is one way to bump up the baseline level of security, for yourself and in the world. Using someone's preferred pronouns is a small thing that can have a major impact on the individual who took the risk to define themselves outside of the culture's predetermined script. It can save lives!

Is There a Link Between Gender and Attachment?

Male and female *role expectations* are parts of the context umbrella that strongly impact our development and our interpersonal relationships.

Cultural norms around gender shape everything from emotional expression, caregiving, managing closeness and distance, to how one gains self-esteem. Those socialized as girls in many cultures must contend with the experience of sexual vulnerability, harassment, and fear of rape, while at the same time contending with gender scripts that promote compliance, passivity, and inhibition. How's that for a double bind?

It's gotten better, hasn't it?

Well, young people today are fabulously open to various gender expressions and beliefs about gender role equity; they challenge gender-scripted fashion and are generally good with understanding and respecting chosen pronouns. Pay equity is incrementally improving in sports* and other areas, and women are making gains politically.

However, gender scripts are stubbornly sticky. The gender pay gap in the workplace has remained stable at 82 percent for the past twenty years. And while the younger generation has indeed become more open, our gendered assumptions are still steeped in the culture at large. In a 2020 survey among opposite-sex couples, those aged eighteen to twenty-four were no more likely to divide household chores equitably than older couples. Gender scripts continue to create pressure that can give rise to unique health and mental health issues and exert that dangerous ongoing stress response that can shorten life spans. However, this can change, and you can be a part of helping that happen.

As therapists we have a unique view inside the private and intimate world of relationships and can tell when something culturally is having an impact. The 2023 movie *Barbie*, directed by Greta Gerwig, is more than a cinematic spectacle—it has proven to be a catalyst for change. Whether or not you like the movie or have even seen it, it's an important cultural moment. We hear some men saying, "I didn't know," and "thank you," and "I'm sorry." They are willing to be influenced (a secure relating

---

*   Megan Rapinoe, a world-renowned professional women's soccer player, has had a profound impact on pay equity in sports and LGBTQ representation. She effectively used her platform to address the unequal pay for men and women athletes, including sponsorships, media attention, prize monies, visibility, and representation. Her efforts have inspired discussion, legal action, and policy reform.

trait!) and are understanding the importance of being allies for women, but also they've opened up a bit to exploring the impact of gender roles and sexism on their own identity.

However, many people were upset, feeling insulted and angry at the depiction of men. Liz Plank, author of *For the Love of Men*, responded to public outcries about the movie. She said, "If you hate the Barbie movie, it's because you hate patriarchy!"* It's an opportunity for empathy development—the systems that enable systematic power over *any* group of people harms us all. Feeling suppressed, unheard, and dominated by another gender feels bad and we should expect more. By engaging men as allies, nurturing progressive values in future generations, and facilitating open conversations about gender equity, we can use cultural moments such as this to create that little ripple of care and security that helps us all.

Perhaps there is no better way to capture the problem of gender for women than to delve into the most talked about portion of the movie, often just referred to as "the speech." In the second half of the film, Gloria, played by America Ferrera, delivered this speech for the ages with confidence, passion, and humor. The speech was so popular because it described the impossible requirements for women to stay on script. We are encouraged to be "healthy" or "fit" but not obsessed with our weight or appearance, yet if our body strays from the standard it's seen as a problem, a sign of disease or depression or "letting ourselves go." What, in fact, have we relinquished when we relax into our sweatpants? Women are encouraged to have a career, be a boss, and to lead yet extolled not to be "too much" and certainly should be mindful not to squash others' ideas or be too overbearing.

In the speech, the character Gloria goes on to say,

> *You're supposed to stay pretty for men, but not so pretty that you tempt them too much or that you threaten other women because you're supposed to be a part of the sisterhood.*
>
> *But always stand out and always be grateful. But never forget that*

---

* For more on Liz Plank's take, see: "You Are Kenough: Liz Plank Joins to Unpack *Barbie*, Secure Relating, Gender Roles & Patriarchy," interview by Ann Kelley and Sue Marriott, *Therapist Uncensored*, episode 211, August 17, 2023.

the system is rigged. So, find a way to acknowledge that but also always be grateful.

You have to never get old, never be rude, never show off, never be selfish, never fall down, never fail, never show fear, never get out of line.

She speaks to the experience for so many women, especially as she expressed exhaustion over watching herself and every woman tying themselves in knots so that people will like them. It is a monologue that has women nodding along in tears or cheering out loud, feeling seen.

The speech ends with the exhortation that "nobody gives you a medal or says thank you!"

So, thank you ladies out there. Thank you, no matter your gender expression, thank you to all of those who have held more than your fair share of emotional and social labor. Thank you especially if you've cared for those who don't or won't or cannot care for themselves. You do deserve a medal! It's too hard! It's too contradictory and nobody gives you a medal or says thank you! And it turns out in fact that not only are you doing everything wrong, but also everything is your fault.

Toxic Invulnerability

Men certainly have a speech like this to give as well. The real battle is not against each other; it's against the societal traps that harm everyone who doesn't comply with their assigned scripts. It is not masculinity that is toxic; it is the unwillingness to be impacted by others that is poisonous in relationships. Again, it's not gender that is the problem; it's rigid defensiveness without a willingness to change and that can be anyone.

However, those raised as men do have the structures that sell young boys' invulnerability and machismo and this harms them. Unfortunately, these wounded boys and men are more likely to turn around and harm others. In a 2023 comprehensive review of relevant studies on the subject, those who conform to traditional masculinity norms were more likely to have violent attitudes and behavior. The limbic circuitry responsible for both violence and empathy are extremely sensitive to social factors and early adversity. Thus, learning gender scripts is both a path toward male aggression and violence and a key place for intervention.

Male-to-male bullying and harassment from peers and siblings often leads to internalized shame that gets embedded in their underlying sense of self. This can lead to depression and rigid defenses and can lead to violence—if you don't stay on script, your dignity, even your life, can be endangered. So, while men—especially white, cisgender, heterosexual men—have been given a hard time about privilege, they should not be vilified and blamed as individuals. They are a product of the culture and context we are discussing, and seeing them as part of an insecure system can help keep all of our green zones more active.

Across races, ages, and socioeconomic backgrounds, men generally have shorter life spans and unique health and mental health issues. They are also more likely to be murdered, be physically attacked, and commit suicide. The term *toxic masculinity* captures the harmful impact that these cultural norms have on men, and society, by teaching them to value competition, dominance, and suppression of their emotions. It by no means is referring to men as toxic. What is toxic is the belief that vulnerability is a feminine quality that should be diminished and stoicism a masculine construct to be revered. We use the term *toxic invulnerability* to capture the harmful impact on any of us, regardless of gender, who were brought up to believe or live in these detrimental assumptions.

Dre's Story

Let's see how this can play out in real life.

Remember Jacki's friend, Dre, who was at Queen's night out?

He is a trans man who is trying to get the courage to come out to his colleagues at the software company he works for. He's conflicted for so many reasons—personal safety being number one. He lives in Texas, historically a dangerous and unwelcoming state for trans individuals. He knows he is safer than his friends who are trans women of color; they face the stress trifecta of racism, sexism, and transphobia. Dre's social status went up, not down, with his transition; however, he's still trans, which makes him a target for overt violence, covert distancing, and personal rejection.

He grew up knowing that he was different, yet had no one who could help him recognize himself or find words and labels to help him understand how he fit in. His early relationships with his parents were supportive and caring, but the social pressures around him kept him hidden to himself and his family. So, he masked a lot to get by and kept his head down.

The legitimate fear of coming out competes against his underlying need and desire to be known, accepted, and loved for who he is. He wants to be liberated from the ever-present dread of getting clocked by a stranger as trans.* Dre was lucky and has always had close accepting friendships, which helped bring a sense of trust and realistic expectations of support to navigate the coming-out process.

Had Dre's early relationships been less positive, it would have further complicated this delicate transition. He might have had an amplified fear and assumption of rejection and abandonment (red sunglasses) or carry an absolute expectation that sharing something vulnerable is not a good thing for him no matter what (blue sunglasses). Attachment strategies are not related directly to sexual orientation, but the well-being of LGBTQ+ people and BIPOC is improved if they have a secure history.

The experience of stigma—which carries the expectation of rejection—is a form of stress that negatively affects the well-being of all those being stigmatized, and this in turn raises the bar of active threat in society. Said the other way, secure relating is about doing small things to convey acceptance of what you consider weird and different.

Secure Relating Reduces Prejudice, Discrimination, and Racism

Don't underestimate this powerful biological tool you are developing—it works inside you and in the world; you just need patience for that long game. It is not about doubling down to convince someone they are wrong.

---

* Not all trans people prioritize passing (outward appearance aligning with their gender identity) because authenticity may be more important than fitting in, but it can be safer to be able to pass. "Getting clocked" means being recognized as not cisgender by a stranger.

It's about being most effective in your attempts to raise the bar of security overall.

When trying to make changes within entrenched systems, do what works—calling in, calling out, boycotting, protesting, voting, organizing labor unions . . . and if you are *effective*, great, keep doing that!* Sometimes, however, people are hell-bent on remaining invulnerable; even though it hurts them and others, there is little hope that they will move out of their discriminatory perspective. You aren't going to win over everyone, so save your time and heart-energy for creating community and joining forces where you can have an impact.

There are many who initially appear immovable, stuck in their armored self-protection system, and convinced of the path forward. Yet, when we stay the course and remain in a more open but determined stance, we will likely have an incremental impact on their willingness to be influenced. Look for small changes, and as long as there is hope and you have the energy, don't give up! This stuff really works!

Again, play the long game—this is a slow process, and remember—it's underlying fear and threat keeping them stubbornly armored up; it will not help to activate their rigid defense system. When we are connected with ourselves, we are more able to co-regulate others toward a more open stance, and it is the best chance that they can consider your perspective. Remember, relating securely does not always mean being nice, ignoring your anger, or giving up your important stance. It means not being ruled by fear and reactivity in the communication process.

Reminding yourself of their humanity and disconnected desire for belonging gives you more areas for joining. With this mind-set we are not out to attack their identity with shame. That does little to move someone unless they actually realize that they care about the experience of belonging. Instead, let's focus on the activated threat—it's their amygdala leading the show. If we stay in reactive fury, it is actually both your amygdala and defenses that are leading the show.

As always, start by protecting your green zone; staying there is your

---

* *Calling in* is a term popularized by civil rights activist Loretta Ross. "Calling In the Call-Out Culture with Loretta J. Ross," *Therapist Uncensored*, episode 168, February 1, 2022, https://therapistuncensored.com/episodes/call-out-culture-168/.

most powerful and influential position. Appealing to their best and highest human nature can help cultivate that regulated, secure zone that motivates others out of self-serving behavior. Just think of the broader implications here, and you can see why this work is needed more than ever.

Pulling It All Together

To foster secure relationships, reflect honestly and openly on who you really are and how you got here. Plumb your various identities. This means understanding the impact of these various sociopolitical experiences on the protective and connective strategies you've developed, weighing their current usefulness, and sorting out your realistic and information-biased impact on specific worldviews.

What cultural and racial messages have you incorporated as a core identity? If you are a Latinx woman, can you feel bias toward you? Do you question your capabilities and perspective? Are you getting the respect you deserve and are you being paid fairly? What stances toward yourself do you carry that you want to let go of? How do you want to be seen?

If you are white, think about your own racial identity. You may be susceptible to thinking of others when you see a discussion on race. How often do you consider the impact of race on your growth and perspective? What cultural messages did you receive related to your identity? If you are straight, imagine walking hand in hand with someone of your same gender identity: How does that feel? Imagine being born a different gender. Would you still be you? How would you be different?

As you reflect on the various systems contributing to your individual attachment map, maybe it's time to reconsider our favorite podcast slogan. Instead of "It's not me; it's my amygdala," perhaps "It's not me; it's *systemic inequity*" might be a fitting motto for when you want to avoid internalizing the negative messages or blaming yourself for conditions beyond your control.

By taking collective responsibility to uphold the worth and value of every human being, regardless of how they are different, we can create better conditions for all. By being on the path toward more secure relating, you join the team of those working to make a difference by being curious about how you may unintentionally perpetuate these problems by not noticing them or not being that interested in them. This doesn't mean the work of social justice is on your shoulders; it's a collective effort that continues through time. Seeing those you don't understand with compassion and curiosity rather than low-grade threat and aversion is a good start. Noticing your aversion helps, and not assuming the problem doesn't exist within you adds to your secure base. (It's not the bug!)

From a grounded, safe space, you are more likely to care about and catch your own unconscious biases—perhaps automatic racist or sexist or homophobic thoughts. We all have them. It's not a threat to know you have them: How could you not if you were raised in an environment that sustains them? They are baked into our lives. If you truly aren't racist or homophobic (in this culture, who could that be in reality?), then it would be natural to be curious and wonder how you aren't subject to these inherent cultural biases. In ventral vagal activation, we can reflect, wonder, and care, and see our negative qualities without collapsing or dissociating or attacking those wondering about it in us. Securely relating doesn't mean we are perfect; it means we are strong enough to know our imperfections and learn how to deal with and grow from them.

It is possible to transcend self-interest, embrace diversity, and be part of dismantling discrimination within our global community. As interconnected humans banding together, we can create a world where equality, fairness, and secure relating flourish, allowing individuals to thrive and reach their fullest—and hopefully weirdest—potential.

Part II:
Reflection—
Building
Agency

8

Warming Up Blue Activation

"Why dwell on the past? That was a long time ago. It's over."

"Sure, my dad was hard on me, but I needed it. We should all do more of that kind of discipline—kids are spoiled these days!"

"Don't worry, it's fine, I'll fix it."

"If you show your cards, people will take advantage of you."

Do these remind you of anyone? Whether they sound like you or someone you care about, learning about blue-leaning activation (the tendency to avoid emotional intimacy and vulnerability) will help. Maybe someone significant in your life asked you to read this chapter—if so, we will explain why they are bugging you to read this and give you some things that may help you understand one another.

There are many of us out there skeptical of therapy-related things, and if that is you, we think you'll appreciate that the gist of this book is about *regulating* emotions and being closer to one another without emotional drama or high defensiveness. The bottom line is if you are even a tad more isolated or lonely than you wish to be or have people asking you for more connection than you know how to give, then learning about what we call blue activation* will likely help you.

Many of us were taught that vulnerability equals weakness, making it hard to acknowledge a problem or ask for help. This isn't the result of stubbornness; it just doesn't even occur to us that we need help. Our high independence and self-reliance tell us that if there's a problem, we should just figure it out and fix it ourselves. We generally assume that we should be capable of finding our own answers. If we can't, people can see our incompetence, and that feels way too exposing. Also, why wallow in self-pity if it isn't effective at solving the problem? Even if others want to help us with something, we may be reluctant, for involving outsiders complicates things and sometimes just adds another person for us to take care of.

Can you tell we get this dynamic personally?

You may be happy to hear that there's no need to start with long-ago childhood memories or historical pain. That would likely backfire anyway because if you lean blue, you may doubt such exploration is valuable and rebuff direct inquiries. And it's not just you: most people aren't that interested in the various underlying mental processes or the long analysis of their history; they just want to feel better. They want their partner to change and stop pointing out problems and insecurities. They want their kids to listen to them and make things just a bit easier. It's easy to feel misunderstood and unseen, especially if we work hard, are faithful, and show up in many important ways.

We may feel emotional expression is the problem and rational thinking is the answer. So, if someone close to us expresses a desire for more emotional connection, we can experience this as an unfair and misguided complaint. If our partner would just be happy everything would be okay, right? Well . . . hopefully you'll come to see the problem in that sentiment by the end of this chapter.

Our strategy of leaning on rational thinking and devaluing emotional

---

* Blue activation is a reference to a neurological and psychological shift toward self-reliance and away from emotional activation explained in short in chapter 1 and expanded upon in chapters 3 and 4 and below.

expression can lead to overconfidence as we are quick to "explain" why the other person shouldn't feel that way. The challenge lies in the fact that our confidence in these strategies may lead us to avoid uncertainty and emotional activation, ultimately hindering our ability to understand ourselves and truly connect with others.

In this chapter we will help shed light on what it is they seek when they are upset or want more of this thing called connection and how to get there.

What Really Happens as We Slide Blue

For those of us who lean blue, our bodies automatically turn down the volume or even shut off emotions in times of social stress. When we perceive others' emotions and needs as "too much," it doesn't feel like an opinion; instead, it feels like an obvious truth.

Let's say your significant person is teary and trying to tell you their feelings are hurt. If your reaction is to empathize and want to know more, then great, likely your person will feel better pretty quickly and you'll add another brick on their trust of you. However, if you have an aversive reaction to that weepiness, it's likely that your neuroceptive sonar* saw the emotional expression as something a little stressful and thus signaled an impulse to pull away or otherwise make their feeling subside.

You think you aren't feeling anything, but that's not true: by definition, *blue activation is a sign of stress.* It means you've left the engaged, secure, balanced green zone, and your protection system (managed in your lower brain) is on deck to manage reactions so that things don't get out of hand.

For example, applying high logic to an important interpersonal situation is often self-protective, not relational. "Fix-it mode" helps us avoid the discomfort with others' vulnerability that may lurk just under our

---

* Chapter 3 will catch you up with all the science behind the framework, if you've missed that. It may be useful to see this isn't just touchy-feely platitudes; it's applied brain science.

surface, especially if we believe ourselves the subject of the emotional upset. Our suggestions may make us feel useful, and if problem solving is what they needed then there is no issue. Often, however, when we are upset, most of us aren't looking to be fixed; we just need to be heard and not feel emotionally alone. This can be good news if we really take it in. Rather than having the answers, the fix is being together, comforting them, helping them talk—the only problem is that right-to-right relating can feel aversive when we lean blue. We often panic and feel shame that we must avoid at all costs.

Another way to describe this common pattern is that we first try to talk them out of their feelings, then we may go with fixing what they are upset about (which gives us relief for sure but may or may not be what they want and need). Beyond that we may begin to withdraw into ourselves, which is actually to avoid the discomfort inside of us, not the other person. If things continue to worsen, we can get pretty cold and withdrawn, or try to shut them down by becoming indignant, or even cutting. Exasperation, eye rolls, and pent-up frustration take over. Good-bye hippocampus and prefrontal cortex: our amygdala-driven stress response self-protection system is now in charge. While our nervous system may be in sympathetic arousal (accelerator), the goal of our behavior is to get away (flee). We are armored up but usually don't even know it. When we are managing by giving unrequested advice, we are getting out of our comfort zone and need something, too.

The further blue we slide and the more activated we become, the less we can incorporate others in our decisions and actions. Frankly, if we keep sliding left and go far enough blue, we lose access to our heart, which means we no longer directly feel caring toward the other person. We are just surviving them now. That sympathetic accelerator may drop into dorsal activation, the last stop on our stress management possibilities.*

---

*   For those who care about this kind of detail: The blue side of the spectrum dips because you can drop into parasympathetic—dorsal—if you go far enough out. However, initially it is sympathetic activation that pulls us away from the green zone either direction. Shifting blue (or red) at all means your sympathetic accelerator is alert and making moves trying to get safe again by either approaching (fight) or avoiding (flight).

Screw vulnerability—in this state of mind, now we are convinced that expressing emotions *is* the problem. Sour or intimidating facial expressions, crossed arms, looking away, and retreating into self-righteousness are common strategies for escaping emotional engagement that feels too intense. Leaving the situation can be common, and once we exit, we shut off our own awareness of the other's hanging needs. Stonewalling is a common response when one person refuses to engage or cooperate with the other and instead withdraws from a conversation by not responding or giving evasive, monosyllabic answers. It's a sign of a perception of lack of safety and emotional overwhelm in the person who is shutting down.

In these moments, we likely don't realize that our body actually feels *threatened*. We think we are just "pissed" or that infamous nondescriptive word "fine." We see the problem as external to us—the irrationality and oversensitivity of others—and often feel trapped and wish to escape the nonsense.

But here is the rub, and we say it with love—fear of emotional intimacy is our version of oversensitivity. Our desire to avoid it at all costs is for us, not them. We are so sensitive to emotions that our body panics and cuts off. While shutting ourselves or others off may bring initial relief, it doesn't resolve anything, grow the connection, or deepen each other's understanding and closeness.

But Don't Take Our Word for It, Look Inward!

Have you noticed any drawbacks from zipping up and staying rational?

Does it bring you the warmth you deserve?
Do your close others love it when you stay aloof, feel like you know best, or try to fix their problems when they're upset?
Where are your needs? Why are they the one who has them all?

Ask around to get feedback on these ideas from partners, friends, and, if they are old enough, ask your kids how you are doing with them and if you could do better, especially around talking and closeness.

You love these people and deserve love; let's make sure you get it. And, just as you deserve love and affection, so do your closest people. This is why we implore you to really consider these questions—this process can truly improve your relationships.

As blue leaners, it isn't that we don't value relationships. We might even dedicate our lives to caring and doing for the people important to us. We can have very high moral integrity. The problem is that our need for self-reliance and our tendency to miss emotional cues and deactivate our own emotions often get in the way of deeper intimacy. Our partners often feel that they are the only ones prioritizing connection, which can create tension and pain in our relationships. We let others hold the emotional weight, but then we're shocked when they weary of that and want to let go. We risk just staying baffled at what else they want from us rather than looking inward more deeply.

We can't emphasize enough how often couples come in to see us, and one person is at their wit's end, feeling they've done everything they can and are ready to exit, while the other is *totally surprised*! How's that for tuning out?

So, please pay attention if someone wants more from you emotionally. It's not a personal attack on you and they aren't just being critical; it means they are invested and letting you know they need something legitimate. If that doesn't interest you, then it might be time to let them move along, but as long as you want the relationship to continue, then dig in! Listen! What they are looking for from you is *good for you*, and healthy for both of you.

Why You Lean Blue

Throughout this book, we've been building an understanding of how biology, experiences, and context interact to form your particular protective and connective systems and, thus, your current attachment map. Let's be honest: we are all complex, and rarely does one thing directly cause another. However, it's helpful to speculate about underlying causes because it builds the secure relating skill of *mindsight* or *reflective function*.* These skills are about growing the capacity to understand one's mind and that of others, which will, by itself, help with managing feelings and getting more comfortable with closeness.

By waking up and getting off emotional autopilot, we'll be better able to keep our higher and more compassionate brain in the driver's seat. This is where learning the *why* of the common blue traits comes in.

In chapter 4 we discussed the Strange Situation experiment, which assessed infant attachment classification. In the experiments, kids in the insecure-avoidant category appeared not to notice when their parent left the playroom unexpectedly and showed few outward signs of distress. When the parent returned, the child didn't seek contact or comfort with the now-reunited parent; they often continued playing with the toys as if they didn't need the parent.

This would be fine if that was the whole story, and initially it appeared that these kids were so secure that they did not feel stressed by their parent's departure. However, upon closer examination (which included measuring their physiological states, such as finger sweating and heart rate), it became evident that these children were showing signs of high internal distress. These toddlers *did* experience the separation from their parent as stressful, *but they were already unconsciously bypassing this awareness.* They no longer sought outside care and nurturance to regulate themselves; they continued playing and did it by themselves.

Let that sink in . . . by twelve months old these kids had already shut down their awareness of their needs, didn't notice their own distress, had turned down their natural attachment behavior to seek others when upset, and they were already assuming they needed to handle things themselves. This is worth stopping for a minute to absorb this and feel your heart.

Think what must have happened for that infant, born with the same needs as any other, that in her environment the most adaptive thing to do was to learn so early to zip up? The children in this group fit the criteria

---

* *Mindsight* is a widely used term coined by Dr. Daniel Siegel; *reflective function* is a term used by Peter Fonagy, a prominent British psychologist and psychoanalyst known for his work on attachment and mentalization-based therapy.

for insecure-avoidant attachment in infancy and, without intervention, were more likely to have behavioral and relational trouble later in life. This is unsurprising because they don't get the same chance to feel their big feelings, learn to name them, come to understand them, and, by extension, be unafraid of others' big feelings as well.

Here is the most important part—it wasn't that these children didn't care to be close to their parents. Instead, they had figured out the right distance to *keep their parents as available to them as possible.* The pattern observed in research was that if they approached their parents directly with arms outstretched, or with tears, demands, whininess, or neediness, the parents often withdrew or showed signs of discomfort or distress. It is not that these parents loved their children less; they likely have their own historical reasons they themselves shut down with this kind of emotional expression and corresponding beliefs about parenting. As a matter of fact, if the kids played happily the parent would show interest and typically engage (it didn't threaten their neuroceptive sonar); it was only certain expressions that caused their underlying threat response that took them away from attunement with their child. The last point here is that these kids didn't love their parent any less, either. They figured out how close they could come without getting rejected—they may play near the parent but with their back turned—so they were actually seeking proximity if you knew what to look for.

To have one's innate need for comfort get rebuffed is extremely scary and painful. While we've all had it happen at times, when it occurs repeatedly and at a developmental stage when our young self is dependent on parental nurturing, it can distort our sense of self and our trust in others, and impact our neural wiring.

To avoid this pain and vulnerability, our young self learns strategies to sidestep the feelings of rejection and keep our parents engaged and available to us. The apparent *avoidance* as it is called is not directed toward Mom or Dad. In fact, the opposite is true: it is a strategy for not driving away the parents by appearing too "needy," thus avoiding rejection.

These toddlers had given up hope of receiving direct emotional comfort and had learned to bypass their awareness of their attachment need as an attempt to regulate themselves.

We can understand this more deeply by considering what these kids *didn't* get in their early experiences. Securely attached kids would be pretty distressed when the parent left the playroom because they had a healthy expectation that their parent would be there for them and felt the anxiety brought on by the sudden departure. They protested and sought them out when the parent left, but when the parent returned, comfort came, and they *felt relief.*

Seeking comfort actually worked for them, the reunion with the parent brought the right harmony of oxytocin, dopamine, and serotonin, the feel-good neurotransmitters and neuropeptides that are associated with pleasure and the relief of distress. This easing of discomfort established a naturally positive association with that parent. When this feel-good association gets repeated, we learn to value and trust relationships. This is the essence of secure attachment and is where this earning security bus is headed.

Unfortunately, children with avoidant attachment to their caregivers miss out on the same sense of relief and the accompanying joy. What's more, because they've become adept at deactivating their attachment system and ignoring emotional signals, the presence of someone trying to offer help may be experienced as unsettling rather than comforting. In such cases, these individuals can perceive offers of assistance as invasive, making it feel like a part of the problem rather than a solution.

If you relate to this feeling, don't assume that you just aren't a caring person or that you don't need people—we all need people in order to thrive. You may have simply learned strategies to shut down that part of your attachment system, like the children described above. For your journey toward growing security, right now we ask you stay open and not blow it off and shut this information out. Lean in and learn more—do your own research. Increasing your interest and awareness is right where you need to be on your path to warm up your attachment system and build more secure connections. It gets easier as you get used to some of the messy feelings—you can actually get good at this! As we continue describing what we know from trends in research, we are hoping to get you curious about your own personal story. Understanding your highly individualized narrative of how you became the person you are today is the point, so as we go, consider the science just fuel for that exploration.

But I Had a Happy Childhood so This Can't Apply to Me?

First, let's not assume pathology. There are many quiet, unassuming people who are secure. Society privileges those who are more extraverted and is not sure what to make of those whose nervous system naturally needs more space to be in the green zone. However it may be that your nervous system has found that withdrawal and avoidance of intimacy is your safest space, and your early experience may have something to do with that.

My parents did the best they could; leave them out of this!

We get it. We aren't interested in assigning blame—it's not helpful and would backfire anyway. **Your parents likely had their own struggles growing up, as did theirs . . . and if we looked for who is responsible, we'd likely need to run it all the way up generational lines.** Your parents did the best they could with the resources they had, and none of us received perfect parenting. If your parents were rough on you, likely they had their own unprocessed pain, which is how these things intergenerationally transmit. We aren't wanting to turn you against them; we are working to help you become aware of what was missing so you can get closer and have the warmth and love you deserve in this life, including with your parents.

Many of us who lean blue recall having loving and caring parents, so understanding how our body learned these avoidant strategies can be confusing. There are many overt and subtle dynamics that can send your body the message that emotions and vulnerability are unsafe. Also, exploring your history can sometimes feel like you are betraying your parents and all that they did for you. Remember, your personal exploration won't harm them and can even make you closer to them. By looking within on this earning security journey, you will be able to see them in more dimensions—their pain, their triumphs, their vulnerabilities—as you gain empathy for your own experience.

In our practice we have had the privilege of sharing the journey with those who lean blue as they warm up and gain more access to their hearts and desire for closeness, and have seen good things come in spades! We frequently see closer relationships emerge with themselves, their partners, children, parents, adult siblings, and even reconnections with old friends at a deeper level.

Also, the scenarios described earlier are most common, but there are many paths that lead to a trend toward blue. Certainly not all blue leaners grew up with overtly dismissive parents, and you are not alone if you recognize yourself as having blue tendencies but recall your childhood differently, even as rather idyllic.

First, remember our whole point is complexity and not putting anyone in a box, so if something doesn't apply, that's okay—there are billions of people; so how can any single idea apply to everyone, right? But also, it's possible that the idyllic childhood moniker is a sign of idealization, not an accurate description of normal family life. Those whose attachment map is blue-shaded often report a happy childhood, but many may actually mean they have nothing to complain about (a common message in these families), so everything was . . . good (nothing to see here, move along).

Their explicit physical needs were met: soccer snacks were packed, soup was offered when they were sick, maybe they had a stay-at-home mom present. Upon further inquiry, though, there may be evidence of needs missing *they didn't know to miss*, such as emotional warmth, comfort when upset, help with difficult feelings, and ongoing physical affection. As adults, blue leaners often focus on the aspects of their childhood that helped develop their strong sense of self-sufficiency and independence, which they rightfully highly value. They often emphasize moments of achievement and success and have a limited memory of experiencing emotional difficulties or an unfulfilled need for closeness.

As children, kids with avoidant patterns tend to protect their relationship with their parents by muting their awareness of their emotional life. Or their parents may have been excessively demanding, expecting nothing but high achievements. To protect themselves from the intense pressure and high expectations, kids in that situation may respond by shutting down their emotional experience—a preferable option to chronic stress and anxiety. Regardless of why, blue leaners learned to bypass their emotional awareness and turn down attachment longings, and this often happened very early in the child's life, thus remaining well below conscious awareness.

For some blue leaners, their parents were indeed supportive, warm and overly loving, but they had a load of unprocessed trauma they've repressed so they can't help steering you far away from your own vulnerability. Their parenting style was driven by their own underlying anxieties and unmet emotional needs. This can lead to parenting that is experienced as intrusive to the child or motivated by the parent's need for affirmation and love. For instance, anxious parents seeking approval from their children can unintentionally burden them with overwhelming emotions, causing emotional overload. The kids' coping mechanism is to distance themselves from their attachment system. So, parents that lean preoccupied can have kids that end up leaning dismissing.

There are many other early dynamics to consider that can promote dismissive strategies, including the influence of cultural and situational factors throughout your life that promoted this high reason, low emotion style. It's not hard to recognize the pressures of gender scripts and other cultural factors that support stoicism and masking emotion—just think of Clint Eastwood and John Wayne!*

As you put together your personal narrative, let's zoom out even further. When a family or community has been through atrocities such as the holocaust, slavery, Indigenous cultural genocide, and land displacement, these traumas will impact many generations to come. The searing pain and coping strategies to survive fundamentally changed the human they happened to. This gets transmitted to future generations through the impact on behavior, stories, beliefs, and through their DNA. Trauma can get transmitted across generations and can easily show up as confusing symptoms you don't understand because nothing ever happened to you directly. The refugee who lost their family and had to leave their home due to violence will be changed at the cellular level, as will the child removed from their parents and detained indefinitely when they tried to immigrate across the border. Thirty years later their grandchild may have unexplained stress responses and without tying in their intergenerational history, they may keep it tucked away (thus potentially passing it down the line).

---

*   Beloved Hollywood characters and humans, but if they are your interpersonal role models, be sure to look up more about their relational lives and explore the "John Wayne syndrome."

Rather than convincing you of anything, our aim is to get you thinking about it and exploring the ideas, not pin you down with ours. No one is more of an expert on you than you. Please just look under the hood for more about who you really are and how you came to be you. Considering these ideas can open up unexpected avenues; just notice what happens as you begin to wonder.

The Role of Shame

It may surprise you to know that behind most emotional avoidance of intimacy lurks carefully hidden shame. Shame is often at the heart of uber-independence. The feeling of shame is so aversive and terrifying that some may keep that messy feeling locked away for their entire lives. By staying away from their longing and the anticipated rejection that comes with it, blue leaners may indeed avoid shame and other uncomfortable feelings that get embedded with their early experiences. But keeping shame and other painful emotions locked up comes at a cost. A sign of this is high defensiveness around any suggestion that they did make a mistake and then harshly blaming themselves when things do go wrong. They tend to take on an inappropriate degree of personal responsibility because, remember, that's what they had to do early on in life.

Cultural Influence in Promoting
Toxic Invulnerability

It is common for messages of self-importance to be unintentionally reinforced by parents who didn't have enough emotional resources themselves (and who likely had under-resourced parents as well), and who have been raised in cultures that promote this myth of "independence."

Often dependence is seen as childlike and independence is seen as more adult, but in fact we will always be mutually dependent on one another through our lifetimes. Peers, parents, grandparents, schools, media, social policy, higher institutions, and businesses can all reinforce this blue-leaning brain dominance over the science-based truth of healthy, integrated, ongoing relationships.

As we discussed in chapter 7, we have labeled these messages as a pull toward *toxic invulnerability* because they promote the idea that we should idealize the independent-minded, judge those that show their need for others, and deny personal mistakes and weaknesses. This becomes toxic as it amplifies our body's need to remain in protective armor. Rather than protecting us from real harm, however, it communicates to our body that we are on our own and shouldn't count on others for our survival—a false and dangerous belief for our individual and community health and relationships.

With this message of invulnerability, we are passing down wiring that deactivates the very part of us that has helped us grow, live, and flourish as a species. It is our interconnectedness that helps us create, nurture one another, and grow into our heathiest selves and communities. Remember, none of this is personal: these blue-leaning tendencies become wired in and reinforced in stereo.

We are not saying that blue-leaning strategies are inherently bad and to be avoided at all costs. In fact, all of us need blue strategies for our ability to cope in this world. We also need diversity, and individuals who lean blue have been a needed part of communities. That said, we are encouraging those who have been socialized to lean blue to be aware of and open up to other important aspects of their emotional world.

Strength of Blue Leaners

Maintaining relational space from others either by dismissing (pushing away) or avoiding (pulling in) as tendencies aren't pathological by themselves. Keeping relational distance can carry many benefits for us individually and collectively. From a broader social context, consider this: if we were a clan of people huddled around a fire outside our cave, ideally some members of the group would be highly attuned to interpersonal danger, while others would be focused on the tasks at hand (blue leaners). It would be useful for some in the group to have diminished access to vulnerable feelings and a keen focus on simply getting things done.

That capacity to rivet your attention for carrying out tasks and tune out emotional information helps in many ways, especially during acute stress. Let's say you receive a call from a breast imaging facility asking you to return for more tests. If you can exert top-down control and manage your neuroceptive shark music—or shut it down entirely—you will fare better as you wait in that otherwise anxiety-filled unknown. It saves your organs from a big cortisol bath! This is why the blue leaning among us see the feeling of control as a sign of safety, while things that appear out of control are deeply threatening.

As a matter of fact, learning how to distract and diminish emotionality is a skill red leaners will need to further develop. Many careers require careful emotional regulation during highly skilled task performance, such as emergency or surgical medical personnel, construction workers in dangerous environments, attorneys, pilots, and athletes. Being able to compartmentalize emotion while making important decisions can be useful, even lifesaving. It can help them be highly focused and productive without becoming overwhelmed by the stress of their work for their country, company, or family. Those in the creative arts or entrepreneurs often need to make independent decisions or take certain risks and not be swayed by others' opinions or expectations, which is another strength. Finally, during emergencies, you would want someone good with uncertainty and change and confident in their abilities to make independent decisions to be part of your survival team.

These patterns have been adaptive in our lives—often even rewarding. When we get a great deal of positive feedback for our strengths, it can be tempting to overvalue the rewards and ignore the related costs. Someone who can tune out stress and focus on work, for instance, may miss the costs to their health and their close and intimate relationships.

It's Not You, It's Your Nervous System

This isn't just namby-pamby therapy ideas. Those darkened sunglasses on the MARS Spectrum aren't just a metaphor—we actually do distort information coming in when we are defensively activated, and blue-zone activation means we are wearing very dark sunglasses that reduce incoming and outgoing emotional communications.

Neuroscience research has consistently found that individuals with dismissing attachment tendencies have different neural processing patterns. Specifically, they tend to be less sensitive to emotional cues in their environment, recall social interactions more slowly and with less detail, and describe associated feelings in a more muted fashion than those that don't have a blue attachment map. As a result, they legitimately miss important contextual cues and show subdued reactions to social situations, including other people's emotions. They also exhibit less visual expression than others.

Researchers call this *minimizing* attachment experiences (blue) versus *maximizing* attachment experiences (red). Physiologically, those with dismissing attachment tendencies show decreased activity in the amygdala when stressed and engage in top-down cognitive control to manage distress. This can be effective at times of high stress and is often reinforced by praise and accolades for their ability to handle difficult situations. However, our best strengths are often our greatest weaknesses. A decreased amygdala response can come at great cost to us personally and in our relationships when our inadequate social responses leave those close to us feeling unseen, undervalued, and dismissed.

When threatening feelings such as anxiety or loss do break through our defenses, we can become extremely overwhelmed and dysregulated because we have little practice managing a range of emotional experiences. Emotions that slip past the rational wall are extremely uncomfortable and disorienting.

For example, it's not uncommon to see a high-level executive with a blue orientation appear impervious to challenging situations, but then when they get fired, their spouse leaves, or their back goes out, they collapse into pain and helplessness. This isn't a moral issue or one of weakness. For instance, studies show that those with preoccupied or dismissing attachment styles have much more trouble managing the real emotional difficulty of loss and chronic pain. In contrast, people with secure attachment histories appraise their emotional and physical stress, loss, and pain as less threatening, rely on adaptive problem-solving strategies, and see themselves as more capable of managing the pain. And, of course, they have less trouble leaning on people for support (catch the pun?).

Signs of Blue Activation

Recognizing signs that we have dropped into down-regulating and deactivating defenses can be *really* hard because the whole point of doing so is to distance ourselves from vulnerability. Rather than feeling discomfort, we shrug and say we actually feel "fine." With those dark sunglasses on, we see ourselves as confident, rational, and often the one needed to fix a problem, while others appear less competent, irrational, indecisive, and blinded by their unnecessary emotions. Feeling so "right" can make it hard to recognize it as a cover-up for your more vulnerable self and even harder to be motivated to shift it. Yet you can imagine how this can feel for the people who are most important to you.

To become more aware, pause and remember what it feels like when you *are* in the green zone (ventral vagal activation) and your best self is available. In the green, you can *feel* your heart, be flexible, patient, and direct without dismissing others or checking out. Eye contact comes naturally and is comfortable; you care for your people and yourself. You can feel safe in your own uncertainty and being connected feels more valuable than being right.

Now feel the contrast between that warmer state of mind and what happens in your body as you slide left, downregulating toward blue on the spectrum. Notice the shift in your pace, your eye contact, and your patience as your protective system gears up and your heart dons its usual armor.

Since it is hard to recognize activation happening while we're in it, we need clear cues to recognize it. Monitor yourself for misplaced impatience, excessively negative thoughts toward others, exasperation, and the urge to roll your eyes. Also be mindful of obligatory caregiving: that's where you take care of the other person to get them to be okay and thus not "need you," or it's when you gratify your own need to be the "helpful" one. Think about the difference between handing them a Kleenex box rather than being present with them or even holding them as they cry.

When heading down toward blue, you can often feel the muscles in your face or body stiffen. The minute that happens, you are more vulnerable to calling on those negative implicit memories to justify your shutting down. Are you communicating with shrugs or a few words? Do you feel trapped by the person attempting to get closer to you? Can you meet their gaze, or are you feeling activated just thinking about it? How about this one, pay attention to how your body feels as we say this: imagine lying on the couch with your head in your person's lap, looking up at them. What's your reaction to that thought?

Remember, we pin the map on a continuum with varying shades of blue. For some blue leaners, lying in someone's lap may feel comfortable, and for others the idea of this much eye-gazing and physical touch makes them want to flee. For some, physical affection feels much safer than emotional intimacy, and for others, physical touch is primarily centered on sexuality, and they may struggle with the idea of touch for connection and nurturance alone. We just want you to move toward curiosity and openness and look for how your relational patterns show up in your life and relationships.

Once you know what blue zone activation is and can tell when and how far you tend to slide into it, it can be scary to realize of how much you hang out there. That's what we mean about blue attachment maps. It's not just a moment; it's a lifestyle you've previously assumed was normal.

What About You?

Remember, whether our map leans blue or not, we all engage in blue defense strategies at times. What circumstances evoke a desire to escape vulnerability or avoid connecting with those around you?

When is it easiest for you to talk more intimately?

How can you tell when you are beginning to zip up? What are your first signs? The more specific you can be, the better.

Take a moment to consider your telltale signals of blue activation. If you are serious about updating your attachment map, then write them down. Quiz those close to you to find out what they've noticed are your tells. The most important part is actually stopping to reflect, and the deeper you go the better, because this inquiry into your inner life may be uncomfortable for you.

The more specifically you understand your own activation, the more quickly you will become able to spot when it is happening and begin managing it. Let's dive into common situations that tend to emerge in relationships for blue leaners.

Common Blue Relational Dynamics (and Ways to Resolve Them)

As we describe these various scenarios and challenges, remember that attachment isn't everything, and no one is all blue, red, or tie-dye. We are a one of one: totally unique. We are looking at trends and patterns that tend to emerge because even solid-blue leaners will vary in the depth and intensity. You may mentally pin your map far to the left—say, navy blue—while others may pin their map closer to the middle, something like baby blue. Either way, if you recognize the blue-leaning struggle or tendencies, we will give you some solid ideas about how to warm your system up and improve your connections.

Strategically Improve Your Listening

Not feeling seen or heard is a common complaint expressed by partners and children of those whose attachment map leans blue. But we understand: listening is not always as easy as it sounds on the surface.

It's kind of strange, but our unconscious can feel a bit threatened if we slow down and really take someone else in. It can feel that listening is too intimate and involves an unconscious sense of losing something of ourselves. When we lean blue, sometimes just ingesting another's perspective can feel penetrating and make us squirm, duck, avoid, justify, and rationalize why we don't easily do this. We just don't have much body memory of this type of **rewarding intimacy** and relying on others in a safe and mutual way. Lacking that natural reward that comes from intimacy, we have often not developed skills of emotional attunement, and this can leave us feeling exposed and uncomfortable. Also, one of our strategies for self-care is to remain task driven. This can leave us vulnerable to feeling like we are losing some sense of time or efficiency.

Do you ever find yourself saying "I don't have time for this!" If you stop and think about it, exactly what is it you are saving your time for? All of this can make really slowing down and listening to others a struggle. This isn't because you don't care—but it can feel that way to those close to you.

If this sounds familiar, we suggest you start by sharpening your focus. Work to hear others' perspectives and hold your own. Just contain it; it doesn't matter right now. Catch their point—listen for their perspective and then show them you accurately heard something they said. It's like putting on their headphones to hear what they are hearing and really listening to *their* music.

If you can reflect what you heard in a satisfying way to the other person and keep the focus on them, you are doing great! "I get it" leaves a question if you truly do, but "I think you want me to do x . . ." or "The thing you are most upset about is . . . Is that right?" works well. The key is that you are sticking with their point and showing them you heard them, not moving on to explain your perspective because you believe it will clear up any confusion or because you think they know you heard them. This may feel corny and rote, but try it in good faith, and you will notice a difference right away.

It's Okay to Make Mistakes—Learn the Art of Apologizing

Another common complaint about those with a blue-leaning orientation is their seeming refusal to admit fault or apologize. Have you ever said a cursory "I'm sorry" simply to move the conversation along? For some, even the idea of apologizing is aversive. Authentic apologies are indeed tough, and most people aren't great at them. Still, we assure you that if you can get this skill down, it'll take the wind out of the sails of the upset person and help you understand your own blocks to intimacy.

Blue leaners tend to approach apologies as a means to emotionally regulate the other person rather than from anxiety, or fear of loss, or genuine remorse. Since we miss a lot of emotional detail and undervalue emotional expression, it is sometimes hard to understand why the person is upset and what we should apologize for. Also, since we feel so über-responsible, we may overemphasize personal responsibility if something goes wrong. This can make us double down on defending our choices or pointing at the other person's misunderstanding. This protects us from the shame of our own imperfections. It can feel like acknowledging faults is akin to losing a competition, and this can feel untenable. These feelings highlight that you are protecting a very young vulnerability in you.

When we are in our most secure ventral vagal state, safety surrounds us, and competition for identity and emotional space is not even on the agenda. Genuine care and a sense of remorse include a willingness to consider our impact on the other person, even if whatever we did "wrong" was not our intention or if we think they "shouldn't" feel the way they do. We have to be willing to experience the world through their eyes, not just our own perspective and beliefs. If we can't allow someone else to share their experience about what hurt them, how can we get to a place of compassion for their experience and truly apologize for what we did?*

One last thing on this: remember in chapter 3, when you learned about implicit right-brain-to-right-brain connection? If your right brain "gets" the other person's pain, it's quite easy for them to *feel felt* and for the repair to happen, with no hoops to jump through or comparisons to make. This is another reason to work toward shifting your body toward ventral vagal green: in the end, everything is easier!

Learn to Ask for Help and Input—How Tos

As a blue leaner, don't you hate it when you're asked what you need?

Answering "Nothing" won't get you very far, but often it's all we can come up with. Many of us just don't think about things like that; we really don't know what to share or what more to ask for. You aren't necessarily opposed to talking; you just can't think of anything to say. You

---

* For more on learning how to apologize, see clinical psychologist Harriet Lerner's *Why Won't You Apologize? Healing Big Betrayals and Everyday Hurts* (New York: Touchstone Books, 2017).

are "fine" (that word again!). Or we come up with things like, I need you to be happy, or to leave me alone, or to give me space. While these may make your system feel less threatened, they don't involve a need for anyone else, reinforcing the false story that you need no one. The problem is, it more likely means that you are emotionally checked out, and the other person carries the emotional load so well that you don't even have to feel it.

A clue to what you need relationally might be found by examining your complaints. You may prefer to suggest what someone can do rather than ask. If you name a problem, try attaching an "ask." This can be hard since asking for something makes *you* more aware that you have needs, and this can hit a layer of vulnerability you prefer to deny.

For example, "We don't have enough sex" is not a come-on—it's not even a request—and it's definitely not sexy. How about telling your lover, "I miss your body and want to be close to you. Can we make time to be together later today . . . maybe some 'afternoon delight'?" You can't seduce if you aren't in touch with what you need and want. To your teen, turn "I never know when you are coming home!" into the more expressive "I like to know when to expect you. Could you be sure to text me if you will be late?" Or to your friend, "Haven't seen you in a while" can turn into "I miss you; when can we get together?"

Remember, hanging in the green means that you feel "good enough" and competent, while having needs and vulnerabilities. You can ask for help, as this does not reflect a weakness in your character or your identity. You trust others want to help out of a sense of mutuality, not as a ploy to gain power over you. For us bluish folks, deep down, we don't believe someone wants to be there for us or that they enjoy giving and don't feel burdened.

Using Humor in Place of Intimacy

Humor and a light punch to the shoulder are often signs of affection, as is the verbal jab. When humor goes well, it's fantastic, and having fun is a huge plus in relationships! But what about when *you* think it's all in good fun, but it upsets other people?

You were just joking, you insist. Why don't they get that? Why do they have to make it such a big deal!

Let us translate what may be going on.

Something can't be "in good fun" or "playful" if *both* people are not having a good time. When only one person is laughing, you can no longer count that as "just joking." Instead, find out if it came across as critical.

When you deny that anything you've said or done should make the other person uncomfortable, you convey that they are the problem, not you. Instead of assuming they are "too sensitive," consider whether or not you are being sensitive enough. Blue zone self-deprecating humor is typically safer for everybody, and if you feel a strong urge to tease someone who may not appreciate it, see if you can find another way to express your affection and connect.

Speaking of which, if you fall into a pattern of using humor as your primary bid for intimacy, it is likely that you are doing so as a diversion from the scarier aspects of emotional connection. For example, rather than joining in the celebration and saying, "Great job!" or "Good idea!" you may be tempted to use humor to express your pride.

"Finally! Thought you would never graduate!" Ask yourself this: *Do I use humor to express my affection, appreciation, criticism? If so, why is it so hard for me to be direct?* When you imagine turning your humor into a direct statement, see how that feels. The direct expression of pride, excitement, hope, and care turns on the feel-good neurochemicals in both you and your child or spouse or friend.

This is a vulnerable step but one that could really make a difference.

Learn the Art of Joining Rather than Blocking

Because those of us who lean blue are less in touch with emotional expressiveness, we can accidentally violate social rules by interrupting others and coming across as brusque. Please do let us know—in a kind way—if we bumble, but also understand this may go deeper than merely correcting poor social habits. Let's take joining for example. *Joining* means signaling to the person talking that you are truly listening and with them. It can be nonverbal encouraging cues or specific wording such as "Great point," or "Oh, I hadn't thought of that," or "I agree."

Joining someone in an intimate way may feel threatening at a lower, limbic level. So, we jump into our deactivating habits (being the expert, teasing, tuning out, talking over) so quickly that we don't even recognize it. Recall, we also get a lower level of pure pleasure (dopamine and oxytocin release) in social interactions. Others can sit and visit and talk about seemingly nothing and get filled with all the good neurochemicals, so the exchange is rewarding. For us, it can sometimes generate anxiety. We may prefer to see the social exchange as transactions—in other words, for a more concrete purpose. We don't mean to be rude; we mean to be useful and efficient.

The good news is that most of us blue leaners are trainable. We can learn how to stay more present and in tune, so don't just let yourself lean in to these tendencies. This is where mindfulness training can be really helpful. Also, if this is something you recognize in yourself, encourage your people to not accommodate you when you jump in too quickly or inadvertently take over a conversation. When *you* bring it up and point it out, it will be meaningful to those who love you, for they've probably observed this firsthand. Also, we suggest intentionally tuning in to the importance of the interpersonal process itself, not just the task or goal at hand. We suggest that you "flip the tasks."

Let's take a mundane, everyday situation: you and your partner are discussing where to go to dinner tonight. Rather than framing the task as Which restaurant should we go to?, try flipping it around. The new task is learning what your partner hopes to get out of the evening together and what they would enjoy having for dinner.

This may be no piece of cake. They may be in the habit of deferring—if so, find out why. Do they simply prefer having you pick the place? Are they nervous you won't like their choice? Or are they just not used to being asked their opinion? All good things to know. If pressed to make the decision yourself, give them a choice of great eateries and then go along with their decision—whatever it is. Take on the task of holding yourself and them in the process and find joy in giving them pleasure (but what they feel as pleasure; not what *you* think they should want). Get them to talk about themselves by asking questions, and then follow-up questions, which show that you're listening actively. Rediscover the person. Enjoy him or her or them.

Use phrases such as:

"Tell me more about that."
"Why do you think that is?"
"What's your favorite part?"
"What has you so worried?"

And by the way, when negative emotions come up, it means they are trusting and turning to you, which is good. All you have to do is *listen*, not fix anything. Just keep them talking and show up for them. It works. Try it! You'll find that once you tune into this interpersonal channel, there is a *ton* to talk about and learn about one another. The "task," if we have to have one, is to put a deposit in your interpersonal bank and fill up your partner with your eyes, your care, and your interest. So you see, the task (if we need one) isn't getting food in your bellies, it's having a connected experience together over a meal.

Update the Myth of Independence and Self-Reliance

We *love* our independence. It's a source of pride, but unfortunately, our desire to be our own person is often a subtext for discomfort with closeness more than it is a sign of security. Ask yourself *why* your self-reliance is such a source of pride and what's the cost of interdependency. Where did those messages come from? Do you want to keep them? It is not just "who you are"; it is a coping style that, if left uninterrupted, actually causes us to become *more dependent*, not less, even if we don't realize it.

If we relate as parents, friends, siblings, and partners from a secure, warm, and open state of mind—the green zone—this is the closest to true independence we can get: interdependence. No one is an island, and you didn't get where you are today all by yourself. It's impossible. So, blue brethren, our choice is to gracefully accept our natural human interconnectedness and enjoy the dignity and many benefits that it brings or we can continue to delude ourselves with the myth of self-reliance.

If you struggle talking *with* those you love, our first suggestion is to say more. Say more of anything about yourself, your friendships, your relationships, your feats or frustration at work, we'll take it! Your people are probably thirsty to know you, so give them sips until you get used to sharing more of your internal world and it flows more easily. They've been carrying the emotional weight; it's your responsibility to help carry a conversation, raise topics, ask them questions, listen, and find out what they need from you. When at the dinner table with your spouse and kids, do you hold up your end of the emotional weight conversationally? This does not mean launching into a monologue or pontificating on how to solve problems. It means reaching out to talk *with* (not at) one another.

Talk about your (or their) difficulty or joy and be there to share in it. You can do it. Feel the feels with them. Talk to them about anything in this book that resonates with you. Again, it doesn't matter what. Something you took offense to, or that touched you, or surprised you. It's not what you say, but just the fact that you're willing to share your feelings and let others get to know you.

Small things matter, as does the fact that you are reading this. You can see the trend in the themes here: more emotional investment, warmer communications, and realizing that you have wants and needs, all of which are good things.

Look for Blue ANTs
(Automatic Negative Thoughts)

Us blue leaners often have some telltale ANTs that run under the relational surface. We tend to see things in terms of black and white and right versus wrong, which can leave us prone to judgmental thoughts about those we love. If your partner was fine yesterday, but today you see him as "crazy," your protection circuit is probably activated. Using labels to wrap someone up as any *one* thing is a sign of black-and-white defensive thinking, even if directed at yourself. When stirred up, we also tend to overgeneralize; for example, one frustrating thing happens, but you see it as a never-ending pattern of defeat. This adds to your narrative that having to escape or shut down is the only option.

Catching these automatic negative thoughts, or ANTs, helps introduce higher thinking into reflexive patterns. Other examples of ANTs might be when you say "always" and "never." Let your brain send up a tiny orange flag: *nothing* is always or never! (Did ya catch that?) Also, if you know that one of your ANTs has to do with pride and personal identity, then beware of activation caused by underlying feelings around receiving feedback. You are prone to hear complaints as a personal insult to who you are rather than focusing on the needs or feelings of others. To correct your sunglasses, you may ask clarifying questions when you think you hear an insult to your character. "It sounds like you think I'm a bad mom; is that what you are saying?"

Also, watch out for "should-ing" on yourself, or its cousins "ought-ing" and "must-ing": "Ugh, I should go visit my mom this weekend." This approach only aggravates your sense of personal responsibility and can add to guilt and resentment. With this as your motivation, you are likely to show up in body but not in spirit, making for a pretty dissatisfying experience for both of you.

Instead of feeling like you have to do something or are obligated, find what you *want*. For instance, rather than just going to visit your mom out of a sense of obligation, and resenting it, permit yourself to explore your conflicted relationship and your feelings about it. Even giving yourself permission not to go may actually lead you to visit Mom with openness and kindness. By stopping the "shoulds" and your belief that your primary value is to be of service, you can find your own desires and wants.

What does it mean to you to "be there"? Turn your focus to warming your ventral vagal system rather than serving your identity as the good son, father, mother, or spouse. This allows you to turn toward the oxytocin-rich relational benefits that can be right there for you.

Here is another sunglass-caused information distortion problem to watch for: when you make a mistake or get approached with feedback, do you automatically feel attacked? If you frequently feel offended or righteous, check for ANTs that are likely protecting you from vulnerability. Why is it so activating to be questioned? When we lean blue, it can feel like asking questions of you is signaling doubt or lack of trust in your capability. When we are in our more secure self, being questioned is not threatening. It is an opportunity to help someone understand, to look more deeply at our own position, or to utilize both of your strengths in a process or discussion.

Your ANTs can be directed at others as well. "She always . . ." "They never. . ." Use your smart, higher, more discerning mind to look for complexity. It's probably not that they *never* reach out to you first, it's that it hurts your feelings that they don't call regularly, and you wish they would reach out to you more. By saying they *never* reach out to you, you could be using this as a strategy to block your vulnerability and as an excuse to cut yourself off from them and your own vulnerability in reaching out. All of these are common examples of ANTs on the blue side of the continuum, but they won't all come up for every person. Try to identify those you rely on most and start your efforts at change there.

Co-regulation—Warming Up Blue Zone Activation

What if it's not you who leans blue but someone you love and you are close to? You can't force anyone into the green zone, but some co-regulation strategies might help gently guide them there. Your beautiful blue-leaning significant person may appear confident, busy, distracted, and self-assured. It's easy to miss their more vulnerable feelings of need and want because of their high motivation to stay the hell away from their feelings and their shame for having them. You are likely desiring more warmth, connection, and affection; keep that as your focus, but let's be smart about it. Despite what it seems, your person needs you to stay connected to your needs. It's better for both of you.

The idea is to help you each have an imperfect self and mutually respectful relationship, and this can apply to any of the significant people in your life—your parents, partners, adult children, and friends. Best case scenario, you and your primary person(s) are on the earning security bus together and each on your own specific pilgrimage, doing your part in healing and growing closer.

Read: this does not apply to one-directional, all-about-them, malignantly narcissistic relationships. Relational trouble is never 100 percent one person's fault or entirely up to one person to fix. If they are on the earning security bus with you, you'll see a few signs that should give you encouragement.

Signs Your Partner Is Working on It, Too!

First, you know in your heart that they are invested in you, too. They are willing to be impacted by you, look at themselves, and grow. Sure, signs of this are:

1. They realize they have an issue to work on.
2. They are willing to work on it (they don't just shrug and say, *Yeah, but that's just how I am*).
3. You can see active steps where they are trying.

Even small efforts really matter. Signals of them trying to work on their side of the street include that they bring the issue up (about their part, not yours), they make visible efforts to change their problematic behavior, they care when they mess up again, they ask for and are open to your input on how they are doing, or they seek outside help for their side of the issue.

Mutuality

Secure healthy relationships require mutuality, where both parties' needs are recognized and valued, both perspectives are heard, and each person supports the other's growth. Humans are messy, and nothing is perfect, but in primary relationships, you each deserve basic mutual respect and shared power and love—not just as a feeling but also as an action-oriented verb. When our protection circuit is in charge, we privilege our own comfort and perspective over others', but that is intended to be temporary, and it's why we are training you to notice when you get activated. It matters.

We all do best when our connection circuit is humming so that our ventral vagal nerve can explore, create, be bored, be sexy, play, and rest.

You'll give and get the best of each other, for regulating each other into safety gives you *both* the most bang for your emotional investment of time and care. Okay, you want more affection? Are you tuning into the expression of affection they *do* give you? Requests, care, seduction, and vulnerability work better than anger, almost always. It is easy to forget that vulnerability disarms defensiveness, and tapping on a person in their defensive protection circuit from your secure state of mind is the fastest path toward more closeness.

Use Statements of Credibility

Threat to personal identity is often a core issue for those who had to learn to rely on themselves alone. DJ was most upset about Mia's questioning his character, though it would have served him better to tend to Mia's desire to spend time together as a family. He could have still expressed his frustration about her booking the vacation without him while recognizing the more powerful dynamic at play. His blue-tinted sunglasses missed the more subtle emotional communication and misread the problem in terms he could understand.

To soothe a blue leaner's danger-scanning sonar, show your care first. Signal safety with your tone of voice, pace, eyes, and words so that their neuroception will stay steady and not perk up seeing you as a threat. The fact is, if you are in the green zone yourself, this will be natural because you are safe. We'd love it if you could have those cute little emojis bouncing around your head with super happy or silly faces signaling that all is well and that the two of you are simply having a normal conversation. It's not pandering; it's smart communication to go for their friendly higher cortex and stay away from the shark music.

Because of their high sense of moral character, and underlying hidden shame, it helps to say *statements of credibility* to assure your person that you remember and can hold their goodness. This has to be 100 percent authentic—no bullshit—or it will strike the wrong chord.

Say "You are an amazing provider . . ." *before* you talk to them about the tight budget or the countless hours they spend at work.

Say "You are such a great dad . . ." *before* you share a complaint about their parenting.

Say "I know you would want to know this, but it's hard for me to tell you . . ." *before* you risk divulging something that will probably upset them.

Working to keep your partner regulated is just part of a relationship. It shouldn't be because you are afraid of them but because staying in ventral-ventral communication is the most effective and powerful frequency for both of you. If you are comfortable in green, this won't be a problem: you aren't losing yourself, you are using your resources to co-regulate into mutual support.

Create a Physical Safe Haven

Animals use places as their safe havens. Think of foxes: when frightened, they dart into their dens. Baby bears start in the den and then have a specific safe tree they hang out in while Mom is foraging. They may play around near it, but that is where they head if they feel threatened, and the space around their special tree expands as they grow. For people, our closest relationships usually serve as our safe haven, but not always. For those with severe blue-leaning tendencies, those suffering from severe trauma, or those who are neurodivergent, using a person as your safe haven can be fraught.

So, if your blue leaner is pretty far out on the spectrum, finding a version of that safe den may be helpful! First, though, call up compassion for their need to be alone. It's designed to recharge them, not to abandon you. You'll receive more from them if their battery is recharged, they will feel loved, and you are disproving any projections they may have of being "trapped" by you.

They may have naturally already created a safe physical space they retreat to, but if not, encourage it! Think about spaces where they can be themselves and no one needs anything from them: a library, the lake, the garage, the quiet porch overlooking the garden. Put a door on the study and dedicate it to them. Let them disappear into the garage or workshop or art studio or local bookstore if that's where they like to retreat.

That said, we do have a few caveats we want to direct to the one needing more den time. Use your safe haven to revitalize yourself for re-entry into the interpersonal world, not to replace it. Watch that your den doesn't become your exclusive source of relief, or it will backfire, stirring up trouble in your relationship. But don't skimp yourself on time there, either; it's better for the relationship for you to get your nervous system back in ventral vagal mode and interested in relating.

However, if your people push back on this, insisting that you're spending too much time hibernating, listen and accept the possibility that they're right. Their needs have equal weight as yours, and this is about rebalancing and recharging, not disappearing and hiding. It's important for you to remain aware of your time away and find your own methods for balancing your needs with those of the ones around you. It's up to you to set times or routines that help you look up and join others, rather than waiting for someone to come retrieve you.

Back to the partners.

We know, we know. We can hear some of you protesting: *Of course they want to retreat, that's all they ever want to do!* Or *I'm afraid if they go to their den, they'll never come out!* Understandable. But worth a try with some important communication along the way. Some people truly can improve interpersonally when afforded their very own space. Giving it to them (with adequate negotiation for your needs) makes it interpersonal and gives them that feeling of support versus if it feels to them like they take it or steal time away in it, which only reinforces that they have to get away to feel safe. As their partner, if this is what they say they need *to come closer to you*, then work together to make this happen in a way that is good to both of you. That does not mean that you let them ignore your needs or those of the family. Working through this together so that it feels like a win-win is what is important.

Put On Your Own Oxygen Mask First

But what if your special person doesn't see a problem with their blue-tinged self-protection? What if they aren't bothered by it being more important than the needs of the couple, thruple, or group? If they aren't that interested in your needs, especially if yours intrude upon theirs, and they won't take responsibility for their part in the emotional relationship, you should consider how strongly you want to exist in that ventral vagal green zone alone—because it's impossible to stay there without your basic safety being assured. If you are left feeling unworthy of kindness and respect or that you should bury your own needs, then we especially want to help you find your bold, sassy, and secure self. Start there, reach out to those who hear and believe in you, and hold strong to your values no matter where that takes you. If their protection system is so rigid, so entrenched, that they remain unwilling to do the work to move toward a more secure way of relating with you, it's important to take care of yourself and put on your oxygen mask first, even if that means ending the relationship.

Final Advice from the Therapist Chair

Okay, if you lean blue, we have a few final thoughts for you. As therapists who see your partner or kid (not literally, of course, but we've seen enough folks who love a blue-leaning person to have a gist of what they might say), this is what we want to tell you: you are probably overestimating the emotional health and satisfaction of your family, and there are things you can do to make it better. We are not saying the other person is perfect, and that only you need to change, but if *they* are in therapy working on themselves and reading books to improve, they are doing their part to make things happen more securely. That's why, with all due respect, we privately need your ear for just a minute and will say what we need to with care. If it doesn't apply, that's okay, just leave it. But for some, these words could significantly improve if not save your relationship.

Imagine for one moment losing the person closest to you. This can awaken your attachment system and help you recognize and feel the care and vulnerability that is already alive and well in there. This is precisely what they seek from you: felt care and emotional connection. Understanding and expressing love and connection is a vital human need, so we urge you not to be complacent. Take a moment to reflect: Are you getting any signals of dissatisfaction? The simple act of checking in will be appreciated even if everything is good, there is literally no downside to inquiring how your people are doing with you, and digging a little to get them to at least say one thing they'd like more of or less of (a great way to take the temperature of a relationship).

Have you written anyone off as chronically unsatisfied or consistently questioning you or letting you down? Reevaluate that assumption, keeping in mind the science that we discussed earlier. Try interpreting complaints as a genuine expression of their needs, their equally important perspective, and a bid for connection. If they are trying to tell you something, that's great. It's when they stop that the relationship is really in trouble, so encourage them to talk to you by helping them feel heard.

Remember, you don't have to actually fix anything or please them. Just be with them and see if you can understand their message accurately. It's much easier to take someone in when we know we aren't responsible for it all. Just find curiosity, ask questions, and be willing and open to doing your own work.

If your first impulse is to refuse or blow this off—that might be the very resistance we are talking about—what's the risk of looking at yourself more closely? What are you really avoiding? What are you afraid of? It's not about judging you, but perhaps reread this chapter with yourself more in mind and see if you can glean any insights. Don't let your fear of vulnerability and an overinflated confidence keep you from taking steps that will bring deeper connections and likely more meaning to your world.

Finally, parents that struggle with intimacy? Your kids need *you,* not just what you *do* for them. You are already enough. Show up and take care of those you love as much as you take care of yourself, and the beauty is that it will return to you in spades! If this is particularly hard for you, give yourself a daily period during which your top priority is to connect with those you love. Put down your phone and close up your laptop. Bring your full mind and body into the moment and let that ventral vagal chemistry come alive between you.

Being concrete can help sometimes. So, think of your favorite person: someone who supports you and whom you want to stick around. Reach out to them directly and let them know how you feel. Ask them to share something tangible you can do this week to make them feel appreciated.

Hopefully, once they trust that you are sincere, they'll respond honestly with a specific request. Then, whatever they tell you—whether it's turning out the lights when you leave, picking your pants off the floor, making kind eye contact, asking about them—do it with a generous and open heart, consistently, for a week.

You can do this. We believe in you because we understand that although you care, you just have trouble expressing it sometimes. You've got this!

9

Cooling Down
Red Activation

Those of us who lean red are typically eager to learn and explore how to improve our relationships. We want to analyze and dig in, so we don't need to spend much time convincing you that deconstructing your tendencies will be helpful. We can jump right in!

As we explore what it means to "lean red," stay flexible in your thinking. Don't overidentify with any labels. Remember, how your attachment leanings show up in your various current relationships is impacted by the felt security in your own history, your present circumstances (for example, the attachment behaviors of the person you are interacting with), and how far out on the spectrum your map tends to lean. The further out on the spectrum our developmental map trends, the more we struggle to feel safe, flexible, and trusting.

Also, a friendly reminder that attachment isn't the end all and isn't supposed to explain everything. There are many influences on who you are at any given time. The best news though is that no matter how dark red your map is, you can shift where it lands on the continuum as new experiences override some of your early implicit learning. It can even vary across different relationships. For example, if you are with a secure partner, over time you'll trend toward holding security more deeply in your body.

***

What Really Happens as We Slide Red

We describe trends to fire up exploration of your own narrative story—so don't take our word for anything, find your own words to describe the arc of your history of how you came to be the person you are today. To help with that we will continue with more summaries of the science.

The descriptor of this "red" style, *preoccupied*, comes from the fact that your body has learned to remain on low-grade alert because of an underlying belief that if your system rests, you might miss something or lose contact with someone, which feels scary. Because of this, it's not uncommon for those of us in this boat to replay conversations or events, trying to understand how things could have gone better. This ongoing review leaves us wishing we could correct the mistake, make things better so that we can avoid the impending judgment or rejection we are imagining.

If you lean more deeply red on the spectrum, you likely experienced fairly inconsistent attunement as a child, and your body has been programmed to look for cues that tell you what to brace for and expect. This creates the common preoccupied theme of relational hypervigilance.

It's common for us red leaners to be vigilant for signs that things might go awry or to anticipate potential future challenges, both for ourselves and for our loved ones. This underlying doubt and worry can make it difficult for us to fully relax and simply trust that things will work out. Instead, we orchestrate circumstances to steer them toward what we genuinely believe will be the best outcome for everyone involved. This proactive approach is driven by a genuine sense of care and responsibility for the people and situations in our lives, but from the outside-in can be felt as controlling and misattuned to the other person's actual needs (i.e., you are responding to your need to manage, not necessarily their need to have your kind interventions).

As red leaners, we often have difficulty managing feelings once they are activated. This isn't you trying to be dramatic or get attention; this is a neurological tilt: you are experiencing the intensity higher than those who aren't activated, those with secure maps, and those whose maps tilt blue. This intensity can cause you to feel compelled to send an unhelpful text message when, deep down, you know you should hold off. It's also why you follow your partner out of the room during a heated argument, when you know it would better for both of you if you let her storm off to collect herself, and why you try to convince your young child to do something rather than direct her as needed.

When stressed, we want to hash out problems *right now* and may be desperate to not lose contact with others. However, this urgency can unintentionally push people away, cocreating the thing we are afraid of. We think to ourselves: *If they could only see* . . . And, boy, do we ever try to get them to see!

While some of us red leaners rush to action, others hold our more intense feelings in and internally ruminate about our deficits and fears. This can lead us to shy away from conflict, merge with what we feel other's want, or avoid situations that could expose our insecurities.

A Few Ideas About Why You Lean Red

Children identified as anxious, preoccupied or ambivalent (depends on the research) want closeness but can't quite trust it. They were loved and cared for, but attunement was inconsistent. They likely had repeated experiences of the caregiver "missing them."

For example, you are a little one and you toddle over to show Mom this cool flower you picked up. She grabs you and picks you up to cuddle, causing you to drop the flower. You try to point to the dropped flower, but she's rubbing noses and not tuned in to what you are trying to communicate. You eventually forget the flower and instead you tune into how she wants to relate. Repeat that enough and you begin to track her interests, forgetting to tune in to your own. As adults, this shows up as being highly responsive to the imagined needs of others and not tracking your own thoughts, feelings, and wishes.

The misattunement isn't random. Research demonstrates that parents of kids with preoccupied patterns tend to miss both positive and negative cues while *overresponding to signs of fear* in their infants. This means joy and distress are often missed, but fear is amplified. While the parent's intentions may be good, they inadvertently teach these kids that the world is threatening and that safety is found through someone else, which exacerbates their need to rely on others. This contrasts with parents who amplify responses to happiness and content play and miss or avoid signs of distress common in kids with dismissing patterns.

Remember this important finding from the Strange Situation studies when it comes to anxiously attached babies? While the kids who were classified with a secure attachment could turn to the parent for support and were soothed quickly *(problem solved! Mommy is back!)*, kids classified anxious would go to the parent *but be difficult to comfort.* Their bodies remained upset, yet they would resist the parent's efforts to help them calm down—hence the classification of "ambivalence" and "resistant." This resistance to comfort was likely due to their body's memory of inconsistency and the residual feeling that they needed to stay on alert. It was as if calming down would release the parent to turn away and leave again, so their body can't quite let go of being upset.

Many of us red leaners can likely relate to this difficulty feeling soothed and the sense we should stay alert for signs something could go wrong. We often hold our worry throughout the day, even if it is just running subtly under the surface. This way, we can track the emotional needs of those we love to ensure that any potential of their experiencing disappointment or rejection is managed. When we do try to completely relax, we have a sense of guilt or feeling that we are missing something very important. Being caring and giving assures our inner doubts that we are important and needed, which keeps people sticking around. It's also why we get thrown off by our partner or kids asking us for space—we experience it as a sign of rejection.

As they grow, kids with insecure-anxious strategies continue to seek physical closeness and not surprisingly tend to hold on tightly. Some may describe this as "clingy," but that points to a negative quality of the child rather than a descriptor of a strategy to keep the parent close. The child is responding to a healthy need for safety and security and has developed a pattern that works to keep their parent available. This isn't great for the child because if the pattern continues, their need for frequent reassurance and physical comfort can evoke negative reactions from others and become part of the problem.

For those parents reading and worrying about their own kids or their own parenting skills, remember that reading this book means that you are working on your reflective skills and thus are working to build more secure relating in your parenting. You are probably *already* highly tracking your kids, so if something is wrong, you'll *know* it. If anything, the risk is probably on the other side. In truth, you are more likely to remain overly aware of their imagined disappointments and feelings of potential rejection, which can intrude on the child's sense of self. Overreacting to minor cues and interpreting them negatively (about your child or your parenting) adds anxiety to the system. Instead of looking through a microscope for signs of a problem, sit back, soft focus, and play the long game. Trust that you are imperfect but good enough; your kid is *already good*. Plus, they probably have it way better than you did, and you turned out okay. Coming from a calmer place will help your accuracy in attunement and protect you from projecting your fears into them.

As a red-leaning adult, you may struggle with self-doubt, fear of rejection or abandonment, or a tendency to lose yourself in others. If so, consider that your body is remembering *something*. You may be unable to point to something specific about your parents or childhood. Still, the body doesn't lie, and most nervous system patterning happens before you develop any conscious memory, which means it would be hard to be "certain" of anything before ages four to five. Furthermore, several factors can lead to misattunement in very loving moms and dads: postpartum depression, substance abuse, experiencing a loss when their kids are very young, job strain, marital strife, living in a potentially dangerous neighborhood, relentless discrimination due to being different in whatever colorful way your parents may have stood out. We aren't looking to blame anyone; we are looking to help you understand yourself more accurately and with loads of compassion.

As you consider your life and history in relation to your red-leaning tendencies, look for intergenerational clues.

How were your parents parented?

What stories did your family tell you about your family history or you as a little kid?

What messages do you get about the world or your ability to handle it? What about your siblings?

The key is curiosity and interest, not necessarily finding solid answers. You are a complex, beautiful person with eighty-five billion neurons and many years of learning and many more yet to come.

Remember, your goal throughout is to grow toward your bold and beautiful right-size secure self, not to find something wrong with you or your folks.

Strengths of Red Leaners

The high value you place on relationships is often the impetus that helps a system move toward self-growth and relational growth. Also, your ability to tune in to others' emotions can contribute to deep compassion and empathy. In fact, your interest in relational learning might have led you to buy this book: you want to understand the struggles that are familiar to you in your closest relationships. Red leaners know how to love and love *big*; we just need to make sure there is mutuality when we give our heart.

If you were socialized female, then your petri dish likely contains many messages about gender scripts, not the least of which being putting others' needs first, holding the emotional weight, and submitting to power. In fact, we are often rewarded for being giving and selfless if we follow the script successfully. So, it can feel rather insulting to discover that these roles, inherent in cultural gender bias, may contribute to what is labeled "insecurity" when it comes to your attachment map.

Like we said in the previous chapter, if we were a group of people in prehistoric times gathered around a campfire trying to survive, we would certainly want people with different strengths to help protect the group, including someone highly attuned to their environment and the relationships within the group. Sometimes, even today, your physical environment is dangerous, and being vigilant about people's relational intentions keeps you safe.

If you are in a relationship slipping toward autopilot and disconnection, you'll likely be the first to notice and respond to get the two of you back on track. Let's say a group with more power than your group (developers, politicians, corporate interests) comes in to try to take your land or convince you to sell your family home—vigilance around who you trust and the ability to read intentions is key. And, most practically, living in a high-crime community calls for relational alertness and vigilance to safety to which you are well suited. That isn't being insecure; it's ensuring safety for yourself and your family.

In other words, your sensitivity can be one of your biggest strengths, once you know how to harness it.

Signs of Red Zone Activation

The red zone is usually easier to identify than the more subtle deactivating strategies of blue leaners and thus often draws more direct attention during conflicts (or in their therapist office the next week). For instance, Mia leaving the restaurant in angry haste is easier to point to than DJ's more dismissive gestures and statements throughout the night. But each of us gets activated differently, and identifying our own "tells" is key to managing that activation.

High stakes activation is a common tell. Do the circumstances feel unnecessarily dire? Look for urgent speech, pressure to connect, or a feeling that depends on a quick response or immediate reaction. Are you flexible about distance and closeness, or do you lean in pretty hard? Anger and blame are other signs we are in an activated state, though this can also indicate either red or blue activation. When you are in the red, your anger is often related to feeling left out, forgotten, or anything that may be interpreted as rejection or abandonment, whereas in blue activation it is more likely that you are feeling invaded or insulted. It is also common for us to feel upset for giving too much of ourselves and feel like we don't get the same back in return.

Information processing distortions (sunglasses on the spectrum) are *real* and are a big part of messy relating. Your neighbor at the potluck dinner says, "Thanks for bringing the potatoes," and you hear, "All you brought were *potatoes*?" This not only adds negativity when there is none, but it also misses the acknowledgment and connected gesture that we long for.

Neuroscience confirms that those of us with preoccupied attachment strategies distort in specific ways, as measured by functional magnetic resonance imaging (fMRI) and positron emission tomography (PET scan), imaging procedures that measure blood flow to the brain, and encephalography (EEG), which uses disc-shaped electrodes to measure the brain's electrical activity. When we lean red, we tend to recall relational events more quickly and with enhanced emotional detail. We are more likely to fill in the blank of neutral or ambiguous information with our worries, which adds negativity to the equation. And depending on our level of activation, we may take it even further by turning positive sentiments into something to worry about, such as with the potatoes. Not only does this add a hint of negativity to a positive exchange, but it also misses the important gestures of recognition and gratitude.

Now try turning your reflection inward. Take that big deep breath in and scan inward. What do you notice? What circumstances evoke *your* more vigilant up-regulation? What does your body feel like when this activation is happening? Take a moment to note the telltale signs of your red activation, and while you are at it, feel free to add green and blue, too. This will help you map out your particular patterns to recognize your state and, through more exploration, map your activation more quickly.

Common Red Relational Dynamics (and Ways to Resolve Them)

We Have Trouble Knowing and Expressing Our Needs

Those of us who lean red might be skilled at reading a room and picking up what we believe others seem to want, feel, or need, but all that external input can cloud our mind and body from listening to our own cues and feelings. Throughout our personal lifetime, it has likely been more advantageous for us to read and meet others' needs than to feel seen. So, learning to slow down enough to tune in to our gut instincts and know what we want can be a real challenge. Instead, we often mistake others' needs for our own.

There are two skills that are essential in our effort to be more direct with others: (1) being able to identify our wants and needs, and (2) being willing to express them directly.

Knowing our needs means that we can hold the external world as separate from us, including the wants and needs of our kids, family, and friends, and instead track our own longings and desires. To want something can feel exposing and selfish, stir fear of rejection, or put us at risk of being judged. This is especially true if we imagine the other person being disappointed and not getting what they want. If your map includes the bodily experience that discontent leads to instability, anger, or rejection, then realizing that you could be the source of someone else's discontent can make you feel quite vulnerable. Instead of knowing and expressing our wants, our needs may come out through complaints, platitudes, or indirect comments.

When working on our secure-relating skills, we need to increase our ability to tolerate the scary activation inside of us when we imagine or experience disappointment in others. Our implicit memory may say *Danger! All hell will break loose! Someone will collapse!* However, if we stay in the present moment, we can remind ourselves that our child's being disappointed is just a feeling; it will pass, and it will not break them (or you). In fact, it may be one of the most important feelings we let them have. We are not helping them grow important relational muscles if we teach them that *their* feelings should be at the center of all decisions, that life should never be unfair, disappointing, or painful. When you can let others be disappointed, you have more room to truly scan for your own desires and put them in the equation of your decisions and choices. This is likely better for all of your relationships, trust us.

Over-Focusing on Feeling Let Down or Disappointed

Our struggle to identify and ask for what we want can have another unintended impact. For those of us who lean red, we can often maintain chronic feelings of disappointment—over a situation or someone else's actions—and this can become a source of frustration for our partners or close others.

Since we often sense what others need, we might believe others can do the same. Remember, your ability to tune in to other people's needs is likely higher than others' in your life, especially if they lean blue. If we forget that, we are likely to misinterpret when others don't respond to us how we wish and often view it as lack of care. We can then put our energy into a negative narrative and ruminate, which only intensifies this feeling. Rather than ask directly for what we want, we hope that those close to us will just "know." If we have to tell someone what to do for us, we might think it "doesn't count." But this is a fantasy, because the only time someone is indeed devoted to intuiting our needs is when we are, well, very young. In-a-crib young. After that, it's all two-person negotiation with active co-regulation. Thus, as adults, we must "use our words" about how we want to be treated. We know it blows up the fantasy of the Hollywood love story we think we deserve, but what you'll get instead is more mutual, and is more likely to grow over time and endure.

Putting your wishes out there and using your words might sound like this: "Hey, babe, I know you think birthdays aren't a big deal. I get that. But *I* kind of do. My big day is next Saturday, and it would mean a lot if you could plan something together with the kids. I'd love a card, also you make great waffles; could you make those for me?"

Give them many ways to get it right rather than a narrow runway that all but ensures they will crash. Beware of setting up subliminal litmus tests to determine if someone really cares. Being open and direct increases the chance of success for the birthday, adds levity, and keeps the stakes light rather than waiting and hoping, then experiencing the dreaded (but not entirely unexpected) disappointment.

For those of you saying, "Wait! I don't always want to be the one to ask for what I want! I want him [or her or them] to know and be thinking of me, too!" We hear you. However, secure relating is not about changing *other* people.

The goal is to develop your own secure self no matter what choices those around you make. That way, if your birthday turns out to be a dud, you'll take better care to make a splash next year. It's staying engaged and dealing with frustrations interpersonally and without big feelings of dread and danger lurking about.

We Can Be Hard to Console—Taking in Comfort

In moments when we are mad or upset with our partner for having done something "wrong," difficulty or resistance to being comforted is a hallmark of preoccupied attachment maps. We may prefer to hold the anger or fear letting it go, saying things such as "Why didn't you think of me when . . . ?" instead of attuning to the person who is there, right now, talking with you, listening to you. Sometimes we do this because we fear losing something if we give up our anger and open up.

If we are upset that our partner has ignored us too much, becoming angry and pointing to the evidence feels less vulnerable than tuning in to our fear that they do not want us. Expressing desires is much more intimate and inviting, yet it leaves us open to disappointment again, so why take the risk?

Staying in the story of "they don't care" can easily reenact the problem we fear, and eventually our partner may begin to dodge us for fear of this reactivity. If you fear being "too much," we get that. Asking for the things you need doesn't typically tax a relationship; it's needing things but *not allowing* the other person to fulfill those needs or never being satisfied by their efforts, no matter how genuine, that puts empathy on a timer.

If you want to be more open to being soothed, you must question your negative interpretation. Remember, overly negative interpretations can be part of your red-tinted sunglasses that watch for anything threatening. We can almost always find what we are looking for if we look hard enough, so imagine the most positive interpretation of your close people and find evidence of how they *do* show up for you. If you are collecting disappointments, that's fine, but be fair: also make a list of what they get right and what would make you sad if they stopped doing it altogether. This can help correct your neuroceptive bias toward fear and its accompanying negativity. It does not mean that your perceptions are wrong; you are tuned in and aware, and your feelings are important and worthy of care. We are encouraging you to be *balanced* in your review and work to express what is important to you without panic, pressure, and fear.

Connect to your agency. Those with red-leaning attachment maps believe the resolution to anxiety or hurt feelings is in someone else's hands.

By calling on your own right-size adult self, you focus on soothing your feelings and moving into the green zone, whether your needs are met or not. Also, feeling that your request is valid and that you are worthy of asking sets up your body to feel more grounded. The added benefit is that it also makes it more effective partly because you come across as safe to your listener. Knowing that you are worth being heard and can find your way forward is not only the truth but also the way to hold your own power.

Do Something! Hold Yourself by Slowing Down

Remember the high-stakes tell we mentioned above? The physiology of up-regulation when feeling threatened sends our body all sorts of messages: *Act! Move! Hurry! Do something!* That's just the neurochemicals talking, and our stress hormones are not what we want to listen to when relationally upset. You want to notice and explore the feeling rather than turn it into action. *I feel like storming off* is way better than hightailing it. Only by slowing down the stress cascade can we entertain important musings, such as: or else *what*?

To build the reflective muscle that slows down the system, say your name either to yourself or if possible aloud to add that reflective perspective. You want to interrupt the urge to act. *Ann, take a breath*, she might think to herself. "Sue, what's the rush?" she might say aloud.

Taking that magic restorative deep breath, or several, is key.

Now visualize your heart beating, your mind alert, and your strong legs ready to carry you forward. Remember that all these bodily reactions function to alert you to something important. You are likely not in any immediate or mortal danger, despite the mayday transmitted by your protection system. It's a false alarm. Yes, you are stressed; no, you aren't actually in danger.

A young, implicit memory may insist that separation or an experience of feeling forgotten is dangerous, but your adult self can handle a few minutes, hours—even days—with emotional distance. Yes it's uncomfortable, but it isn't dangerous—you can tolerate it. Visualize yourself on the spectrum of activation and remind yourself that in the red, your body is overstimulated and underregulated; this is the pressure you are feeling, not the action or inaction of someone else. "It's not Sue that is a huge problem right now; it's my amygdala," Ann might tell herself.

Try to become what we affectionately call "an amygdala whisperer." When triggered, we react to our emotions over our thinking, so we need to cool off our protection system. Use your thinking to prime security: "I will take myself seriously and don't need to plead or explain."

To be super geeky, you could even say, "My left amygdala is firing to keep me safe; I need my right PFC to calm that sucker down." Also, you can use time as a tool because remember, if the amygdala is in charge you've lost the present and future. By calling up your sense of time—you haven't always felt this way, you won't always feel this way—you are automatically engaging higher parts of your mind such as your hippocampus and PFC, even if the amygdala is still active. So, visualize yourself and the object of your ire a few hours later, after things calm down.

Let's say your eleven-year-old stomps down the hall and slams their door. If you can fast-forward in your mind, you can realize that in an hour, this will pass, and they'll be bugging you for a bite of whatever you are eating. You can visualize their puffed-up energy having dissipated, and by not following them down the hall and fighting with them, you allow them space to regulate their aggression and see that the anger passes. The trick here is that it doesn't matter if they do calm down or not: by thinking more secure thoughts, you prime *yourself* out of your own activation and back into the green zone. So, rather than jump into action, notice the feeling and hold it. You will be okay letting it run through you rather than pushing forward with it. Wait, don't react, and let time pass. Then, with your fuller embodied mind, you can move for a place of connection.

Mushy Boundaries—Find Your Clarity First

Do you make decisions by committee? Run informal polls to figure out how you feel or what you should do?

If you trend red, your body may feel best when those around you feel safe, good, and in agreement. For example, it's not uncommon to be sincerely happy at almost any restaurant chosen by those you care about as long as everyone else is happy. If they feel good, then all is good in your world. It's often not that you know what you want and choose to ignore it, but you've learned to tune in so quickly to the wants and needs of others and find meeting those needs so gratifying that actually stopping to know what you want can be the real challenge. As a matter of fact, if someone insists that *you* choose whatever *you* want, this can present an embarrassing challenge. Claiming yourself is a vulnerable act. If you stop to notice how much of your own perspective you've given up, it's painful.

When insecurity looms, it can feel like the right decision is out there, but you just don't know it. The more choices we have, the more we risk making a "wrong" decision, which is why we look externally for answers. Building confidence in your sense of authority is a process, but once you realize that you can be as much of an expert as those you seek input from, turning inside becomes a bit easier. How can anyone else know what you want or need better than you?

Form a thought you've wanted to say to someone but haven't yet. Visualize yourself asking for something important to you. Say the words in your mind or out loud.

"I want to talk about who does what around the house."

Say it, whatever it is!

"I think it's time for a raise."

Keep going!

"I want you to initiate sex with me this way."

You get to ask for anything, and they get to respond or have a feeling or otherwise not deliver, and that's okay! We are focusing right now on you being able to put it out there.

By forming those words in your mind, you're building new neural connections. By saying them, you're building new motor connections. Even better, you can keep going. Imagine your person having a *negative* reaction: let's say that they sigh deeply and look down, or they shake their head no and begin telling you why. That's fine, let it play out in your mind's eye, but this time, stay engaged. Your next move is the most important in the exchange. Rather than responding in reactive upset to their head shake or their protest, stay clear to your need or goal. This in itself is holding a boundary. "I hear you don't agree with my thoughts on this. I get that. But whether you agree or not, it is still important to me." Boundaries are often thought of as limits or rejecting borders. We prefer to regard boundaries as *clarity*. Being clear with yourself first, then with others, and holding that in importance.

Giving your body the memory of holding your own is surprisingly effective.

Your challenge today is to find clarity in what is important to you and let the other person have their feelings about it. Trust them. They can feel hard feelings, it's okay; you just hold tight. Tolerating someone else's anger or their let down will be a game changer. You can hear it—even have compassion for their experience—without being responsible. Boundaries are about clarity of what you need and want, not about rejecting anyone else.

Sentences, Not Essays

Speaking your truth is usually a way to claim power, but when we are activated red, we can get quite verbose and have much to say, unconsciously undermining our message. No matter how well meaning, no one can really hear and take in *essays* of your perspective. They need bullet points and fair turn taking. And to be honest, by the time we are verbally going on too long, we often are not very connected to ourself, either, so it makes sense that people drift away (because we aren't present, either).

Making your point concisely requires you to consider your needs more deeply to help you eliminate all those extra words that unintentionally flood the other person and increase the chance of your getting pushed away. Clarity in your points and phrasing is more likely to be effective and get you what you want, which is the whole point of communicating.

So, if you want something, you don't have to justify why you feel the way you do or explain the backstory leading up to it; you can *just say it*.

You do not have to be right to have feelings. This is a critical point. We red leaners doubt our perspective and experiences, so we hold back, trying to decide if what we are feeling is accurate or appropriate for the occasion. Using caveats and extended justifications exposes your uncertainty and your need for the other person to be okay with your words. This can consciously or unconsciously lead you both to continue focusing

Figure numbers in this insert correspond to the figures in the text.

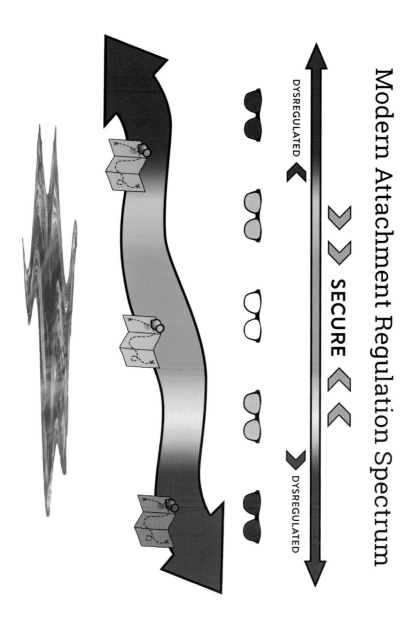

Figure 1: The MARS Framework

The Spectrum

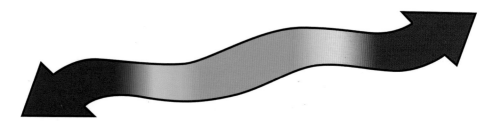

Figure 2: The MARS Spectrum

Connection System (felt safety) or Protection System (felt threat)

Figure 3: Connection System or Protection System
We often aren't aware that we are in a threat response,
so learning to distinguish these states is important.

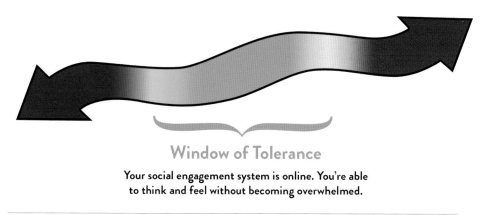

Window of Tolerance

Your social engagement system is online. You're able to think and feel without becoming overwhelmed.

Figure 4: The Window of Tolerance
Adapted from Dr. Dan Siegel's *The Developing Mind*, 1999.

The Spectrum (States of Mind)

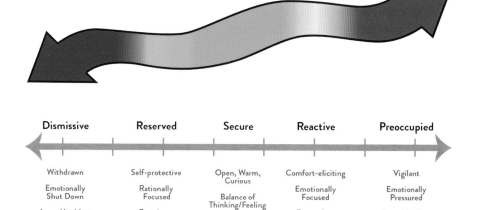

Dismissive	Reserved	Secure	Reactive	Preoccupied
Withdrawn	Self-protective	Open, Warm, Curious	Comfort-eliciting	Vigilant
Emotionally Shut Down	Rationally Focused	Balance of Thinking/Feeling	Emotionally Focused	Emotionally Pressured
Angry/Avoidant	Emotions Minimized		Focused on Others	Angry/Anxious

Figure 5: The Spectrum
Common state activation along the spectrum.

BAMA	Development Window	Primary Discipline	Common Assessment	Key Ideas	Common Nomenclature
B Biology of Attachment	Prenatal - Lifetime	Affective Neuroscience / Interpersonal Neurobiology	fMRI cortisol/oxytocin heart rate variability	Protection/connection systems, polyvagal theory implicit memory, right-to-right relating	amygdala HPA Axis hippocampus prefrontal cortex
A Attachment Patterns (child)	3 Months - 18 Months	Developmental Psychology	Strange Situation	Behavioral attachment patterns, caregiver/infant relationship, not individually diagnostic, relationship strategies	Secure Insecure/Resistant Insecure/Avoidant Disorganized
M Maps - Attachment Maps	3/4 Years - Lifetime	Developmental & Clinical Psychology	AAI Adult Attachment Interview and AAP Adult Attachment Projective	Internal Working Models IWM + embodied culture & context	Secure Preoccupied Dismissing Disorganized/ Unresolved
A Adult Attachment Styles	Adult - Lifetime	Social Psychology +	Experiences in Close Relationships - Revised (ECR-R)	Adult Attachment Styles Anxiety/Avoidance dimensional measures Self-report	Secure Dismissive/Avoidant Preoccupied Fearful/Avoidant

Figure 6: BAMA Framework

Adult Attachment Styles

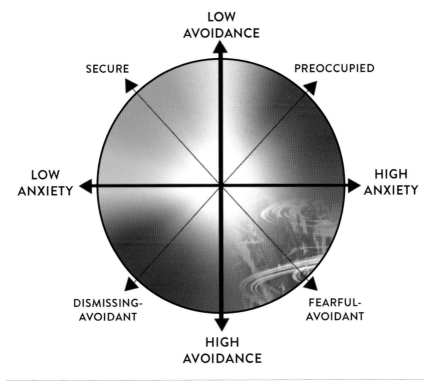

Figure 7: Adult Attachment Styles
Adapted from Brennon, Clark, and Shaver, 1998.

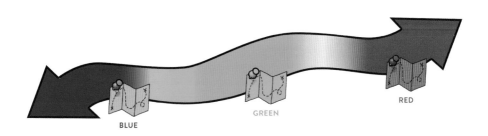

Figure 9: Maps along the spectrum
Attachment maps are more stable but can be changed.

What Shade is Your Map?

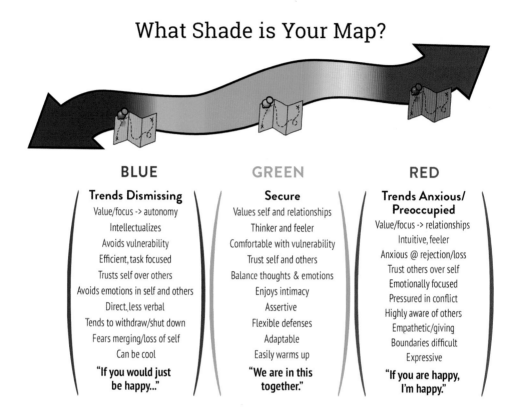

BLUE	GREEN	RED
Trends Dismissing	**Secure**	**Trends Anxious/ Preoccupied**
Value/focus -> autonomy	Values self and relationships	Value/focus -> relationships
Intellectualizes	Thinker and feeler	Intuitive, feeler
Avoids vulnerability	Comfortable with vulnerability	Anxious @ rejection/loss
Efficient, task focused	Trust self and others	Trust others over self
Trusts self over others	Balance thoughts & emotions	Emotionally focused
Avoids emotions in self and others	Enjoys intimacy	Pressured in conflict
Direct, less verbal	Assertive	Highly aware of others
Tends to withdraw/shut down	Flexible defenses	Empathetic/giving
Fears merging/loss of self	Adaptable	Boundaries difficult
Can be cool	Easily warms up	Expressive
"If you would just be happy..."	**"We are in this together."**	**"If you are happy, I'm happy."**

Figure 11: Common characteristics by color
Identify where you trend and signs that you've left the green zone.

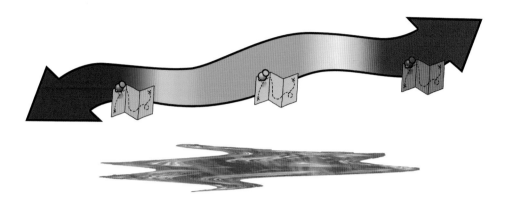

Figure 12: The Tie-Dye Puddle
The puddle represents temporary dysregulation/disorientation—
the goal is to get back up anywhere on the spectrum.

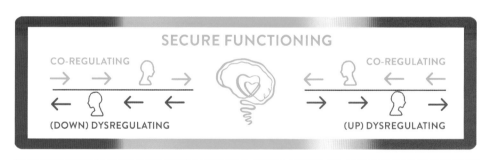

Figure 14: Co-regulation/Co-dysregulation
We can move one another into more secure functioning or more dysregulation.

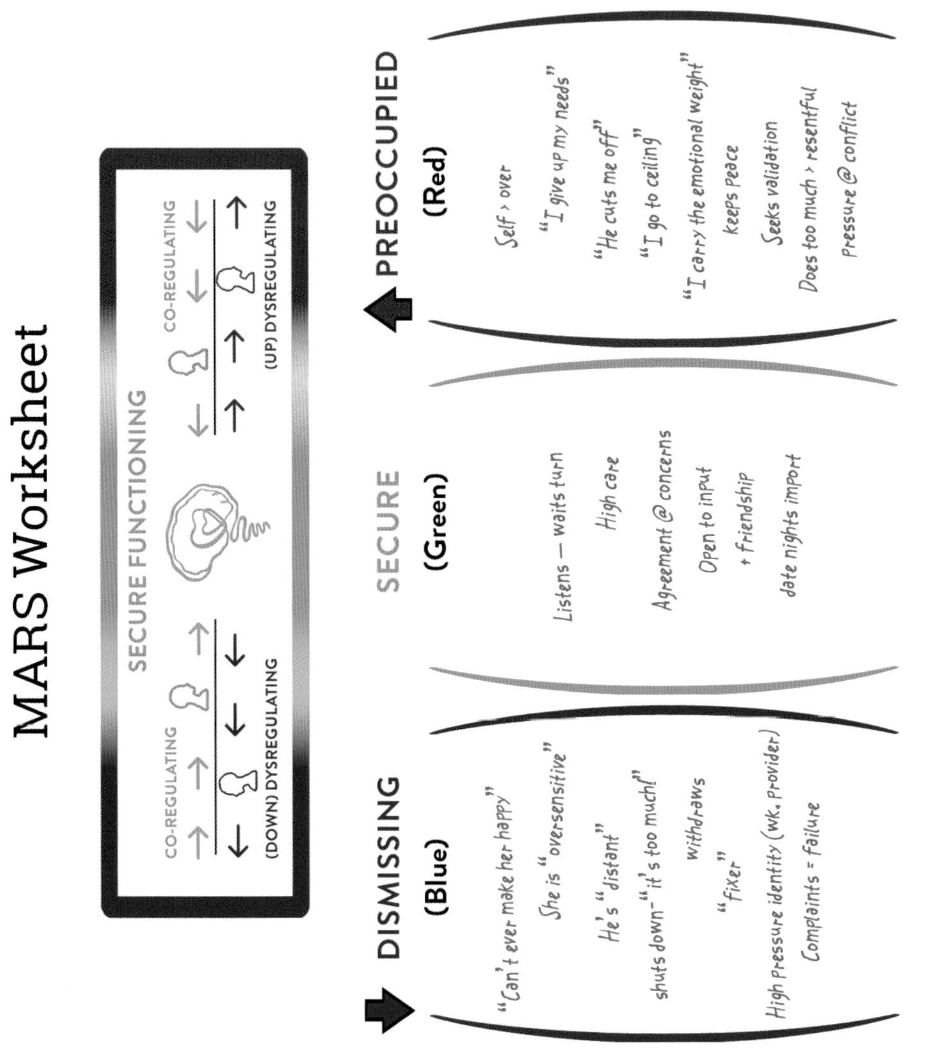

MARS Worksheet

SECURE FUNCTIONING

CO-REGULATING

CO-REGULATING

(DOWN) DYSREGULATING

(UP) DYSREGULATING

DISMISSING (Blue)

"Can't ever make her happy"

She is "oversensitive"

He's "distant"

shuts down – "it's too much!"

withdraws

"fixer"

High pressure identity (wk. provider)

Complaints = failure

SECURE (Green)

Listens — waits turn

High care

Agreement @ concerns

Open to input

+ friendship

date nights import

PREOCCUPIED (Red)

Self > over

"I give up my needs"

"He cuts me off"

"I go to ceiling"

"I carry the emotional weight"

keeps peace

Seeks validation

Does too much > resentful

Pressure @ conflict

Figure 15: MARS Worksheet.
Example of notes taken with signs of the various kinds of activation

on their thoughts and opinions rather than your own. It's as if we are trying to *prove* that our needs are important enough to be considered.

Pay attention to your voice: Is it high pitched and pleading or intense, angry, and accusatory? These are the physiological signs that you have shifted to self-protection and are not in your more green, secure self. We aren't saying to stuff a sock in your mouth—quite the opposite! We are saying to take yourself seriously and consider what's most important. Slow down your nervous system (breathe, pause, let your prefrontal cortex and thinking mind catch up and steady your voice).

Ask yourself what you want, what is important to you and what may be blocking you from speaking your truth.

Why am I afraid just to say it without defending it?

If I skipped the backstory, what core takeaway or idea do I want them to know?

These calming measures are intended to get your green zone, ventral vagal activation going, which means you are aware of your worth and take what you have to say seriously. This signals others to do the same. So, take a moment to organize your thoughts and visualize your powerful, best self to earn yourself the respect you deserve. If someone says you're being "too sensitive," rather than defending yourself, claim yourself.

"Whether it feels too sensitive to you or not, it is important to me, and I need you to know that."

Holding Your Own in Conflict

You may have noticed that the theme in most of the conflicts above centers on learning to hold your own: your own feelings, needs, desires, perspectives, limits, and decisions. Learning to hold yourself with compassion, care, patience, and confidence does not mean forgetting others. Quite the opposite. It means holding self *and* others. Here are some general ways to practice holding your own daily.

Containment is power. If you struggle with saying things too quickly, too frequently, or too intensely, practice seeing something and *not* saying something, at least not immediately. By containing that first impulse you can find your second and third thoughts and strategize what, if anything, you want to share.

Have they earned your trust to open up?

Will they reciprocate?

Especially hold your tongue if your impulse is to tell them what they are doing wrong to make you feel XYZ. The goal is not to change the outside world in order to avoid your internal activation. Instead, take a moment to feel the feelings, be aware that you can handle the experience, then ask yourself, *What is the activation about?*

Imagine a sizable, gorgeous wood-grain salad bowl, and let that be the container of all your beautiful, worried musings. Keep things safely *in the bowl* until they are processed enough to be shared, and then serve reasonable portions so that your guest can enjoy your incredible mind.

Recognize Your Red ANTs (Automatic Negative Thoughts)

Since anger and frustration about being let down or left out is such a common red-oriented complaint, it stands to reason that it would be important to begin to mindfully reconsider your certainty about your read on relational situations. Notice any automatic repeating thoughts.

Big ones include feeling as if you love them more than they love you or feelings of being dropped, not important enough, rejected, abandoned, or left out. Other experiences include the feelings of looking in from the outside, not fitting in, fear of being judged and rejected, fear that they really don't want you there, and fear that they really don't like or love you after all. What matters is that you find and name your favorite repeated bully patterns.

Be specific: What runs through your brain when you are activated? Is your ire firing at you or at the other person? Either way, look for repeated feelings and patterns—those are your ANTs.

Remember, you undoubtedly will be missed, dropped, ignored, and left out at one time or another. It stirs a primary experience of rejection that once meant mortal danger in our survival, but now, it's just a feeling. If you can't contain yourself, you are either forcing the other person to merge with you in the morass of your feelings or you are pushing them away, which is not, deep down, what you actually want.

You are important and special; hold that tightly.

Co-regulating—Successfully
Soothing Red Zone Activation

Oxygen Mask on You First

If someone you know gets activated red, the first order of business is to stay regulated yourself.

This is easier said than done because as the recipient of their heightened emotions, you may be in the hot seat, and, as you've learned, humans can easily co-dysregulate. The minute you notice someone getting agitated (including yourself), do a few things right away. First, take a couple of those good regulating breaths, focusing on the slow inhale (count to four), hold it (count to four) and then release it (four beats again). Then gentle shake out any tightness so that your arms are limp, you are sitting heavy in the chair (versus getting ready to spring up), your eyes have a soft focus, and make sure your tongue is not touching the top of your mouth. Doing these things tricks your sonar system and directs it toward calming down.

By forcing oxygen into your body and slowing your breath, you ensure that when your neuroceptive sonar sweeps to see how you are doing it'll notice plenty of oxygen, which is a sign of safety. So are loose limbs, soft eyes, and unclenched jaws. Within at least twenty seconds but for sure in a minute or so of this intentional softness, you'll literally feel it begin to work and your body calming down.

Now you have room to imagine how your best, highest, wisest self would respond. This is a version of "security priming" and calls on your prefrontal cortex to help out. Picture yourself fully immersed in your green zone self, full of warmth, strength, and compassion. Remember, the goal isn't to talk someone out of their feelings, it is connection and safety. There is no rush.

Now that you are on firmer ground, you have more resources to share to help cool off what's coming at you. You might picture the activated person as young and genuinely upset—it can help you stay compassionate. Remember they are seeing things through their sunglasses that tinge everything a bit more extreme—they aren't making it up, they really are experiencing the world that way.

Soft shields help us stay in the green zone sometimes. You may want to prepare yourself for accusations—often with them centered on feelings that you don't care enough about them. This is an unskilled, activated bid for connection, not an attack on your character. This can be especially challenging for blue leaners, who are often extremely protective of their identity and can focus heavily on facts. If the red leaner in your life amplifies when upset, they aren't being intentionally manipulative. Instead, imagine that they had to make things bigger to feel they were being taken seriously. Also, know that they feel hurt big-time, not because you are so bad but because feeling hurt is hard! So, don't dismiss their emotions. Their vulnerability is hanging out there, and they need you to fly cover for them if you are closer to the green zone than they are. Bear in mind that they are trying to tell you something important. If you dismiss it due to the intensity, you will shut down vital parts of your relationship.

All that said, their activation isn't a license for you to be bullied. If your partner can't take in your sincere efforts to help them regulate at that moment, you should protect yourself. Putting your oxygen mask on first might mean taking a break or letting them know you are not in a good place to listen, so you are taking a short time to gather. Step outside for a bit or take a walk. It is very important, though, to make it clear that you will return and let them know when, since one of the deep-seated fears for people living in the red is the threat of abandonment. This will help your partner's body feel safe rather than getting more highly activated by your departure. They won't like this, but it'll give you both some breathing room for your nervous systems to cool off.

As soon as you are ready, move toward them instead of pushing them away. Find ways to reassure this beloved person in a way that they can take in.

Be straightforward with them and use clear messages such as:

"I'm listening."
"That's helpful to know."
"I'm glad you are checking this out with me."

Be the bigger person and apologize first if you can mean it. If you put on their sunglasses and view the situation, it's easier to say, "Oooh, I can see why it hit you like that. That isn't what I meant, but, yeah, your reaction makes sense if you heard it that way."

Give them credit whenever possible and convey a "You aren't crazy" message because they aren't. Your warmth and desire to soothe their protective system is important. Remember, if you run blue you may be withdrawing and dismissing in ways that are a big part of their activation. They are upset because connection with you is important. So, warming up both systems with your facial expression, tone of voice, and pace is important. One of our roles as primaries is to be an amygdala whisperer, a huge sign of progress on our own earning security journey.

Use a Third Person (Real or Imagined)

Don't let pride get in the way of your more mature, secure self. To maintain access to your green zone, imagine listening to the argument like a third person: perhaps a wise friend, therapist, or any respected other. Seeing yourself reflecting with them in the future, after things settle, can help you lower the stakes of the moment. Pretend you'll have to relay this to a friend, or to a real or imagined couples' therapist—that kind of witnessing can help us regulate if needed. Or, more simply, imagine yourself the next day. From this place, listen for what the other person needs from you. Assure them you are willing to talk about it, you are available, but may need time. Or you may need them to lower the volume so you can hear them better.

Finally, use your words to create kindness, love, and respect. "I'm right here, I'm listening; can we slow down? Can we just cover one thing at a time? I'm getting full but want to listen; can we give this another five minutes, then can we wrap up this part of the conversation together? We can come back to it later." And, if you say that, mean it! In short, be their advocate, not their critic. This helps fire up their ventral vagal system and return to that more generous and enjoyable green zone.

Our learned protective and connective strategies can be our biggest strengths once we understand them and learn to use the best parts for our greater secure self. Think of it as a social and emotional workout. We are putting a set of weights in your hands to strengthen the parts of your system that haven't received enough protection and need more time, attention, and care.

Being highly attuned to others, being in touch with the value of relationships, and having access to your emotional self is awesome! Take these strengths, hold on to them, develop the muscles that have been under-functioning, and enjoy the powerful combination that follows. Our goal here is to help you build on your foundation to grow an even more powerful and secure self that can be effective and influential in all of your relationships and communities. That is secure relating.

10

Resolving the Unresolved

The Tie-Dye Puddle

This attachment category has the most variable language and descriptors because it is so complex, and we suspect it consists of multiple subcategories caused by different early experiences and perhaps by different neurological leanings. We like how Crittendon says these children are not "disorganized" but doing exactly what they need to do to stay out of danger—the opposite of formlessness.

We use the tie-dye puddle to represent the dysreglation and at times disorientation that occurs due to what has been called early infant disorganization. So, as adults it might look like a devoted mom who startles at her child's touch or has difficulties managing time-sensitive tasks such as getting the kids dressed and off to school. Or a seemingly unflappable cop who loves his job and community but can get disoriented quickly and go into a rage when his fear circuit activates. It's the teacher who has internalized so much fear for her own safety that she cannot set limits with her students and has trouble focusing on preparing course material in a clear and organized way. It can even be a CEO or politician who perceives an internal threat to their personhood and worldview of success, which can cause dysregulation to the point of existential rage and divisive despair.

Having a history of trauma or having post-traumatic stress disorder (PTSD) isn't the same thing as having attachment disruptions that lead to tie-dye dysregulation, but they are indeed related. Trauma can happen to anyone, regardless of their attachment security and relational history. When trauma symptoms emerge in the present, it's an indication that the trauma is not fully processed, and it continues to impact your stress response system. You may occasionally fall into a disorganized pocket if your trauma gets triggered, but with a generally more secure attachment history, it's rare and will be specific to the trauma experience.

However, if as a child you had experiences that were so chaotic, threatening, or unpredictable that you could not find an effective strategy to keep your parents available to you, you may struggle with a more ongoing state of dysregulation. You likely developed a coping strategy involving a mixture of preoccupation and avoidance that doesn't follow the recognized coping response patterns.

As you learned in chapter 6, unresolved attachment strategies can emerge for any of us if our experiences of stress or trauma outstrip our ability to cope. Still, what this kind of unpredictable dysregulation looks like can be hard to pin down because the very nature of trauma makes it difficult, if not impossible, to put into words.

None of us are entirely immune to tie-dye moments, and our nervous systems are often so good at protecting us from the memory of unprocessed overwhelm that we aren't even aware we have a pocket of trauma hibernating in our limbic-level basement. Symptoms are present, but we think they are normal idiosyncrasies. We fail to see how they relate to our tendencies to avoid specific triggers or overreact when that limbic bubble gets tickled.

It can feel confusing. Perhaps you go beyond just being in a light trance for a short time and uncomfortably disconnect from yourself and have trouble grounding. Or perhaps you feel like your thoughts are spinning and it's difficult to get out of it, or your body flops to more of a freeze response and you aren't feeling much of anything.

When we find ourselves in a state of severe overwhelm, it can feel like we lack control over our circumstances, causing our bodies to enter a passive survival mode by any means necessary. This can lead to either overcontrolled reactivity or a dissociative disconnection from reality, both stemming from an overwhelming sense of distress. If you've experienced significant early-life danger, your nervous system might have learned to switch off abruptly, like a breaker box rather than a more gradual dimmer switch. This can make it easier for you to disconnect even in situations where there isn't imminent danger; those neural pathways are simply more accessible due to your history.

In other words, if you learned to dissociate and enter a state of dorsal vagal immobilization to survive, you may find yourself prone to dissociation even in less threatening circumstances. It may not take much stress to trigger dissociation in your present-day life.

One of the healing objectives is to regain control over this process, like finding the "light switch"—even installing a dimmer—so you can regulate more fluidly. This means learning how to stay present in your body and grounded when facing stress. Dissociation itself isn't necessarily harmful, and it can offer comfort in certain situations, but the key is to be aware of the experience, even be able to choose whether to dissociate or not. Being capable of returning to your body, feeling your feet, regulating your breath, and orienting yourself in the immediate environment helps shift you into a more present moment, away from that tie-dye-tinged state of disorientation.

Why You Fall into a Puddle

If you have been exposed to emotional or physical neglect or overwhelming feelings of danger or had a significant unprocessed loss as a child, you are more likely to have developed a mix of coping strategies that worked best at the time. Witnessing domestic violence, experiencing parental separation or the loss of a parent without social support, and living in extreme poverty or an unsafe neighborhood can increase the risk of disorganization, since the system is not supported enough to facilitate optimal child development. Also, having a depressed or substance-dependent caregiver or having a primary parent with unprocessed and unresolved trauma is a risk factor for disorganized attachment. Many avenues can impair a parent's ability to reflect on and empathize with a child's thoughts and feelings that can leave a child feeling alone, overwhelmed, and unsafe. Of course, experiencing direct physical or sexual abuse are all potential contributing factors that increase the risk of disorganized attachment.

If you are in this boat and reading this book, we consider you a sturdy survivor! As you read please remember we are covering statistics and probabilities, not talking about your experience specifically. Our goal is to help you over time and with others piece together your life story so that it comes together and makes sense, letting go of old narratives that are harmful, and coming to believe what is actually true about your worth and value. It's a hard topic but way more common than you might think, so we will continue but are holding in mind all the sturdy survivors out there.

Kids identified as having disorganized attachments with their caregiver didn't get the chance to develop healthy coping skills, so they are at higher risk for struggles as they age. They spent their energy surviving and didn't have help sorting out their feelings, so naturally they aren't great at understanding and managing emotions. This sets them up to be more likely to struggle with anxiety, depression, acting-out aggression, substance abuse, and self-harm.

The cycle of abuse is painful, and most abuse occurs in families that have multiple risk factors already. For example, neglectful and/or abusive parents often have a history of severe relational conflict, postpartum depression, significant loss (like the loss of a baby at birth or soon thereafter), depression, and other psychiatric concerns, any of which impacts the parent's capacity to raise an infant. In addition, one review of studies found that living in environments with accumulated socioeconomic risk factors (family living in severe poverty without job opportunities, mental illness in parent or sibling, financial strain from divorce or incarceration, for example) can also be so disruptive to a child's development that it is associated with disorganized attachment absent any parental abuse.

The context umbrella cannot be overstated here. See these kids and their families within the context of larger systems that fail to provide material support, healthcare, mental health care, and economic opportunities. Ah, the webs we weave, which is why holding your own while also focusing on broader system issues matters so deeply.

Signs of Tie-Dye Activation

Tie-dye activation can take many different forms. If, when activated, you drop into dorsal activation (parasympathetic brake, down-regulation, flop), it can feel like walking in molasses or floating in outer space. Physically we may be slumped or slouched, our bodies shaped like a C. In more severe activation, our limbs and head can feel heavy, and our movements and breathing slow. We have natural opiates coursing through our bloodstream to protect us from impending pain. Your facial expression will be flat and not give away much, and inside, you may feel "nothing" or numb.

Because the puddle is a tie-dye mix of strategies, we may also sympathetically up-regulate when overwhelmed. In that case, we might get physically tense as we contain overwhelming feelings, or those big emotions might just come spilling out all over us and anyone nearby. If you could identify feelings, they would likely be intense, be they terror, shame, fear, self-loathing, or silent rage toward someone else. Patterns in this direction are associated with having experienced overwhelming fear as a child (versus neglect). Your amygdala will be highly sensitive to cues of that threat reoccurring.

In the puddle, you may feel certainty one moment and self-doubt the next because you will have difficulty trusting your mind and others. You may secretly hope that someone will come to take care of you or rescue you but cannot signal for help. Finally, you may engage in destructive behaviors you don't understand, such as intentionally harming yourself or unusual compulsions that you find soothing.

When you're marooned in a puddle, your neurotransmitters may be out of balance, aggravating the sense of danger and fear of self and others. As you can imagine, these dysregulated puddles can get in the way of intimacy and connection in relationships, especially when the other person doesn't understand what is happening.

When you become aware that the fear and turmoil you're experiencing in the present moment is rooted in past events, a remarkable breakthrough occurs. This awareness by itself takes you out of the immediate experience; your PFC can help you think, name what you are feeling, and wonder what it's about. This PFC activation taps down the feeling already.* By embracing compassion, you disrupt the harmful cycle of dysregulation and self-criticism. This compassionate attitude makes room for curiosity and fosters new learning opportunities—i.e., you can encode something different, new safer experiences, rather than just re-experience the pain as it was. Acknowledging how unresolved attachment or trauma has shaped your current coping strategies is a significant accomplishment, as it empowers you to consciously update your ways of relating to others. Instead of relying on automatic protective and defensive responses, you can now engage your higher cognitive functions and your newer safe connections to develop more secure attachment patterns.

These illuminating moments, reminiscent of a lightbulb flickering on, carry immense relief and excitement as we unravel patterns that were once elusive and shame inducing. Termed "organizing the disorganized," this transformative process replaces the sense of chaos with comprehensible insights that cultivate genuine self-compassion. Armed with the comforting realization that we are not alone, we are ready to navigate our journey more confidently, relying on a better-organized internal map and a compass guided by empathy. We can trust this bus ride a little more and continue our pilgrimage.

Strengths of Tie-Dye

Children who have experienced traumatic loss, endured emotional abuse, or feared for their lives know how to appreciate love and life and the feeling of security when they find it. Their difficulty with trust makes building relationships with them slow going, of course. These individuals are often described as hard on the outside and soft in the middle, but it can be so rewarding when you get to their middle! Their depth and insight can make all that work worth it.

If you are lucky enough to be involved with someone who has done

---

* "Name it to tame it," popularized by the venerable Dr. Dan Siegel, is a common phrase used in trauma therapy.

and continues to do their deep trauma work, they will push you and expose the areas in *you* that need healing and attention. This person is working super hard, which means you have to do the same to keep up with them. These relationships can be challenging, but they can result in a deep and profound connection. Professionally, bonding with clients who have gone through such pain and have come out the other side is the most rewarding and humbling experience in our careers.

Those of us who spend a lot of time in our tie-dye puddle have all the strengths of those who carry blue and red attachment maps because we readily use both sets of coping strategies. Suppose you've experienced adversity to the level that you've developed a tie-dye coping strategy and survived. In that case, you can be highly attuned to signs of danger and will not immediately feel overwhelmed when the unexpected occurs. Research suggests that those with insecure and unresolved attachment histories who have worked toward gaining attachment security can heal and parent well. In fact, because they've worked so hard on themselves, sometimes their capacity for active and accurate reflection can be greater than for those who come by security naturally.

There is also an evolutionary advantage for those who learned early to cope by dissociating. Dissociation effectively pauses traumatic memories, which can reduce hypervigilance, normalize cortisol levels, and reduce sympathetic emotional reactivity. These adaptations can continue to benefit individuals as adults, when they have important tasks to attend to that would be disrupted if overwhelming emotions surfaced uncontrollably. Our bodies know what they are doing, and although the cost of dissociation is high, it does make sense in some cases because it can help prevent trauma survivors from feeling submerged in a tsunami of emotions.

Finally, regarding treatment prognosis, there can be an advantage to a stronger tie-dye orientation over those that have a more organized dark blue, dismissing attachment map. The further blue you lean, the less aware you are of feeling emotional distress. Without pain or distress, there's no motivation to undertake the uncomfortable work required for change, but considerable motivation to avoid revisiting your emotional inner life. Conversely, if you find yourself frequently overwhelmed by emotions, you will be more directly aware of the need for help and more motivated to obtain it. This makes you more emotionally accessible, which is a wonderful precursor for healing, growth, and secure relating.

Common Tie-Dye Relational Dynamics (and Paths to Resolve Them)

Perpetual Stress

When you have more entrenched, unresolved trauma, your stress response system is on alert full-time. It wants to protect you from even feeling a desire for social connection. After all, the vulnerability of a desire for closeness has proven dangerous in the past.

This protectiveness can be overt, characterized by arguing, overexplaining, blaming, defending, and justifying, or it can be friendly and agreeable on the surface yet resistant and noncompliant underneath. If you've been mistreated and are terrified of the thoughts, feelings, and memories of this abuse, you are probably pretty angry in there somewhere. Staying angry can help defend against those unbidden longings. But if you can help your close people decode your patterns, they won't mistake your hard-shell toughness or anger for all that you are.

Your choice is to stay walled up and "safe" but trapped, or work to slowly discover hidden aspects of yourself that will give you your deserved human care. Professional help can come in many forms, such as individual therapy. But if that is inaccessible (for financial or cultural reasons), there are other options, including group therapy and programs offered through community YWCA and nonprofit organizations. Even online peer or professional support can make a big difference.

Managing When the "Safety" of Closeness Can Be a Source of Threat

If you identify with the tie-dye leanings we've described, you might, on the surface, mistrust others, but you also feel a longing for connection. You might be slow to warm up and actively test new connections because you assume that people will hurt you, but once you establish trust with someone, the bond can be intense. As you let people in, a new level of threat emerges that is deeper than what you've been used to: You've let down your guard, so you feel like a turtle without its shell, relying on someone you could lose. What is most familiar to you is the fortress you've constructed around your heart, so letting someone in could put you in uncharted, turbulent waters, which can lead to that painful "come here, go away" dynamic for you and your close others.

It is unlikely that whatever happened in the past is happening in the same way now that you are an adult. As a child, you didn't have resources or agency, but you absolutely do have more resources today than you did then. There is no way that exactly what happened to you then can happen to you now. Ever again.

The people you have allowed close to you are likely in the "safe enough" category and can be much more helpful to you than you realize—so the more you can be open with them, the safer—and happier—you'll be. We know that just reading this will not be enough to shift your internal experience to one of trust, but if you involve a safe other (if possible a professional), science is on the side of hope. If you keep trying in tiny increments trusting just a little bit and seeing how it goes, we believe recovery, discovery, and the awe of life await you.

Turn On Your Oxytocin Pathways—Face Clean Pain

If your history of attachment disruptions impacts your nervous system, then social and emotional connections may not give you the natural high that they do those who have had an easier time of it. Instead, intimacy and connection are fraught—so aloofness becomes a solution to avoid even the hint of rejection. Isolation is associated with fearful attachment, and while being alone may bring temporary relief, it becomes a harmful trap. Prolonged isolation creates structural changes in the brain and negatively impacts stress response systems.

In this isolated state, your protection circuit gets activated but gets no relief. That neurochemical dance gets dysregulated due to alterations in the dopamine and serotonin systems, and your immune system gets jacked up, producing atypically high inflammation in the body and brain. Also, a lack of social stimulation can lead to cognitive decline, as anyone who came out of Covid lockdown and found it difficult to reengage with other people knows well.

If you have barricaded yourself from risk through isolation or keeping people at arm's length, push yourself to expand a tiny bit out of your established safe haven. This may mean facing the dread and excuses that keep you avoiding others or changing the practiced schedule that keeps you regularly avoiding real connection. Small risks create new felt experiences and lead to new, more expansive learning. It won't go perfectly, but you will learn to trust *yourself* more to manage if things don't go as you hope, and as that comes on board, your life can really open up.

Staying engaged and pushing yourself to take small interpersonal risks is hard, but that kind of difficulty is what we call *clean* pain. Giving up in defensive avoidance or despair is *dirty* pain. Clean pain is essential to human relating: the unavoidable discomfort from facing life's challenges. Dirty pain is the additional suffering caused by staying in a defensive, cut-off, and dysregulated state. The unnecessary suffering comes from resisting or struggling against clean pain. There is no way out but to charge straight through, so stay in your labyrinth and keep plugging along, knowing that with support, you are strong enough to handle the clean pain path and the growth that comes from that. It is in the clean pain that others can bring support, connection, and compassion.

Mourn Significant Losses

We mean this on two levels.

First, the concrete: At times, instead of embracing the reality of death or the conclusion of a relationship, we shield ourselves from the pain and sorrow by staying mired in other feelings instead. Feelings like anger and regret may serve to hold on to the person, hindering our ability to properly grieve the loss. Whether it's the unwillingness to acknowledge that a relationship has reached its natural end or the haste to move past a significant death as though it were inconsequential, these actions block the grieving process. Refusal to accept that the relationship has run its course traps us in the known dirty pain and unrequited love: an approximation of closeness but without the threat of *actual* closeness.

Losing a parent or significant attachment figure when you are a child often contributes to the development of this protective pattern. It makes sense that significant loss is highly correlated with disorganized attachment strategies because so rarely at that age are there adequate supports in place to help the child process the loss. If possible, when losing a parent, kids need age-appropriate information as the loss is happening, active and ongoing involvement with the family's grieving process, and these kids need to have a surviving parent or trusted substitute be present and available to help in processing the loss. It is easy to imagine situations where these conditions are not met, and the child is left to manage and make sense of these huge feelings on their own.

Second, mourning a hidden loss. In most instances of attachment disruptions of any sort—blue, red, or tie-dye—the symptom itself is a compensation and signal of something painful not processed through. For those more buttoned up as a strategy, coming to see their history as neglectful, for example, has to happen before there is even a chance of grieving what they lost. They have to recognize there was something missing they needed. And for those who tend toward the anxious side of the spectrum, letting go of some of the more vigilant defenses to finally feel what is underneath is necessary to mourn and heal. Carol George describes this as Failed Mourning (for clinicians we recommend her book, *Working with Attachment Trauma*, 2023).

Other experiences that don't always register as a loss include things like: a caregiver having a life-changing injury or being diagnosed with a serious illness, the loss of a sibling, the death of a grandparent that causes the child's parent to become consumed by their own grief, losing a beloved home due to disaster or eviction, and having to flee their state or country due to danger or disaster, just to name a few. Many of these types of losses will only increase as climate change and the warming of our planet continue to wreak havoc on weather patterns, contributing to a growing number of raging storms, massive fires, and unprecedented flooding.

Sometimes we have to set aside acute pain to deal with life as it comes. But eventually we need to confront those feelings and reengage with the healing process if we want an integrated nervous system that doesn't get caught up in these dysregulated puddles. Fortunately, the grieving process is finite: although you may certainly miss a departed loved one forever, grief eventually transforms itself as it become integrated in your understanding of life and love. Having big open secure hearts nearby can help us through it, so we encourage you to go find one and lean in!

Disempower Disappointment

As we've mentioned, many kids with disorganized attachments adapt to their circumstances by engaging in a role reversal. Instead of expecting their parents to care for them, these children take on the caregiving role themselves; it's as if they're saying, "If you can't, then move over, I've got this." These adaptive kids can be pleading and pouting, or confident and demanding, but each strategy of course has different effects on both the child and the parent. The kid may pack school lunches, manage the calendar, have trouble trusting the parent to remember things, and generally attempt to regulate themselves and the parent. This isn't possible, of course, but it is a common adaptation when you are little and your parent cedes his or her responsibility. As an adult, if you find yourself in the overcontrolling category, have curiosity and compassion for how this may have developed, and challenge yourself to explore your history, learn to lean on others, and work to rewire this early learning.

For some of us with unresolved attachment strategies or histories of trauma, assertiveness can feel too frightening and is avoided at all costs. In those scenarios, a common strategy for getting needs met without facing the vulnerability of actually asking for help is to feign helplessness. If you find yourself hoping for rescue and attempting to communicate your needs via telepathy (or other creative indirect methods of communicating distress), this may be why.

Challenge yourself into new experiences where you begin to hold your own at whatever level you can tolerate. The person who doesn't pick up on your wishes isn't ignoring you. Remember, the goal is to grow your green zone and your capacity to stay engaged despite having big feelings, so that when disappointment happens, you can tolerate it and not amplify the distress. In the end, it's just a feeling. It'll pass. By learning to accept disappointment, you'll be more likely to get your needs met and help your body learn how to manage even more distressing feelings.

Children growing up in a double bind—confronted with an incomprehensible lose-lose choice—is a common theme in the tie-dye puddle world. For example, an intoxicated parent yells at their child but then asks immediately for a hug. The child's body screams no because they are terrified, but it also urges them forward because it needs comfort and fears not complying with the parent's request. There is no win here; the child's nervous system is urging both *Run away!* and *Run toward!* simultaneously.

If you can relate to this, it's a theme that likely repeats in your adult life. You want to get close to people but are afraid and don't believe they want you. You want to speak up for yourself but are terrified to do so.

Just knowing that this is a recurrent theme in your life will help you find alternatives to this false felt trap. There are always more options, degrees of opening up, and adjustments to your choices after the fact. When you feel caught in a trap, look for how you've collapsed options. If the stakes feel high—if you sense urgency and high anxiety within yourself—then you are likely activated and seeing the situation through your fear-filled sunglasses. You'll want to steer back toward green, which might just mean waiting, sleeping on it, or talking to someone to get perspective. Just don't believe the urgency, because *you* are in charge now.

Sue used to work as a line cook at a barbecue restaurant, responsible for making baskets of delicious thin-sliced fried onion rings (shout-out to Luther's!). She was new and trying to do a good job, but the orders kept coming in faster than she could keep up. She couldn't hurry the fryer, so as she waited and the orders stacked up, she began to panic. A manager noticed her stress and, like a wise Yoda, commanded kindly in a God-like voice, *"You control the onion rings, they don't control you!"*

This greasy mountaintop moment stuck with her, and now she uses that line whenever she gets herself in binds that, in reality, are not binding at all.

Co-regulating Successfully

Have we said it's about felt security (not just safety) enough times yet?

The key to co-regulating someone in a tie-dye puddle will always be to regulate *yourself* toward a secure state first. If the other person's body becomes significantly activated, and you join them, it's as if you are confirming that the world is not a safe space, and soon each of you will be on the ceiling, cutting off or running for the hills.

Setting clear boundaries can be challenging because it might feel like the other person will fall apart. If you're used to giving yourself to this person, boundaries can feel like you're rejecting them or leaving them in a time of need. However, when set firmly, not reactively, boundaries can send a message of strength. There is no need to get mad at the person asking something of you—they get to do that—as long as we can hold our own and comfortably say no when needed.

Think of yourself as the pole in a tetherball game that stands and maintains the grounding force even as the ball wings around you, first this way, then—*Pow!*—that way. As you stay sturdy, the ball comes to a calm center.

Keep in mind that establishing boundaries is about establishing what you will tolerate, not telling someone else what they are doing wrong. Telling someone they're being defensive often sounds accusatory and activates a more protective response.

A compassionate approach to bringing attention to their activation might be saying in a kind tone, "I don't think you mean to, but you sound a little angry as you are talking. Are you?" Or: "I must be coming across more critical than I mean to, are you feeling criticized?" And a ninja communicator might put it this way: "I'm finding it hard to connect with what you need, but I really want to. Can you say it again or in a different way so that I can understand?"

If someone has grown up with an undercurrent of "You're lazy!" and "You're always messing up!," they go on autopilot to prove this isn't so. Underneath, they're saying to themselves, *If I don't defend myself, I have to accept I suck, I'm broken, and I'm always doing it wrong.* Give them prompts that speak to this core: "I know you work hard, and I know you don't mean to do . . ." This allows their nervous system to calm down and hear what you actually are communicating, not what their limbic system is throwing their way.

If you can see someone you care about in a tie-dye puddle, you can truly support them. If they're in a puddle and nobody recognizes it, they risk being traumatized repeatedly. Carmen recognized this for Beth. Rather than keeping up her self-righteous anger about Beth's failed promises and relapses, she sent her the phone number for Pastor Ben, her previous safe haven. Carmen could see Beth living in her trauma protection. This didn't shift her need for boundaries, but at least Carmen recognized that her partner was not *choosing* to relapse or have trauma emerge in her actions. She was not responsible for her addiction or her painful disorganization. That said, Beth was the only one who could hold herself accountable and take responsibility for gathering the support she needed to recover.

Beth's Backstory—The Origins of Tie-Dye

Beth's mother believed that old myth that you would "spoil" a baby if you picked them up when they were crying. That was how she was raised, and like her mother, she had the capacity to emotionally block out Beth's cries. In addition, as a single mother with limited income, she had to rely on childcare that was sporadic and inconsistent. Finally, since she was a night nurse and had to sleep during the day after her shift, she often wasn't available for Beth when she needed her.

Initially, Beth would protest being put down in her crib during the day and cry intensely for her mom, but this did not help. The pain and fear were all-consuming, but there was no way to feel better by herself. Eventually she gave up trying to keep her mother from leaving her unattended. She was still in despair, but she had withdrawn into herself in resignation.

The terror, shame, and rejection she was experiencing were an amorphous cloud of disorganized pain since she had no way to understand what was causing the overwhelming feelings. Like all kids in similar situations, she had no choice but to internalize those feelings and encode that pain as being *about herself.* This is one way people develop an "un-thought known," or a deep sense of utter "badness" or "worthless."

In the worst-case scenario, Beth could have detached from her attach-ment system and not even acknowledge that she needed affection, love, and attention, much less worry about how to elicit it from others. Think of Dr. Harry Harlow's experiments, discussed in chapter 4, involving baby monkeys raised without their mothers or even peers; that is classic infant disorganization.

A challenge in Beth's healing journey is that her early traumatic experiences couldn't be stored in her autobiographical memory because she was too young to recall any of it—remember, the hippocampus takes a while to function fully. Instead, these experiences were deeply embedded as unprocessed pain in her limbic system. As an adult, she won't recall the specific details of her distress, but the intense fear and disorganized terror remain in her body and can be unexpectedly trig-gered in the present.

This is a common way in which intergenerational trauma is trans-mitted. Unprocessed childhood pain stored in the body can resurface when someone becomes a parent. Even well-intentioned individuals who have experienced past maltreatment may inadvertently pass on these un-processed emotions to their children. Even small triggers can tap into a parent's buried memories and cause overwhelming emotions to surface.

For instance, if a child's cries trigger an early painful implicit memory, the parent may react negatively without understanding why. This can lead to confusing verbal or physical reactions toward the crying infant, or it can lead to dissociation, where the parent detaches emotionally and thus cannot parent from a place of warm attunement. This was certainly the case for Beth's mom.

Often either the baby is afraid of the parent, on whom they are depen-dent, which is horrible, or the parent is afraid of the baby, which is just as awful for the developing child. Naturally, any of these scenarios are terribly confusing and frightening for the baby and could set up risk for the next generation if there isn't intervention and positive experiences of security to update their attachment maps.

If you are like us, reading about how parents might invertedly harm their children may make your heart hurt. So, here is an important note to parents: don't jump to any conclusions by reading a few paragraphs on this topic. These are complex matters summarized for the general public; we aren't talking about you specifically or any particular family. If you have questions or concerns about this, please seek professional guidance. Pain and love and heartbreak and children . . . it's too much for any individual person to process alone.

In this very moment, you are reading this book, which means that you are making the effort to explore your own story and to develop reflection and sensitivity toward yourself and your children. Most people (unless you lean very dark navy blue) are more secure than they think, so start with the premise that you are *already good enough* and work from there to get even better.

Your own parent probably didn't have enough resources to get help, engage in therapy, or actively worry about their impact on you, so it's likely your kids already have it better than you did. It's easy to assume that our kids' experiences of distress are similar to the ones we experienced when we were young, but that's us projecting ourselves onto them. Instead, work to see them as they are: separate from you, likely better off than you were, and with more internal security than you had.

Beth's Healing

After her call with Ben, Beth was more motivated to seek help. She joined a tight queer women's 12-step group and began working the program intensely. Her nightmares worsened at first, but with her sponsor's help, she qualified for and joined a local nonprofit mental health network. After several false starts, she found a therapist affiliated with the nonprofit, specializing in trauma-informed therapy.

Beth's therapist didn't encourage her to address any childhood abuse initially. Their primary goal was to form a stable, trusting bond, which, he explained to Beth, was working on her trauma in the most direct way possible by creating a stable attachment base. During her treatment, Beth learned about neural Wi-Fi, trauma, and unresolved attachment. Once she understood that what was wrong with her wasn't just "her"—it was what happened to her—she could begin to understand in the moment as she dysregulated what was happening. It didn't stop floods of feelings at times, and the nightmares didn't totally stop, but since she had the scaffolding to understand her mind a little better, these dips improved. She'd use the dream or the dysregulated incident to add to her understanding of what was triggering her and what her body needed.

With her therapist's urging, she began weekly trauma-informed yoga with the YWCA, which eventually led her to joining their women's softball team. Her safe social circle grew and as her schedule stabilized, she eventually was able to give up her last drug of use—pot.

This change helped her more than she ever imagined and was a result of her feeling more care and compassion for herself. She felt less alone than ever. She'd never had such honest and supportive attention, and life became more manageable. Her mind was quieter, she felt safe, and as she stayed sober, she felt good about herself for maybe the first time in her life.

As Beth and her therapist began to use EMDR to relieve her nightmares, memories surfaced, and she slowly began to make sense of some of her symptoms and dreams. As painful as it was to acknowledge what her body was telling her, it came as a relief to finally develop a basic understanding about what haunted her. Her recurrent dream images shifted into basic templates for events she had blocked out. She still felt like a mess—but a new mess. And, not *only* a mess. She tried a women's self-defense class and excelled so much she soon began to teach. She loved being able to harness the power and finally kick the way her body needed her to in a constructive and satisfyingly powerful way.

When Beth reconnected with Ben about eighteen months after that fateful phone call, she was in her body in a way she had never experienced as an adult. She wasn't in a rush. She didn't feel furtive; she felt clear. She was most excited to tell him about the surprisingly positive effects of the psychedelic-assisted therapeutic experience she had just completed. Her therapist was part of the MAPS network and helped her get into a clinical trial that was testing the effects of consciousness-altering molecules such as psilocybin and MDMA on addiction and treatment-resistant PTSD. The general idea is that these drugs, which are illegal at present, quiet the default mode network and the amygdala and allow the review of significant life memories with a healthy dose of oxytocin on board, creating safety and compassion for her memories.

As a result of all of her work and her new secure relationship with her therapist, Beth no longer felt like a puddle without form. While she continued to struggle with trusting others and expressing her emotions, she felt more organized inside herself and with those close to her. According to Beth, she felt truly alive for the first time in her life.

Part III:

Rewiring— Creating Deep Change

11

Deepening Security
Inside Ourselves

We've discussed shifting our activation back to a more balanced green state and establishing secure connections in specific moments. But the ultimate goal—what real healing looks like—is shifting your whole attachment map toward green, basically operating from more secure base assumptions. This goes beyond course correcting when we have veered into extreme distress or detachment and coming back to regulation—it's growing our capacity to stay grounded and centered in ourselves and our relationships. This is individual healing, and degrees matter. If your map is darker blue or red or swirly colored and you can move it to a lighter shade even a few degrees toward green or develop more predictable strategies, it can have profound impacts on the quality of your relationships and your emotional and even physical well-being.* **Any reliable shift toward secure functioning matters!**

Don't underestimate the internal changes that may already be happening while reading this book—small, in-the-moment shifts toward staying regulated, repeated over time, are enough to alter and improve our neurological wiring. You are teaching your amygdala and the stress response system that it can calm down, that it doesn't have to take over, and that the stories it brings are often tired old narratives that are likely no longer true. *I'm too needy* (limbic-driven implicitly learned) can become

---

* Remember that relational security is associated with a wide range of physical health benefits likely due to a less reactive stress response system—including immune, metabolic, and cardiac functioning.

I have needs—not too many and not too few; they are just needs. Of course, based on my history, the feelings of these needs are scary to me. How we experience and express these needs can shift, along with the narrative we tell ourselves. Can you see how upgrading your self-talk and adding some compassion helps calm down, or at least not aggravate, your prickly amygdala?

But it's hard because that old wiring is strong. The old thoughts are like freeways that we drive down without thinking, the pathways are so automated. The great news is that intentionally cultivating new relational experiences can create new neural connections and wire new paths—like little country roads off that high-stress freeway. You have to pay more attention to where you are going to stay on this undeveloped road, but over time it'll grow and become more comfortable and automated.

Many strategies and therapeutic approaches can help you gain deeper insights into how your body holds your personal and systemic history, how this impacts you and your relationships, and how it can help you engage in the process of growth that feels most meaningful to you.

Some of this journey involves strategies we've mentioned throughout this book: pausing, reflecting, and intervening on your own defensive activation; recognizing your own ongoing protective and connective patterns; and learning to regulate yourself emotionally to widen your window of emotional tolerance while staying connected to others. Creating a strong cognitive map and compassionate understanding of your struggles is vital—it changes your thinking and thus your experience. It adds permanent scaffolding to your understanding of yourself and others and provides footholds when things go wonky. These top-down changes in thinking are essential for growth, and the rewiring we discuss below relies on it.

From here, we move to bottom-up processes to get these changes percolated down into your relational wiring so they are more natural and thereby more permanent. While we have touched on this throughout the book, in this chapter we will dive much deeper into the potent process of engaging with your body's sensations to promote healing and growth toward a more secure foundational map and continue to point you to paths to continue your growth and exploration beyond this book.

Jacki's Post-Blowup Session

Let's take a peek into Jacki's therapy session right after her evening out with friends that you read about in chapter 5. For context, Jacki has been in therapy for a while and has made incredible progress, so the blowup was a setback. But she wasn't ready to admit that yet. At her next session with Dr. Horowitz, she takes her time filling him in on the details of the evening.

"And Grace still hasn't spoken to me!"

She receives no sympathetic nod or soothing therapist affirmation as she tells him about the group text she sent impulsively and the barrage of repercussions that followed. Still, she can feel his care and openness; he's just not going to engage with this story in the way she wants him to.

They've both been through this before, and Jacki is stalling. She can feel two parts of herself now: the fighter who had taken charge of the evening and was still standing ready, and a softer, younger part full of shame and embarrassment.

She lets her talk fade out* and sits quietly, her eyes looking out the window at the budding maples. Even she is tired of her "Can you believe they did that to me?!" stories. She can hear herself doing it, and it's not as gratifying as it used to be. She begins to sink into her body and connects to what feels true by pausing her words and closing her eyes.

Instead of righteousness, she feels a wave of grief. Ugh.

"Your eyes look sad," Dr. Horowitz noticed, encouraging her to stay with the feeling.

After several minutes of silence, he asked softly, "What's your take on what really happened, Jacki?" his expression inviting her to let down her guard.

In the past, Jacki might have argued, "I did tell you what happened," keeping the focus off her actions. And she was tempted to do so again. Who wanted to be sad? For some time, her sessions were filled with energetic and even occasionally convincing vitriol, but lately she's become

---

* Note that it's easy to be responsive to stories of being done to, and joining those can sometimes be supportive, but at other times the best intervention is to let an old narrative pass and stay focused on the inner experience of the person talking.

much more adept at slowing down and looking deeper inside herself. She thinks that is why she has gotten so much better, and she's ashamed she jumped right back into it so convincingly

She grabs the pillow beside her and hugs it to her chest, signaling she will soften and let Dr. Horowitz help her.

"Grrrr," she protests as tears filled her eyes. "I didn't want to cry today."

Dr. Horowitz's body relaxes with her; in this opening, their neural Wi-Fi starts to sync, and their hearts become more connected. This safe mutual syncing is how Jacki's body has begun to experience the care she desperately craves. From this connection, they resume their life-changing work together.

This Earning Security Voyage Can Feel Rickety

Reexamining your life story and your ongoing narratives is daunting and will no doubt be uncomfortable. You'll need a good dose of compassion and courage, but we are compelled to pilgrimage because not working on it leaves us stuck reenacting old stories and responding to misfires of threat and danger. If you actually let yourself feel your heavy armor, it's lonely and exhausting. To beat back our protective system and make room for our hearts and real connection, it soon becomes self-reinforcing because as you do it, it begins to feel good!

Jacki knew instinctively that her triggers caused her trouble in close relationships, but now things had gotten really interesting—she was moving from intellectual insight to more exploration and bottom-up processing. Because she'd been practicing this for a while and let herself get so close to Dr. Horowitz, she'd already been nudging her now crimson-colored attachment map toward the middle.

The key to this deep bottom-up change is being open enough to take in the experience of security in close relationships. It's this risk of the uptake—the vulnerable believing it as you receive care and attention—that really sprouts new learning pathways and helps you internalize new safe relationships.

This pushing yourself out of your comfort zone is often signaled by feeling, well . . . awkward—and that cringy discomfort is a sign you are taking a risk—your growing edge.* However, did you know that feeling "awkward" facilitates accelerated learning? It can stop us from learning, if we avoid it, or if we push past it, can accelerate new learning.

Dr. Andrew Huberman, a neuroscientist and professor at California's Stanford University, reports that novelty, challenges, and discomfort trigger neuroplasticity. Rather than stopping when you feel self-conscious, move through the feeling and let yourself feel the discomfort. Rest assured that your brain is making new connections in that moment. It's learning, and it learns fast.

A friend of ours recently recalled one of her own painful processes of emotional change that happened years ago. Her mother taught her how to play tennis when she was young, and she'd always felt fairly confident. As an adult, our friend decided to take lessons, and although the instructor complimented her abilities, he told her that she was holding the racket wrong, hurting her game. Eager to improve, she changed her grip—but this new approach totally threw her off. It felt awkward and she hated playing for a while and almost quit. Then, with practice and persistence, her new grip started to feel more natural, and her game took off. This is what individual healing looks like. Engaging with the world and yourself in a new way will feel weird before it feels normal, but once you push through the discomfort, you will become stronger on the other side.

How Change Happens: The 3-R Healing Framework—Recognize, Reflect, and Rewire

The 3 Rs—recognizing, reflecting, and rewiring—are not steps in a linear process, and how one works through them will vary widely. Throughout the book thus far, we have focused on helping you recognize and reflect

---

* *Growing edge* refers to that spot where your skills are being challenged, the frontier between what you already know how to do versus uncharted territory to lean in to.

on your history, your protective system cues, and ways that you can make different, more insightful, deliberate choices. We can create and rewire new pathways by repeating and deepening these skills.

Let's recall the 3-R healing spiral of change. Throughout the process of learning about ourselves, recognizing our patterns, and working to pause and try different strategies, we are building our reflective muscle and helping to expand our window of tolerance.

Figure 13: The 3-R Healing Spiral of Change

Let's make the 3-R spiral, or process of change, more concrete by going back to Jacki's moment when she walked up to the table and could sense that people were talking about her, to see how it might have played out differently. What if, instead of demanding accusingly, "Did I interrupt something?" she'd taken a moment to notice the sharp spike in her attention. What if she'd tuned in and *recognized* her bodily shift into activation—that feeling of a carbonated exclamation mark in her chest and stomach? In therapy speak, we call that recognizing "an urge toward action." Rather than acting, this time her opening move would have been to . . . pause.

Why is pausing a "pro move"? Because it is one of the first regulation steps. It interrupts the action and allows the rest of the system (higher-level cortex) time to catch up, helping to keep our hands on the steering wheel of our reactions. However, we need more than just a pause to understand what's happening inside us.

Building Our Reflective Muscles

Recognize, pause . . . then reflect.

Reflection can mean thinking, considering, feeling, or wondering about what is happening in your body and in your environment. Remember, your protection circuit only hijacks the connection circuit if it perceives a sufficient threat kicking in. Just pausing and naming what is happening can help signal that you are "safe enough," which steadies the autonomic fight-or-flight response that is always standing by. We don't need our protection circuit to take over if we feel we can handle the stressor or if help is nearby. Because of that, we need to know how to connect with our internal resources and deepen awareness of who else we can turn to for help.

One powerful thing you can do—something that is available to everyone free of charge—is to turn to the endnotes and look at all the resources on how to develop a **mindfulness-awareness practice**. It's not just meditation, although that helps, too. Mindfulness is a specific practice working the muscle of your mind and is scientifically proven to create the kind of neural changes that bring us into secure relating. A recent meta-analysis demonstrated that using smartphone apps to access mindfulness meditation exercises has a significant and positive impact on negative emotions with the general public.

There are many other effective strategies that can help in this process, but a simple step we find rather effective is using your imagination to **add a third perspective in your mind**. See the situation from your best friend's or a real or imagined therapist's perspective, or consider how your grandmother would feel about how you were acting. The idea is to pull up and above the action to shift your perspective and open up the frame. Again, it invites more help from the prefrontal cortex. By the way, from this perspective, add the support and care you would likely receive for the powerful feelings you are having. Imagine your grandmother's soothing voice or your friend's warm smile and caring nature. These can add a dose of calm to the process along the way.

Another way of adding a third perspective is to **perspective shift** with yourself. For example, Jacki's pause allows her time to quickly envision the answer to this question: *What would my best self do right now?* She might also channel Dr. Horowitz, her group members, her higher power, or even visualize the right side of her frontal cortex—her wise mind—the part she calls upon when she needs calm wisdom. That wise part can turn to her lower left limbic system that is on fire and begin to cool it off with assurances and kindness.

And how about DJ? What if he would have paused in the car when he sensed Mia was upset, rather than just staying cut off from his emotions? What if he'd had enough self-reflection that he could have challenged himself to show up more? Even in hindsight this can work. If DJ goes through his version of the evening looking for moments he could have responded more helpfully, that builds out new, more secure images of himself in his mind. He could see himself staying inside the house and feeling more like a team with Mia as they embarked on their date. He could imagine realizing that Mia was upset in the car or at the table and see himself reaching for her hand. He could hear himself saying the things we know in hindsight could have helped.

***

A cousin of adding a third perspective is **time-shifting**.

When you are in a state of high threat, your limbic activation causes you to zero in on the immediate moment, thus losing your ability to foresee a more secure future. This is why we feel compelled to act quickly in a moment of desperation, with little regard for the later outcome. When you cool down and wonder regretfully *Why did I do that?*, just know that you were acting on your evolutionary instincts.

So, we need lots of repetitions calling ourselves into our more developed and wiser mind. Engage your hippocampus and its regulatory friends by imagining the hours before and after this exact moment. You might also imagine a day when you can see yourself responding calmly to stress. You have to put in the reps to build the muscle, even the muscle of your PFC staying in charge. Practice, practice, practice.

When Beth imagines herself in the future sober and connected, she is *security priming.* In security priming, we attend to words, thoughts, and images that evoke safety—for instance, picturing your grounded secure self snuggling a cute puppy or connecting with a special person. A recent study reviewed a collection of research findings and confirmed that security priming is effective at enhancing positive feelings and reducing negative ones. Done over time and with mindful attention, we continue building new, more secure pathways in our wiring. Did we mention it was important to practice?

Just because we pause and don't react doesn't mean we need to stay passive if something upsets us. We can address the issue at hand, but now we are going for thoughtful effectiveness, not just letting our amygdala run the show. *Curiosity takes out the urgency*—wonder is like oxygen for a connection system deprived of air.

Jacki's reflection when standing at the table in the restaurant helped her identify feelings in the moment that were familiar to her: the fear that people were talking about her, and if they were, that it was hurtful, and she was being left out or rejected. These were her automatic negative thoughts, or ANTs. It didn't mean that her perceptions were entirely wrong—in fact, her friends *were* talking about her, and she *was* being left out—but if she'd noticed that she was filling in the blanks with her familiar ANTs *I'm being left out because people don't want to be with me*, and *If I don't say something, they will think I don't know it!*, she could have been pretty sure that the volume was turned up even if the channel was correct.

ANTs are often linked to our attachment maps, and by labeling them ANTs (small benign sugar ants) instead of trusting them as true perceptions of current events, they go from threatening to just annoying. They are *not* connected to our survival—we can lower the sense of looming danger. In this case, Jacki could have noticed that she was feeling some familiar ANTs, and because of that, she could have made the wise decision to sort through her thoughts and feelings before pushing forward to find out what was going on. It's not all her, she may have legitimate reasons to be hurt or angry, but by taking her time she can find that clarity and assess how she feels about her relationship to Grace in particular. She will be taking herself and her needs more seriously and be treating herself with the respect she deserves.

What Is Bottom-Up Processing?

The 3rd R—Rewire

Had Jacki taken her breath and its related pause, tuned in, and been able to reflect, taking the time to feel her body's response, she would have been using some of the core aspects of *bottom-up processing*. *Bottom-up* means using sensory input and small bits of data from your body to then build up to thoughts and explanations. When faced with a potential threat, our higher cortical thinking mind believes it understands what's happening and begins incorporating practiced cognition and rational intelligence to manage the crisis. We hear a loud noise behind us and begin to run instinctually; then we tell ourselves that we ran because we were afraid.

According to amygdala expert Dr. Joseph LeDoux, we fill in the blank that we were afraid because we were running (top-down); we don't run because we feel afraid. Our body sensed the threat and acted before our mind had time to interpret that we felt fear (bottom-up). Dr. LeDoux's research and writing continues to shed light on how our bottom-up activation impacts our emotion life.*

We hope that much of this book has added to your top-down process and increased your insight and understanding of yourself and those around you. This is great. Once we are effective at the top-down, curiosity, wonder, reflection part, the next step is to include more of our body and get closer to the core of our limbic system.

From a nervous system perspective, it goes more like this: our ventral vagal internet circuit picks up an experience—let's say a sensation in our stomach. So far, it's unprocessed and just in the spinal cord as it travels up to the bottom right portion of our brain. That part detects the signal and begins to form some rough representation of what the signal is: a generally positive or negative valence—in this case, positive so far—a motion, a gurgle, a squirt . . . but these are general concepts, not words, and there is no conscious awareness of it yet.

Next, the sensation moves into the middle limbic area, which gets a

---

* To learn more, turn to his book *The Deep History of Ourselves: The Four-Billion-Year Story of How We Got Conscious Brains.*

hold of the general concepts caused by the sensation and begins to sort them out based on comparisons to previous experiences. It still isn't thinking yet, just comparing the new experience with what it has felt before. This brings the sensation into the sphere of symbols and images in preconsciousness. Only then does it cross over and up, and symbolic language begins to form: *stomach, ache, hunger, gas, excitement.*

Finally, it gets up to conscious cognition, at which point it dawns on us: "I'm getting a little hungry!" or "What I just ate isn't agreeing with me!" or "I'm anxious (or excited)" depending on the data gathered on the way up. It's not a direct line from stomach to awareness of hunger, but our conscious rational mind likes to think it is. If it were a direct line, we likely wouldn't find ourselves staring into the pantry when feeling stressed and actually not really feeling hunger.

Our thinking mind creates stories to make sense of things it doesn't understand or doesn't want to face. That's why therapists are trained to listen to more than just the words a patient is speaking, and it is the reason that *Why?* questions are often not helpful because they invite logical, left-brain dominant fabrication.

For instance, "*Why* are you late?" sets the stage for a quick answer. Typically, we'll automatically say the first thing that comes to mind: "Horrible traffic." There may or may not have indeed have been unexpected and unpreventable traffic that accounts for the lateness, but it usually isn't the only thing. In addition to a little traffic, if we listen for more understanding inside ourselves we may find that the real reason we were late was that we felt ambivalent about coming in for this morning's session and took our sweet time getting ready. Or, perhaps we arrived late because we don't like sitting in the waiting room; it makes us nervous. Or because we didn't like something the therapist said in the last session and are dreading talking about that or avoiding our hurt feelings. And so on . . . the exploration gets much more interesting.

In bottom-up processing, you focus on your current experience, taking in any sensations, feelings, emotions, memories, and images, and without passing judgment. By combining our senses, emotions, and thoughts, we can slowly start making sense of things not already in our conscious verbal awareness. It's a way of collecting data and even reshaping hurtful memories that were previously scattered. It often doesn't make "sense" because it's not cognitive; it emerges from farther down the brainstem before reaching the portion of the brain where language forms.

Your first answer to the question "Why are you late" was top-down, a conscious thought telling an appropriate social story that makes sense. An example of bottom-up processing would be to regard the question as an opportunity to explore more deeply, so let's see how that could go.

As you reflect on your experience of getting to the appointment, you remember that you left your apartment not in a hurry, knowing you were already running a little behind. Hmm, okay, what's that about? This morning not only were you casually late, but you stopped to grab coffee on the way. Now you are intrigued . . . Curious, you tune in more deeply and then feel embarrassed, realizing your therapist no doubt noticed the fresh cup of coffee you walked in with, so they probably knew you weren't trying to get there on time.

Now you feel a little exposed and cringy; you weren't meaning to be rude by ignoring their time. What may you have been communicating though?

You realize that you never even thought about what your therapist would think or feel about you taking your time. Your desire to stop was more important, no one can control you—you get to stop if you want to!

Oh my God, you muse, *I'm making myself defensive in my own head*. Your discomfort increases as thoughts flood in. You often cut corners relationally and expect people to wait for you. If you have to wait for them, it feels disrespectful—a power play—so is your lateness also a power play? Finally, you find you are ready to respond to the question about being late:

"Because I think my time is more important than yours, and that if I have to wait in the waiting room, you win," you admit, kicking off a productive relational therapy session where you examine your fear of being controlled and your more aggressive feelings about relationships.

Beth's Bottom-Up Processing

Once Beth began therapy, her counselor, Arden, had to help her become more aware of her unconscious resistance to the process without scaring her off. For instance, in her sessions, Beth would wedge herself into the far corner of the couch, as far from Arden's chair as possible. She sat slouched and made little eye contact with him, signaling "Keep your distance!" Her body's protection system was in full, familiar swing, as she wanted to connect but was afraid to.

Arden was aware that asking Beth to engage more directly might be too much for her, so he decided to "join the resistance": rather than coaxing her out of her shell, he assured Beth that she could keep her shell on as long as she needed. The goal of therapy was to help change the system, not change Beth. She needed distance? He respected that. He then continued to promote enough safety in the system (the room, the relationship) that she felt seen and honored, even if just on an unconscious, gut-felt level.

As they sat quietly, Arden encouraged her to avert her eyes for as long as she liked, but to notice the experience and perhaps share a thought or feeling about it. Beth felt awkward at first, but after a while, she took the risk to share a simple thought.

"Disappear?" she said unsteadily, more of a question. "Disappear," Arden repeated.

Don't see me, Beth thought to herself. Then, when the words formed clearly and stayed strong in her mind, she said out loud, "I don't want to see."

"'I don't want to see' . . . Do you have a sense of what you don't want to see?" Arden asked gently.

Beth broke out of the experience and looked directly at him, surprised by what had happened so quickly. She was impressed by how easily he could get her to feel things she tried to avoid. Her respect and trust of him increased, and she felt nervous but hopeful about the work.

Over the next several months, they continued to slowly work from the body up, Arden rolling his chair closer and closer until Beth made him move back. "Farther," she instructed, but laughing. "Farther. Farther." Eventually Arden's back was against the far wall. He laughed along with her.

"Okay, now closer, a little closer," she said. "Okay, right there, stay right there. That feels good." This wasn't rational and cognitive, but a body-felt experience, and Beth instinctively felt his collaboration and respect of her personal power. He also respected that she knew what she needed.

By collaborating about closeness and distance, Arden was directing her to more awareness of her body sensations that gave her a safe way to tune in, rather than cut off and disconnect, as she learned to do as a child experiencing abuse. You can see how this type of work is critical when trauma or overwhelming emotions hinder cognitive processing. Without it, Beth could never have mustered the courage to tell Arden to move away; she would have just disappeared inside herself. Instead, they collaborated on this and many other things as Beth gained more and more trust in the relationship and in her own capacity to have agency.

So many of the interventions meant to cultivate security have to do with feeling safe, accurately understood, and comforted. Despite what we see here with Beth, it wasn't the counselor's wise insight that created such change; it was that magic safe connection that did most of the work. And this is good news because it doesn't require a paid therapist to make safe connections materialize—anyone can do it, so long as they allow themselves to be vulnerable, with someone safe, and let those new experiences all the way in to perform their magic.

For people who run blue, like DJ, and have disconnected their own sense of vulnerability in favor of relating more intellectually, learning to tune in to the sensations in your body is essential to improve most of your significant relationships. Rather than reacting with impatience, shutting down your and others' emotional vulnerability, shifting your personal map involves leaning in to recognizing your own gut-felt activation.

By feeling your impatience smolder, you can recognize the volume of the reaction and noise coming from inside. You may also notice it is out of proportion. Returning to a frequent blue-tinged refrain, "I don't have time for this!" you can now more readily experience this as an implicit threat activation putting pressure on your nervous system. *Your sense of impatience and activation is coming from inside the building, shall we say.* As you tune in to the experience, the discomfort and pressure may begin to fade, giving you more room to open up and explore the rich emotional information that is at the core for you, and at the essence of what you need for true connection.

We know it is not always easy for any of us to tune in to what our body is saying, but it can be especially difficult when your history has taught your body that it is much safer to spend your adult life in emotional disconnection. Knowing how to turn up or down your awareness of your body and turn up or down your activation will increase your sense of safety to explore more deeply.

Mind-Body Techniques

The Power of Your Breath

The fastest and easiest way to do that is your breath. Focusing on inhales (adding oxygen) is a way to bring your energy up and gather resources to engage, and slow long exhales (releasing carbon dioxide) slow your nervous system down. A quick technique to reduce stress you may be holding is to take a full breath through your nose if you are able, then add an extra fast second inhale to force oxygen all the way into the small sacs of your lungs. Then slowly and steadily release the breath through your mouth. Try it—you only need to do it once or twice to feel your body respond.

Sometimes you aren't sure how to breathe right, so just *box breathe*. That means inhale deeply for four seconds, hold for four seconds, exhale slowly for four seconds, pause for four seconds, repeat. This controlled breath exercise stimulates vagal tone and helps you to manage whatever is coming next without leaving the green zone. If you are down-regulated, add oxygen to the system by focusing on your inhale, in for six, out for four; to down-regulate focus on the exhale natural breath in then long slow exhales for six beats. Play around with what works for you, but it's a powerful free tool linked directly to your protection and connection system.

Sue's favorite breath technique is the fake yawn. Try it now—just pretend you are yawning, give it a big go—open wide, make all the sounds, enjoy it! Bonus if you get a real yawn out of it—it's like a micro-meditation it's so effective in cooling off your limbic activation.

Correct Information Distortions (Clearing Your Sunglasses)

As you recall from chapter 5, sunglasses in the MARS framework represent information distortion, an unconscious tilt in the experience of interpersonal events that happens at the neurocognitive and hormonal levels. These sunglasses distort differently based on our coping patterns, either maximizing attachment-related information (red zone) or minimizing it (blue zone). See chapter 5 for more specific details.

One of the toughest steps in this journey is *first acknowledging to yourself that you are distorting information.* To update our attachment maps, we need to continuously work on clearing our biased sunglasses. There are many avenues to correcting information distortions, but talking about painful experiences and shifting the memory significantly is an effective starting point. This can mean *reviewing recent memories from a more updated and accurate perspective* so that you allow your body to lay down different emotional experiences.

For example, Stan Tatkin, developer of the Psychobiological Approach to Couples Therapy (PACT), suggests an effective technique.[*] Mia could learn to *replay her story* about what happened between her and DJ at the restaurant by slowing it way down and working through it frame by frame to really explore her version of events. This exercise would help her correct for her tilt in interpretation, and she would likely shift the negative downward spiral of her beliefs about DJ, her marriage, and herself. We might encourage her to tell the story from the waiter's point of view or from a fly-on-the-wall perspective. Or, we could go all in and ask her to describe the whole evening from DJ's perspective, encouraging her to explore possibilities other than her interpretation. If pressed, what are other explanations of what happened? Just introducing nuance is a shift away from the certainty embedded in information bias.

Further, while Mia is turning over the story in her mind, we could

---

[*] Personal communication with Sue Marriott, August 16, 2023, In Each Other's Care interview, www.therapistuncensored.com/tu212.

invite her to **search for and amplify *positive* moments**—no matter how small—that feel real to her from that evening. Looking for moments of connection or success is another way to security prime. In addition, we might ask her to imagine how she wished she'd responded. If, for example, she said that she wished she'd have taken DJ's hand in the car, we would linger there and ask her what that would have felt like. Speaking of lingering, we are lingering here because rewiring requires new actual experience, so helping Mia have a new experience—not just thoughts— will help form new connections in her body.

The idea is to shake up her history of insecure memories that are more embedded in her experience and allow her to create new, more positive ventral vagal experiences from her imagination. For Mia or Jacki and others whose maps lean red, we would compassionately confront her negative assumptions and the tilt toward her negative interpretations of events.

We would repeat something similar for DJ, who leans blue, but with a different goal: by slowing down his recollection of interpersonal events, we would help him catch things he missed or blocked out and reinterpret and help him *learn to read social interactions more accurately*. We would also encourage him to challenge his assumptions of being in the right. By gently confronting his information distortion, we can enhance his interest in his own feelings as well as other people's.

Therapeutic Approaches/Techniques

Working with Memory

Neuroscience findings over the past decade suggest that another way to update an attachment map is to *alter a limbic-stored memory entirely*. We used to believe that memories held in your limbic system, especially traumatic memories, remained there forever. The best we could do was to create a bevy of new safer experiences that lie on top of the challenging ones and basically override them (until something triggers the old memory, which remains). However, new neuroscience suggests that previously consolidated traumatic memories can be modified, updated, reorganized, and restored in the brain. One way to use this new neuro-science in therapy is called *memory reconsolidation*.

To understand memory reconsolidation we turn to therapist Bruce Ecker, co-founder of the Coherence Psychology Institute and author of *Unlocking the Emotional Brain: Eliminating Symptoms at Their Roots Using Memory Reconsolidation* and a comprehensive PDF primer for the subject. In a paper published in 2020 called "How the Science of Memory Reconsolidation Advances the Effectiveness and Unification of Psycho-therapy," he makes the case that there is an empirically reviewed process of transformational change.

Clinicians applying the science describe how existing memories be-come temporarily unstable when retrieved, potentially allowing for the memory's modification, or updating. Reconsolidation therapy attempts to use this window of memory vulnerability to intervene and shift trau-matic memories. It involves accessing that limbic-stored implicit memory that is driving symptoms, calling it up, and then altering it with new information before it settles back into long-term memory. It is a com-plex and delicate process but is worth learning about for those deep into working on trauma.

Working with Imagination to Heal

A common theme in many of the interventions we recommend is the use of active imagination, a powerful therapeutic technique that uses the complexity available in our nervous system to unlock the creative realm of the mind. It allows us to create new secure stories rather than repeat old narratives.

Remember that neuroplasticity goes both ways: if we repeat disturbing self-talk, it reinforces these beliefs, but by creating and practicing new internal connections, we can update the neural wiring. For example, you can *use the power of your imagination* to move out of the painful present and access the past when you were in a secure state, or the future when you will be again. You can establish internal boundaries and control, access other parts of your mind or self to protect you, and create transformative symbols to help you further resource yourself. For nightmares, you can "redream" or "finish the dream" with a more secure ending.

The idea here is to begin building a new, more secure relationship with yourself. Talk to yourself as you do your loved pet—"Aww look at this soft and sweet tummy" you would say while rubbing your belly. While that can be funny, the point is important—seeing yourself compassionately and accurately (not through distorted sunglasses) develops your secure functioning self. Resistances to self-kindness should be explored as part of your old attachment maps—inaccurate learning from your history that you repeat today.

Ideal Parent Protocol

One of our favorite evidence-based bottom-up therapeutic techniques that leverages the power of imagination is the *Ideal Parent Figure Protocol,* developed by David Elliott and Dan Brown, coauthors of *Attachment Disturbances in Adults: Treatment for Comprehensive Repair.* We will describe it briefly but encourage you to follow up to learn more; for example, see two podcast episodes and detailed show notes featuring Dr. Elliott, including a direct demonstration of the technique in episode 120 (linked below).* He offers in-depth training to therapists and we encourage you to look him up and check those resources out.

Using guided imagination, the main goal of this technique is to access a "younger" experiential sense of yourself as a child, such that you become in touch with the feelings evoked by sensing yourself as a young child. The therapist then actively works with you to help you create imagined ideal parent figures, who can be there for you in ways that you missed, that you yearn for, or that you learned to cut off. Through collaborative cocreation with both of your active imaginations, you and the therapist support experiences of these new and different parents attuning

---

* See "Treating Attachment Difficulties with Dr. David Elliott," interview with Ann Kelley and Sue Marriott, *Therapist Uncensored*, episode 34, June 21, 2017, https:// therapistuncensored.com/episodes/tu34; and "Finding Security and Healing Attachment with Dr. David Elliott," interview with Ann Kelley and Sue Marriott, *Therapist Uncensored*, April 27, 2020, episode 120, https:// therapistuncensored.com/episodes/tu120.

to and responding to you in ways that are deeply nurturing. Through this process, you develop new, positive attachment experience, which is encoded in the deep limbic structures of your mind. When this connects, it creates a powerful new embodied experience that facilitates bottom-up neural change. This helps to create new, more secure internal working models that can be developed and expanded for well-being in adult life. It's a delicate process, but a powerful tool.

Research on using the Ideal Parent Figure Protocol during stabilization for individuals with complex PTSD has found encouraging results. It decreased symptoms of attachment traumatization and increased quality of life! Encouragingly, at an eight-month follow-up assessment the positive changes remained.

What Is the "Best" Therapy for You?

Bottom-Up Therapy Examples

There are many techniques to discover and therapeutic approaches that can help tune in to your body sensations and work from the bottom up. See appendix 4 for a more extensive list of professionally based options, but some well-known approaches are Eye Movement Desensitization and Reprocessing (EMDR), Sensorimotor Psychotherapy, Somatic Experiencing (SE), Internal Family Systems (IFS), Group Therapy, and Psychobiological Approach to Couples Therapy (PACT). With the plethora of encouraging research studies and effective treatments, it is beyond the scope of this chapter to cover all the robust options available.

And finally—informed consent. Bottom-up rewiring typically involves sharing lots of big feelings with someone you trust, and may entail evoking unexpected but needed tears and pain as your heart unfolds. For many of us, willingly doing something that will create intense feelings you'd rather avoid is a tough ask, but we are confident it will help you, so let's just consider it informed consent. It hurts, but it is life changing.

We are agnostic when it comes to recommending an exact therapeutic approach. The most important thing is that it is accessible to you, that you find a good working alliance with your therapist and that you connect.

There are many non-European models and many healers with no official academic qualifications that have been successfully growing and healing their communities for millennia. In many communities around the world, healing involves spiritual rituals, sweat lodges, vision quests, tonics, medicinal plants and molecules, the guidance of healers and diviners, ancestral reverence, dance, music, storytelling, connecting the physical, spiritual and natural realms, and trained peer-to-peer support. An excellent example of this is The Friendship Bench, an evidence-based intervention developed in Zimbabwe that uses trained grandmothers to address *kufungisisa* (which means "thinking too much" in Shona). These respected community volunteers provide a supportive place for talks on discreetly placed wooden benches around the community. This delivers deep and accessible care for their community, effectively helping to bridge the gap in mental health availability.

Therapy treatments for adult attachment insecurity include some sets of principles and methods that can be termed therapist-as-good-attachment-figure. This relational context is widely and appropriately accepted as a foundation for any attachment-focused therapy. Fortunately, what works is consistent among many modalities: they all involve some level of bottom-up processing; safe, supportive authentic relationship(s); and access to a realm bigger than our personal gain.

Nourishing Mind, Body, and Connection in Your Everyday Life

Remember, one of the goals of your map work is to learn to connect and coordinate your body and your mind, to have more agency in regulating your emotions, promote ways to reduce stress, and to engage in connections with others. The good news is that many everyday movement activities can be powerful tools in this process. For instance, when you engage in activities that promote rhythmic left-right motion—biking, swimming, walking, running—especially if you exert yourself to the point where your face turns pink and you're beathing so hard that it's difficult to talk, this simulation gives your brain regular doses of soothing neurotransmitters that aid in general well-being and healing. The effect is as strong as some mild antidepressants.

The repetitive and predictable nature of the movement has been found to reduce stress and anxiety, restore balance, and regulate emotions during times of heightened emotional states. You can also reap these positive effects without even breaking a sweat, through back-and-forth rocking and swaying. Yoga, tai chi, and Pilates facilitate body-brain integration and moving in unison with others, and dance, martial arts, and even just walking in sync with someone creates that right-to-right syncing so many respected trauma therapists highly recommend.

Writing also works. Think about it: in order to write, you have to notice a feeling or experience, organize it enough to describe it, and then express it. It's the same way that talk therapy works, by integrating your brain with experiences of your body and feelings. Writing helps you shape a narrative, whether that's in the form of journaling, creative fiction writing, writing letters from your perspective as a child or writing loving assurances to your young self. You might also write to the parent you wish you had. All of these exercises activate your imagination and allow implicit stories that you are unaware of to emerge. In fact, all of the creative arts—music, drawing, painting, dance—can easily bypass our reasonable conscious stories and get right at that lower limbic truth of experience held without words.

Finally, social experiences can also be extremely effective, including activities such as improv, drama, and volunteering in a way that matters to you. Improv is one of Ann's favorite recommendations for those who struggle with joining. Here you practice moving from the reflexive block along the lines of "Yes, but . . ." to training yourself to join first with a "Yes, and . . ." All of these activities can prime the oxytocin pump and actively engage your mind and body quite dramatically.

Integration Is the Key

According to Dr. Dan Siegel, whom you met in chapter 1, *integration* is postulated to be the central mechanism by which health is created in mind, brain, body and relationships. He describes neural integration as the linkage of differentiated parts. It is your various nervous system circuits maintaining the integrity of their individual jobs but working cooperatively. The protection and connection circuits work in concert with each other to do their jobs, the brain's left and right hemispheres coordinate happily, and the neurotransmitters dance together, activating and resting in the right levels at the right times. When our different brain regions and mental processes are integrated, we can experience a sense of wholeness, balance, and resilience. It's also a key factor in developing healthy relationships and cultivating compassionate and empathic connections.

Rewiring is an integrative process, as our emotional heart comes online with our body being present, our thinking intact, and all the parts of our nervous system beginning to work together more fluidly. Think of a song featuring perfect four-part harmony: different voices blend together and create magic not by losing themselves but by joining one another. They create something bigger than any of the four voices alone—they are interconnected.

Signs of Progress (and Trouble) in Therapy

First of all, one thing we know is that therapy works. Neuroimaging studies confirm that therapy can shift one's attachment patterns, and it is associated with measurable changes in brain activity, endocrine activity, and neural wiring. Even though we know that long-term embedded stress wreaks havoc on our nervous system, it is also true that altering how we perceive and respond to stress can positively impact our system as well. We are happy to report that there is incredible hope and capacity for change. It ain't over till you quit trying!

We also know therapy doesn't heal everyone, and the institution of mental health delivery has focused at times too much on the individual and not on the systems of exploitation and discrimination driving harm to individuals we treat. Many people will never cross the threshold of a therapist's office for many reasons, including lack of access or cultural inhibition. This doesn't mean healing is out of reach. But for those who regard therapy as an important healing space, let's dive in and have a fireside chat about this weird and unusual and special intimate relationship. Maximizing your healing requires understanding best practices and what to look for.

Some therapeutic relationships can go very deep and feel incredibly intense. That strong bond and deep work are often an essential part of healing for those with more attachment neglect or disruption. This deep work includes transferences, which is when the limbic-level early experiences get activated and experienced as if it is happening in the present with the therapist. For example, let's say the therapist forgets a long-term client's spouse's name. Ick. The client's internal reaction may be to quickly brush that off to protect the connection with the therapist, or a host of other interesting responses. The client may feel hurt or angry, they may pretend they don't notice, they might immediately question the therapist's value and wonder what the point is, or they might not even notice, because they would never expect important things about them to be remembered.* Each of these reactions has a flavor that, if repeated, may reveal themes embedded in the client's attachment map that they project onto the therapist. So, it is driven by stored implicit memory and can reveal important elements of the deep learning embedded in someone's attachment map. It also makes the intense feelings that emerge in therapy particularly important. Because of the sometimes-confusing intensity of the relationship, a few words of care on what is expected versus signs of trouble.

First, your therapist should stay in the role of your therapist, even if you love them like a long-lost parent or are angry at them because it feels like they aren't helping you. These are all normal human feelings that are therapeutic if explored in the safety of the session—in the professional

---

* Therapists are given a hard time about "making a mountain out of a molehill," and we certainly do sometimes! But the reason we listen so carefully to tiny things like small internal reactions is to welcome communication from your deep limbic that doesn't have language. Also, side note—sometimes eye rolling the exploration of deeper meanings can be a blue-tinged move to avoid the vulnerability of exposure.

office, during your scheduled time that you pay for regularly, and with the focus on you and your healing and growth. It's common to regress in deep healing and rewiring, but overall, you should get better. Look at your outside life: Is it expanding, deepening in authentic connections, and are you taking risks toward change and growth? If your therapist comes across as an expert and does not seem open to your perception, that could be worrisome or even dangerous.

Mental health professionals have training and expert skills, but their job is to amplify *your understanding of yourself*, not to amplify doubt in you or overwhelm you with their expertise. What we encourage is working with a therapist who raises your awareness, even challenges your stuck places and old narratives, while still promoting your secure sense of yourself and your value.

Your therapist gives you feedback, right? Well, you can give them feedback, too! If it's about authentic relationships, then you will eventually have to because two humans can't exist very long in close quarters without having to work things out on some level. Let them know what was helpful in the last session, what you feel toward them that you are scared to say, what you liked or didn't like about what they said, how they are missing this or that part of you, or how you felt disappointed by something they said. If you are often the one in charge in your everyday life, do you find this happening in your therapy as well? If so, can you be open about your fear of being influenced and challenged? Let them know when you feel deeply seen and whether you feel you are being challenged to grow. Let them know if you feel there is not enough direction and that the two of you are merely chatting about life events.

Your goal is not to direct your therapy; it's to take risks and show up authentically together. A therapist isn't likely to answer all of your questions and, hopefully, won't do everything you want, but that isn't the point. The point is to allow them to know you, and to celebrate these new parts of you as you grow. It can be hard for any of us, including therapists, to be challenged, but embracing your voice and your risk in speaking up is part of the process. Most therapists will respond with curiosity and with care to your open communications with them; if they don't you might consider that a gentle flag. Most therapists want you to bring your full self into the room and will honor your input.

Is the relationship "real"?

Absolutely! Your vulnerability opens up their hearts, and their interest and care stimulate yours. This right-to-right syncing up is a dance that can't be fabricated.

Yes, you pay for their time, but the magic within that time is highly individualized.

If a close relationship does develop, it's real. You can't pay someone to "care"; that happens naturally when you are taking risks and working together so closely. It's not for everyone, but a good, safe therapy experience can be both harrowing and beneficially life changing.

Whether you are in therapy or not, we encourage you to keep working at these efforts at individual healing and keep taking small risks in all your relationships to allow yourself to grow. That's how you learn, so take the wins, even if they are small. Incremental change is how it mostly goes. You may feel as if you are hiking up a steep mountain, its summit shrouded in clouds. You're slugging along, looking at your feet and feeling like you're getting nowhere, but when you stop and look up and around—wow! You've come a long way there, friends. Keep at it!

12

Deepening Security
Between Us

Think about the most significant connections in your life: romantic partners, children, friends, family, coworkers, ancestors, beloved pets, special
groups where you belong, and even nature itself. All your work to cultivate a healthier relationship with yourself will inevitably reverberate to
these other connections.

Throughout this book, we've focused largely on how your nervous system picks up cues and communicates with those around you *outside of
your awareness*. Now let's focus specifically on how to consciously harness
that knowledge and improve how we relate with our most significant
people.

We will dive into what secure relationships look like next, but first we
need to share the science of why this matters so desperately.

The Dangers of Isolation Are No Joke

As it turns out, engaging in close relationships promotes psychological
and even physical health! A US surgeon general's report released in May
2023 outlined the eye-popping statistics on the negative effects of social
isolation: in sum, it's terrible for everyone's physical and psychological
health and well-being. The effects of social isolation and loneliness on
mortality are comparable to *and in some cases greater than* those of risk
factors such as smoking, drinking, being sedentary, or having chronically

high cholesterol or blood pressure. For example, poor social relationships were associated with a 29 percent increase in the risk of heart disease and a 32 percent increase in the risk of stroke. Poor social relationships can increase the risk of dementia by approximately 50 percent in older adults. Since most of us fear cognitive decline and isolation increases that risk, do we have to say much more to encourage you to open up and show up? Sadly, the report goes on and on, outlining the serious negative health and psychological risks of disconnection and loneliness.

Fortunately, it works the other way, too: social connection is protective. The positive effects of social relationships are stronger than high blood pressure medication and rehabilitation interventions. Positive connections are related to economic growth and a reduction in income disparity. In 148 studies that followed thousands of people and followed up with them about seven years later, social connection increased the odds of still being alive at follow-up by 50 percent. With more close connections, we can even reduce the rate of murders by 20 percent.

How can something that seems so benign be so good for us?

It's what we've been talking about all along in this book: close relationships help us in many ways. First, there's the biology: closeness buffers the effects of stress and increases our immune functioning. Second, there's the psychological component: feeling seen and heard by our close connections affirms that we exist and that we matter. Most people say that their relationships with their family and friends add meaning and purpose to their lives. Finally, our relationships affect what we do. Without others, we are more likely to sit too much, eat crappy food, and sleep too much or too little and at the wrong natural rhythms of our body. (Poor sleep alone can account for a high degree of the increased stress load on our bodies, so, at the very least, work on your sleep hygiene to give you a little more energy to take risks to break old habits and begin to open up your life again.)

If you are finding yourself prone to avoiding connections or staying in isolation, it isn't about you; it's a human thing. When we become overwhelmed, many of us tend to draw inward and isolate. But we can get stuck there. It feels like our situation is somehow uniquely bad or we are especially unworthy. Loneliness has the wicked effect of causing us to blame ourselves and is associated with shame, which can exacerbate our use of our favorite protective strategies that keep us stuck.

If you lean blue or tie-dye, you may convince yourself that people require too much effort or energy. That is likely your protective strategy stuck in avoidance. You may need to reach out more just knowing it is good for you. Don't wait for the desire to emerge first. You don't need a partner or even a best friend to connect just a little bit more! Sign up to volunteer for *anything* you are interested in, check out a study group at your spiritual center, join any competitive sport or game—kickball, pickleball, backgammon—show up at neighborhood activities, check out the residents' association. If you have roommates you never see, hang out in the living room rather than your bedroom to catch them and show them you are interested.

Connecting with others with similar interests, beliefs, struggles, or experiences allows us to develop networks that offer validation and meaning. Everyone else there is probably as lonely and awkward feeling as you are, so they'd love you to say hi! Even a weekly yoga class where you don't talk to anyone can help impart a sense of community and a reminder that your journey is likely shared by many.

Okay, with that dire warning under our belt (can we call it enthusiastic encouragement instead?), let's focus on security and what it can look like.

Secure Relationships Are Not Necessarily Nice and Neat

Even the healthiest relationships are messy and frustrating a lot of the time. This is a function of being humans trying to get along and not always due to a problem with the relationship itself. The belief that a relationship is supposed to be any certain way often keeps us focused on what others should be doing differently, and this can become a major source of frustration.

We suggest thinking of most of your relationships in terms of pass-fail. It's best to keep the bar realistic; if most of the time you give and get most of the things important to you both—authenticity, connection, mutual support, passion—consider that good enough. We shouldn't shoot for perfection.

In "good enough" secure relationships, each person has *mostly* made peace with the other's quirks and idiosyncrasies so that they *mostly* love and accept each other as they are. Her clothes on the bathroom floor can be annoying, but you recognize you haven't bent down to pick a single weed in the yard this year. Or, you're annoyed by your therapist's scheduling errors, but when you zoom out, you recognize she's been there for you for years and you can deal with her quirks, including some calendar messiness. Arguments and disconnections still happen and can even be ugly, but the bounce back typically improves over time so that it happens more quickly and with more flexibility. Repairs when we screw up are given and received imperfectly, but you get there.

Partners in good-enough relationships can generally count on each other and effectively soothe and comfort each other when distressed. When you drive up, and the other person's car is there, you feel happiness or relief rather than dread or disappointment. And if, on occasion, you do feel disappointed, you can take a moment to reflect and be open with yourself and them about what is going on. Even when you can't *stand* how they put on their socks, you hold them inside your heart and mind in a solid, valuing way. This is *love* the verb, not just the feeling. It's doing the harder thing because you love them—the right thing for the *couple*, not just for you.

Finally, different perspectives can coexist in secure relationships and are treated equally. You don't have to deny role-induced power differences—parents and therapists can retain their authority—but you do have to engage mutually, recognizing and taking responsibility for each of your parts in disruption. It's natural to hold agreed-upon power in some areas more comfortably. For instance, someone may control the TV remote, but they know this, do not take it for granted, and can share it fairly easily when asked. They also have areas where they feel comfortable ceding power and are open and at peace with allowing themselves to be influenced.

Understanding the good-enough relationship can help you stay off the hamster wheel of always trying to reach the "perfect" relationship. We promise, there's no such thing. We simply want to help you be increasingly comfortable in emotional situations, to stay free to have your thoughts and feelings and not shut down, and be as close to others as you want.

Here is a way to practice. The next time your partner complains or asks more of you, take it as a compliment. They are leaning on you and trying to communicate something, even if it's unskilled. Getting offended or upset just adds negativity to the exchange. *Allowing yourself to be influenced is a sign of security, so hearing complaints without becoming defensive is a powerful green zone move.* By coming to you, they're saying you're important to them, that they are invested in the relationship, and they want to grow *with* you.

Now, this all assumes basic mutuality and a shared desire on each person's part to grow toward more security together. In those cases, dropping defenses and working toward more risk and vulnerability makes sense. However, if you aren't fundamentally safe, that is an entirely different story. If you are in a situation that threatens, belittles, intimidates, or scorns you, then holding your own may mean holding on to your protective strategies until you can find the necessary safety and support to address the issues.

In a good-enough relationship, each partner should be aware of something they can do to improve things, be willing to work on it, and demonstrate ways they are actively growing. If you both agree that you are the problem and only you need to fix something, that is not mutuality. Find support and make space to hear yourself clearly. Some part of you knows what you need.

Natural Relational Conflict

In any important intimate relationship, there may be extended periods of disillusionment and doubt and even the experience of loathing,[*] but

---

[*] We first heard the term "marital hate" from Michelle Obama in her *Becoming* tour, Austin, Texas, March 2019. She publicly talks very candidly about the struggles in her idealized marriage to help a more realistic picture of a good-enough long-term relationship.

in the end, the love and security hold, and you find your way back to each other. In romantic relationships, couples and thruples may fight like banshees or be quiet and unassuming, having minimal conflict, and neither is a mark of a problem in itself.

You might think this goes without saying, but ideally, you actually like each other and are good friends. You have more positive than negative interactions, and you can repair and work it out when things go upside down. High-conflict couples work if both are okay with the passion, and if the fighting doesn't emotionally harm either person. What matters is that you come back together feeling close and secure again. A good fight can be a kind of purge of built-up feelings or misunderstandings: the two of you feel awful during it, but it was needed, and afterward, you both feel better.

While most of us realize that some friction is natural, we typically don't expect the growing frustration and pain that arises when we get stuck in repetitive conflicts. At the beginning of a relationship, we are drugged with those feel-good neurochemicals oxytocin and dopamine, and we are happy to make changes to show we care. But as time passes, the excitement (and dopamine) fades, and we return to our natural baseline. This is when differences surface, and formerly cute quirks suddenly irritate. Once we begin engaging with each other about what *isn't* working, we might either split up or move to the natural challenge of resolving conflict, which is when the relationship may mature into a deeper attachment bond.

Everybody Needs a Primary

We've come a long way since attachment theory first emerged with its focus on mother-child pairs. Today we understand that it's close relationships in general that grow security, and that includes a whole host of configurations and the idea is that you don't just have one special person; you can have multitudes. However, it's helpful to pull back and think about your closest, most primary attachments today.

Primary relationships are the first person we turn to when we get that terrible news or diagnosis. They serve as our confidant, our safe haven when in real trouble. Who is primary for us isn't always obvious—it may or may not be our spouse, for example. It's about the quality of the relational experience. It can be your sister, your best friend, your former partner, your adult child, a parent, or your therapist. We don't consciously pick them; the rapport occurs naturally as we trust them and turn to them.

Primaries can and do change. For example, as you age and perhaps lose your spouse, the primary relationship may shift to your adult child or sibling. It isn't always reciprocal. In the case of an elderly parent, they may view you as their primary, but they may not be your go-to person in return. Your therapist may be your primary, but, hopefully, that role is not reciprocal! Having a primary helps us ground to the world in a safer, more secure way. It is not a dependency; more often the dynamic is one of interdependence, helping us explore, take risks, love big, and go through hardship with the feeling we are in this together.

The idea of a primary becomes even more interesting when you begin to consider less traditional configurations of bonded people.

Ethical Non-Monogamy

In relationships such as *polycules*, characterized by multiple partners and creatively negotiated power dynamics, the notion of "primary" takes on an intriguing dimension, potentially involving multiple individuals. Nontraditional relationships, including those embracing *ethical non-monogamy* (an umbrella term that includes polyamory and open relationships), have typically been excluded from discussions on securely attached relationships, which have historically focused on parent-infant and adult pair bonds, usually within cisgender heterosexual couples. This omission overlooks the diverse dynamics and attachment experiences present in nontraditional relationship structures and other configurations of family and kinship.

The narratives surrounding "family" hold great power, but can, at times, create a deceptive sense of security. Conventional elements such as legal marriage, home ownership, sexual exclusivity, and children form an interconnected system that can provide a stable foundation that helps keep us committed to and working on our relationships rather than acting hastily when our natural protective system kicks in. However, it can be difficult to disentangle and differentiate these systems from a true felt sense of core security in the relationship. Ensuring that we continue to work for and toward authentic and open connection is an important element in all relationships.

Polyamory challenges the embedded assumptions of traditional structures, providing an opportunity to confront and explore both the secure and insecure feelings within ourselves and our relationships. The 3 C's associated with ENM are good for everyone: communication, consideration, and consent. By shining light on relational assumptions and insecurities, many of us can gain important insights for ourselves that can foster deeper growth and transformation, even as we remain happily monogamous.

For instance, polyamorous relational structures often intentionally shed traditional views of roles within relationships, with some holding clear roles for primaries and others practicing *relational anarchy*. Secure relating in both monogamous and polyamorous relationships includes openness, honesty, and consensual agreements and requires a high degree of emotional intelligence, self-awareness, and a willingness to prioritize the well-being of oneself and one's partners. For polyamorous relationships, these qualities are typically prioritized, discussed, and actively renegotiated, and the expression and honoring of feelings are an active part of the relationship success.

Research suggests that attachment styles, both secure and insecure, are found at similar rates across different relationship structures, but some studies indicate a higher percentage of securely attached individuals in polyamorous relationships. These nontraditional arrangements often engage in higher levels of emotionally honest communication and greater intimacy and can have higher relationship satisfaction, all factors in secure functioning.*

We are not romanticizing ethical non-monogamy (ENM)—those practicing it still struggle with natural friction and are imperfect humans trying to get along with other imperfect people. However, the framework that challenges societal norms under which these relationships develop can provide valuable insights. For example, a common value of those practicing ENM is to actively work on overcoming jealousy by embracing *compersion*. Compersion involves wrestling with your jealous and possessive feelings and even finding joy when your partner finds happiness and fulfillment in activities that do not involve you (gasp!), which is only possible in relationships where each of you have put in a lot of work getting comfortable with your sense of security. This practiced mind-set is rooted in empathy and mutual growth, and built on the belief in abundance rather than scarcity.

People in ENM relationships value norms being challenged and reconsidered, thus cultivating an expansive and generous perspective within their connections. We are not suggesting that valuing monogamy implies a belief in scarcity or that compersion is only about opening your relationship to others. Your relationship with your partner(s) is unique to you and represents your own personal beliefs and values. Cultivating a generous, honest, compassionate, and mutual relationship is the goal of secure relating.

If you would like to learn more, we recommend Dr. Elisabeth Sheff's books *The Polyamorists Next Door: Inside Multiple-Partner Relationships and Families* and *When Someone You Love Is Polyamorous: Understanding Poly People and Relationships*. If you are interested in more on the intersection of polyamory and attachment, see Jessica Fern's *Polysecure: Attachment Trauma*

---

* Interestingly, this same study indicated that attachment expectations shifted with each partner; you could be secure with one and lean red with a different partner simultaneously. It's not only you; it's the relationship and what it evokes in you. This validates the dynamic and interactive nature of adult relating we will continue to discuss. This is also different from deeply held internal working models, which are not being studied in this sort of research.

and Consensual Nonmonogamy and our interview with her on *Therapist Uncensored* (episode 176).

Interactive Regulation

Humans are inherently wired for co-regulation, effortlessly perceiving and responding to subtle changes in other people's facial microexpressions and physiological cues such as pupil dilation, flushing, and respiration. Interestingly, we are quicker and more accurate in detecting these changes in others than in ourselves. As you know from chapter 3, this neural synchronization acts like a Wi-Fi connection, promoting a sense of safety and connection. It allows us to share another's excitement and enhance their positive mental state. Conversely, we can also synchronize and amplify feelings such as stress, anger, and fear.

The following image, Figure 14, reminds us of how we can impact each other as we co-regulate or co-dysregulate. Do you ladder each other up into distress or ladder each other back toward the green zone? When we are able to hold ourselves, remain more grounded, turn toward each other, and engage, we invite corresponding engagement and pull each other toward a more secure state of mind. The middle image—an integrated brain, heart, and gut—represents secure functioning.

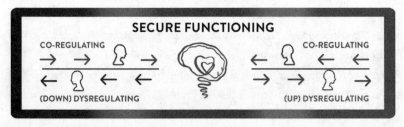

Figure 14: Co-regulation/Co-dysregulation box

Neural Wi-Fi and co-regulation aren't just about reacting to each other in the moment. These processes are embedded with anticipated stories from previous experiences—so much so that our brains use pattern recognition from these experiences to predict what's about to happen. It is not only our immediate experience but also our built-up anticipation and stories and our attachment map that create our response or reactivity.

Let's say that Andre knows that his partner, Barrat, has been frustrated with their sex life, so Andre has been thinking sexy thoughts in the afternoon and trying to crank up some desire and excitement. Meanwhile, Barrat is on his way home, expecting the same lukewarm reception he always gets. He's feeling neglected and uninteresting before he even walks in the door.

Andre, anticipating his partner's arrival, is nervous but ready to warm things up between them. He waits at the door to welcome Barrat home with a long kiss, something they haven't done in a long time. When Barrat arrives, Andre immediately feels his partner's low energy and notices his unfriendly face but goes in for the kiss anyway. Barrat pulls back slightly, surprised by the attention and not trusting this new development, which Andre registers as a recoil—so he ends the kiss much more quickly than planned and turns away from Barrat, embarrassed.

Cringe.

So, what just happened from a Modern Attachment perspective?

Both partners in this scenario want more closeness, but underlying trust issues emerged, information bias intruded, and fears blocked their connection. Barrat went on with his night, unaware that he'd missed Andre's attempt to reach out and angry that all he got was a fast kiss and nothing else. His neglect story stayed intact, and he remained unaware of Andre's bid for connection or the hurt his partner felt for being rebuffed. As Andre's quick embarrassment indicates, he struggles with shame and his attachment map includes a deep belief that he's not desirable and that his desires are aversive. Both partners were entirely unaware of their parts in the missed opportunity. This all happened quickly. Before either had said a word, they were filled with the story each partner already had in his body.

The problem in this interaction wasn't Andre's lack of desire or Barrat's reaction to his partner's sexual approach; it was the missed connection between them. That disconnect is where the true conflict resides, and then it takes on a life of its own, becoming bigger than either of them—almost a third party in their relationship.

It can be hard to communicate effectively when we see our relationship problems only through our own sunglasses. When we try to explain to our partner what went awry, we will naturally focus on what *they* did wrong because that is often all we perceive. This finger-pointing will invite resistance in return, and then we're off to the races, overexplaining ourselves and defending our position. But what are we defending? Who are we even really fighting with?

What About You?

Let's continue to integrate all that you have learned and take stock of what protective strategies you use with your primary people.

How does your coping style impact those close to you?
What ideas do you have to help regulate your close people and to teach
   them to help regulate you?

As you reflect on your repetitive points of tension in your relationship, can you relate them to energy patterns in your attachment map strategy? Look for your automatic negative thoughts as a pointer to your unconscious working models.

Now is an excellent time to do a practical exercise to make your attachment leanings more concrete. The Experiences in Close Relationships (ECR) is a free online tool that measures conscious thoughts about adult relating. Before you do it, though, a word of clarification about what it's assessing: self-report and self-observation, both of which are used in this tool, yield different results than open-ended assessments looking for more deeply embedded early limbic learning.

As you learned in chapter 4, your attachment map is held partially in conscious semantic memory, where you have words and can consciously think about it. Those are your thoughts and assumptions about yourself and other people. The ECR will assess this more conscious part of your attachment map, which is very helpful but often not surprising because it is self-report. We encourage you to take it in relation to different figures in your life—you'll score differently thinking of your mom versus your partner versus your ex—it's stimulating to see the degrees of difference and validating to recognize how highly interactive attachment styles are. *It's not just your amygdala; it's theirs, too!*

Another part of your attachment map is held in your implicit memory, embedded in your nervous system and automated unconscious coping patterns. Typically, specialized open-ended projective assessment, or deep relational therapy, is necessary to truly uncover those implicitly embedded early limbic learnings. Also, since they emerge under relational stress when the protective system activates, we all look pretty good when we are safe. That is part of why we are so heavily promoting this green zone relating—it brings out the best in us regardless of our history. The most accessible early attachment pattern assessment is the Adult Attachment Projective (AAP), about which you can find more information online at attachmentprojective.com.

But you don't have to be professionally assessed to peek at your more unconscious leanings. The recognition, reflection, and rewiring we've discussed is all about building awareness and curiosity about these more subtle signs of attachment system activation. Journaling; reviewing your memories; interviewing your siblings, childhood friends, and family; exploring photos and old letters; recording dreams . . . these are all ways to understand and update the important narrative of our life story.

Also, recognizing what activates your defense department and what protective strategies you rely on in your relationship can give both of you great insight into your assumptions about yourself, others, and the values you hold that impact your relationship.

As you've read through these chapters, what examples do you relate to? What thoughts do you have about your primary? The more you can understand your map and your protection system, the more agency you have to build security within your relationship.

Relational Therapy— Promoting Security and Relational Health

Working with your primary to grow more security in your relationship can amplify progress for both of you. A couples counselor can help each person dig into their personal history and discover what is under their specific pain and trigger points. They will also help establish greater safety and connection along the way. This can make the difference in any of your primary relationships, whether with your partner(s), child, aging parent, sibling, or friend. Having an objective and supportive third party can remove some of the fear, frustration, or even shame that may be building between you.

Of course, getting your primary other into the room with you can be tricky. **Couples often wait too long to seek relationship assistance because they think couples therapy is like hospice care—reserved for the end stages when nothing else has worked.** If you're hesitant or think your partner will be skeptical, we encourage you to think of therapy as more like going to the gym: a way to *enhance* your relationship, not fix something broken or tap the final nail in the coffin. Rather than an admission of failure or weakness, it is a courageous step of openness and an expression that you value the relationship. After all, enjoying solid relationships is the crux of building deeper security in ourselves.

Let's take a look behind the scenes to understand what couples therapy might look like and how it can benefit anyone looking to grow in their connection and communication.

Mia and DJ's First Session

Mia and DJ are sitting in the waiting room awaiting their first couples therapy session, which Mia scheduled after their blowup at the restaurant.

On the surface, DJ appears typically distracted with emails on his phone. Inside, however, he's tense and full of dread, resenting Mia for making him go through with this. Mia can feel DJ's discomfort and is anxious herself. She has repeatedly suggested they see a couples therapist, but DJ has never been interested, insisting that they were doing fine and didn't need someone else in the middle of their relationship. Mia had let the idea go—even just mentioning therapy seemed to agitate DJ, and she didn't want to force something on him. However, after this last episode, she felt differently and doubled down on her insistence until DJ agreed reluctantly.

It doesn't take long for their therapist, Carolyn, to pick up on the

dynamic between Mia and DJ. After many years of working with couples, this initial tension is familiar, as relationships are one of our most
private spaces, and talking about intimate struggles with a stranger can
feel exposing and threatening. However, once they decide, schedule an
appointment, and sit together in the therapist's office, couples often find
themselves pleasantly surprised by the helpfulness of the process and how
quickly positive changes can occur. This is particularly true for those who
seek therapy before their relationship patterns become deeply entrenched
in resentment and animosity.

Sitting on the couch, DJ turns to Mia and signals for her to begin.
After all, it was her idea to come here. Mia shares her worry about their
level of disconnection . . . she wishes they could discuss things and have it
go well, but lately she's stopped trying. In fact, she says, it's getting easier
to spark a fight and harder to recover. Mia looks at DJ, and with his nod
of encouragement, she continues. She speaks hesitantly, as if she's feeling
her partner out, but ultimately takes a risk and says more.

"He often feels so distant, yet he says he's fine. The more I try to get
him to open up, the more frustrated he seems. We're fine as long as I
seem happy and we do things together. But things go south when I get
upset or want more from him." Mia pauses and turns to DJ. "I feel like
I've gone too long ignoring what I need just to keep the peace. I don't
want to do that anymore."

DJ becomes visibly agitated as Mia speaks, so she pauses, returning
her eyes to Carolyn, looking for help. Carolyn is tracking what's happening and knows she needs to help DJ come in.

"What's happening for you right now, would you share your thoughts,
DJ?" she asks.

After a long pause, he says, "Yeah, it seems like I always disappoint
or frustrate her," he says to Carolyn, already a bit defeated. "No matter
how much I do, it's never enough. I don't think I'll ever make her happy."

Carolyn is aware they are both talking to her, not each other, but she
feels it's too early to turn them toward each other. Instead she encourages
both partners to keep speaking. As they do, she isn't listening for who
she agrees with or which side has validity. Instead, she's trying to learn
their patterns by tracking *how* Mia and DJ talk to each other and allow

the other to impact them. She's also looking for moments of connection to amplify.

They unconsciously feel Carolyn's interest in their perspective and begin almost immediately to let down their guards. Since DJ is the most hesitant, Carolyn tends there first. Rather than focusing on the details, she empathizes with his frustration, understanding his sense of overwhelm and desire to be recognized for what he brings to the relationship. DJ's fear of being ganged up on and criticized begins to wane; he's sensing that this could be helpful to him. And deep down, he really does want help.

Eventually Carolyn weaves in what she can see as each of their body's natural response to the other and takes the initial shame out of their dysregulation patterns. She focuses on creating a sense of space and calm, assuring that there is enough time for everyone here, and they have taken excellent steps already. They leave the session buoyed.

As sessions continue, Mia and DJ unravel several repetitive, more entrenched conflicts. Carolyn doesn't always use the MARS worksheet, but for them she incorporates it into a session to show visually how they are each triggering the other into threat rather than safety. She shows them her basic notes toward the end of the appointment and solicits their input and insights about the accuracy of her observations. She discusses their natural use of protective strategies as a way of coping with fear and overwhelm. She talks caringly about co-dysregulation, normalizing the push and pull they have been experiencing. Let's take a peek at her notes (see Figure 15) to get a glimpse of what aspects of their protective and connective strategies she has been noting. You can find your own blank worksheet to explore your dynamics at www.securerelatingbook.com.

Focusing on the biology of their responses worked to release tension for both partners. As Mia joked about "going to the ceiling," DJ was playfully amused as he started to recognize some of his strategies for distancing. In the safety of the session, they could observe their dysregulation patterns and realize how much their protective defenses were driving the conflict. This process also helped them put words to what was happening between them, creating a shared language they could understand.

MARS Worksheet

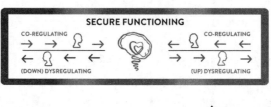

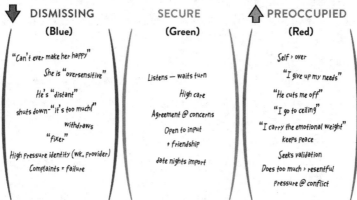

Figure 15

For example, once DJ recognized his pattern of shutting down emotions, rather than focusing all his energy on Mia's "oversensitivity," he could speak to his internal overwhelm. Instead of telling Mia what she *should* be thinking and *shouldn't* be feeling, he learned to say things such as "I think I'm reaching my limit" or "I'm starting to feel defensive." This may sound like a small shift, but it spoke volumes to Mia. It also helped DJ understand how this same shutdown pattern impacted other relationships, too—he winced thinking about his kids especially. This gave Carolyn the key to help him explore where this pattern of emotional shutdown came from, and his vulnerability deeply impacted Mia.

As sessions continued, DJ became gradually more comfortable opening up to Carolyn and Mia, and this gave Mia a window into DJ that had been previously closed to both of them. He seemed relieved to gain insight into how other aspects of his personality could be linked to his early history and attachment map, including the pressure he put on himself at home and work to have all the answers and solutions. He connected that when Mia expressed dissatisfaction, it left him feeling like a failure, and this panic increased his desire to silence her.

The most powerful part of this process was not the insight but the process of living in his own imperfections *with* Mia and feeling care, compassion, and even increased value along the way. This is the impact of relational work. **When we dive into the parts of us that we fear the most, in a safe and loving relationship experience, our body gets to rewrite and eventually rewire the old scripts and build new, more secure-related experiences.**

Although we kept our focus primarily on DJ's process just now, rest assured that Mia embarked on her own equally impactful self-exploration and growth journey right alongside him. *Vulnerability begets vulnerability. When one partner opens up and looks at their own process, the other more often than not feels compelled and motivated to do the same.*

Mia did the work of learning how her own early history taught her to give up her needs to keep things safe and others present. She learned that her red attachment map often left her watching for signs of loss, rejection, and disappointment. She tended to express this mostly during activated distress, which triggered the defensive shame and withdrawal response in DJ.

Underneath, she doubted herself and often sought validation about her perspective or worth. She realized that one of the reasons she often felt taken for granted was related to her fear of asking for what she needed from the kids and DJ. Through their work together, Mia began to risk holding her voice and expressing her needs more, building her capacity to handle DJ's frustration without fixing it or surrendering her needs.

The stronger she felt in her voice, the deeper security she felt in her own body (or one could argue it was the other way around). With this felt security, she could express herself to DJ with fewer alarm bells and less panic, which in turn helped DJ stay in his more open and connective system as he listened. This joint journey between Mia and DJ strengthened their connection and remarkably impacted and promoted healing for each of them individually and relationally.

Watch for the Rebound

A funny thing that we've noticed after years of working with couples is the impact of the first blowup following a significant period of growth. After working hard together and growing closer, we want to believe that past patterns are in the rearview mirror. Thus, that next big fight where the old patterns reemerge can feel devastating. Before, conflict was expected and almost routine and you were rather numb to it, but now that you've grown closer and more open as a couple, conflict feels like a fall from grace.

Many people mistakenly believe that this setback means the change wasn't real. The letdown after feeling good is more painful because you've reinvested in the relationship. This reinvestment and hope is a good thing, even if it stirs more hurt and discomfort. Revisiting fights as if they are new is just how humans work. You might even be having the same argument you've had a million times, but something *has* changed between you, so beneath the surface, something is different. Remember, the 3-R spiral is a spiral for just that reason. We will return to the same sticking points, but as it comes back around, we're approaching from a slightly more advanced place.

Real change takes time and patience. We are working to shift long-term wiring, and that will involve getting triggered toward old patterns. By anticipating this and reminding yourself that it's natural, you can avoid sliding toward threatened hopelessness and focus instead on compassion—for yourself and your primary partner.

Holding Your Own with Relational Anger

Robust relationships have a wide range of big feelings, some of which we are more comfortable with than others. Anger, specifically, is an essential part of relationships that many of us confuse with aggression and avoid at all costs. Or, we assume we shouldn't be made to feel that way, as in *"Why would you do that if you know it makes me angry?"* If you stop and take that in, there appears to be an assumption that, (1) you shouldn't feel angry and (2) others should modify their behavior based on your emotional response.

Rather than working so hard to avoid the experience of anger, consider it a valuable source of information about what is important to you or someone you care about. Let's say your child who just graduated doesn't want to go to college anymore, which makes you furious. Rather than focusing on what your teen should do differently to make you feel better, investigate first why their choice is so triggering to *you*.

You've already identified the feeling: you are angry, pissed off, put out. That you are feeling it at such a high volume indicates it's a threat response, so *what feels threatening to you*? That your teen is directing their own life, and it isn't your script? Maybe you feel embarrassed imagining other parents' judgment. Deepening into the anger, maybe you discover other feelings, such as fear. Fear for your child's future? Fear that they won't be able to make it on their own? Fear of being out of control? And *what* are you out of control of, exactly? This kind of exploration often deepens even further. Maybe you'll get to the dread and panic that you've failed as a parent? Or your own disappointment for your loss of something you wanted. You get the idea. Anger is vital information that inspires these questions.

Sometimes expressing anger just feels good, and you may just want to vent. Sharing with your loved ones is great, but if you get home from the office every day and go on a tirade about what ails you at work, you're unleashing a lot of emotion onto someone else without necessarily considering how it affects *them*. You feel better, maybe, but what about them? Are you talking *with* them or *at* them? Stay curious about this. Ask them their experience of your downloads. Does it bring you both closer or do you forget to actually see them in the process? The very act of having this conversation together is adding bricks to your relational foundation.

Approaching your partner with a simple "Do you have ten minutes for me to unload?" can make a big difference to how they react to your anger or any other intense feeling. This way, the person to whom you're venting will feel seen, and it's more of an interpersonal exchange. Plus, you are more aware of what they are doing for you in the act of listening, and that can feel vulnerable. You're a step closer to feeling your need for them. But once your partner feels seen and acknowledged by you, they're more likely to want to hold the burdens along with you.

Strength in Numbers: The Power of Group Therapy

Paul is a sixty-seven-year-old retired attorney. He enjoyed individual therapy for years, but his wife still complains that he doesn't open up enough, and now that he's home more and not working, they've been arguing. Even when they are okay, he is increasingly uncomfortable and morose and doesn't understand why. Separately, his doctor gave him an article on the health impact of isolation, and he was motivated to stay healthy, so he agreed to the doctor's recommendation to join group therapy. (Smart doctor!)

What else did he have going on? he figured.

In the group, Paul was encouraged to put his thoughts and feelings into words, which was a challenge. By being immersed with others who were much more articulate—and not nagging him—he began to enjoy the group and attach to the members.

Over time, though, he began hearing the same complaints from the group members that he heard from his wife: He didn't share enough. He didn't listen well. They weren't sure he cared about them, and some began to get angry that they'd invested so much in him without getting much back. Paul was taken aback that his charm and other usual strategies didn't work to keep the group members at the right distance where he felt comfortable. He considered leaving the group; maybe it wasn't for him after all, but then what? The longer he stayed, the more he desired to really become part of the group.

When Paul finally began to open up and really talk, he came in hot. He was surprised by his pent-up resentment and also surprised by how much better it felt to be directly angry. He could especially do that with these members, who could get mad at him in return. Their comfort with their own aggressive feelings helped him know they could take it and would not crumble or reject him. It wasn't long before Paul was actively working, taking risks, and having a range of emotions. The group had been the vehicle to help him wade through the 3-R process, and by taking risks, getting vulnerable, and eventually attaching to the group and its members. Paul was actively rewiring his nervous system and moving his attachment map toward that warm green zone.

Sue especially can't help but get a little evangelical here for a moment—she's led ongoing process groups for decades and has grown by being a member of group for years. Sue and Ann both participate as members of ongoing groups, and it is still rewarding and challenging.

Group therapy is a uniquely powerful vehicle for change when it comes to family-of-origin issues and attachment-related struggles, and here is why. *Individual therapy is like the heart of the watermelon: so juicy and lush, who wouldn't want that?* It is exactly what is needed for many of us. However, going from individual therapy to group therapy is like going from the lap to the playground. It is harder and stirs up our not-so-great habits and unexamined blocks because it focuses on *interpersonal relating* rather than only internal (intrapsychic) exploration. Our experience is that when people do both group and individual and want to stop one, they often stop individual and continue with their group.

Think of it as a real-life laboratory where the very issues you grapple with in the outside world manifest live, right there in the group. Trust issues, identity, loss, conflicts, and commitment dilemmas all unfold in the moment. Surprisingly, this immediate exposure can be the most effective way to learn and grow. It's like learning a new language through immersion—you learn how to have productive conflict and deeper intimacy, i.e., to more securely relate by actually doing it.

This open communication process leads to greater self-acceptance, personal breakthroughs, and a profound sense of belonging. Group therapy provides stability and continuity in one's personal life—and it is a much more affordable option than individual therapy. Regular meetings and interactions within the group establish a reliable support system that helps individuals navigate their challenges more effectively. The group's sense of community and structure creates a solid foundation for personal growth. If you are interested in exploring this option, find more at the

American Group Psychotherapy Association, www.agpa.org, or the International Group Psychotherapy Association, www.igpa.com. You can also hear Sue, Ann, and others discuss more about group on our podcast (episodes 22 and 7).

Building Relationships Through Community

Above we are referring mainly to interpersonal process groups—closed ongoing groups that are not topic-centered but flow with in-the-moment interactions. However, there are many forms of groups that exercise interpersonal relating skills—work-related task groups, time-limited groups, reading and study groups, knitting groups, walking clubs, civic groups, and gathering your friends each week to watch the latest episode of your favorite series counts as a group. We are easy that way—interacting and sharing space with other people in a supportive environment is just plain good for you. And yes, online live human interactions are good, too—so turn on your camera, look at each other, and don't multitask to get the benefits. Seeing pixels is just different than being live, but it's way better than being isolated, so whatever level of interpersonal interactions you have right now, just see if you can stretch it to get a little closer.

There are many ways to find relational healing and connection that are powerful, free, and do not involve a professional counselor or therapist. As we saw from Beth's story, Carmen found amazing strength from attending a regular support group for family and friends of individuals struggling with addiction. There are many such 12-step groups, all free. Besides Alcoholics Anonymous (AA) and its siblings focused on drug or substance addiction, there are also Al-Anon, Gam-Anon, CoDa, and ACA (Adult Children of Alcoholics). These groups are hierarchically flat, peer led, and work through mutual support. It's widely accepted in these groups that you get better by helping other people, so newcomers have lots of phone numbers right off the bat, and oldcomers provide that support because they know it helps them grow, too. If 12-step programs don't speak to you, there are often a host of community-based support, meet-ups, and non-AA recovery programs available that might feel like a better fit for you or someone you love. There are groups for almost everything if you dig enough—spiritual, political, civic, social, reading, crocheting, sipping whiskey, walking . . . we bet there are people out there for you once you are able to open up and find them. Growing your support system from these and many forms of community groups can be a powerful avenue for deepening our sense of security.

Advice from the Therapist Chair

When working with individuals and couples, we have noticed a few things that may be helpful on your path of relational growth. First, don't be afraid to jump in and try something new, whether it's talking more directly with your aging parent, attending family therapy with an adult daughter, or asking your partner to read a book about relationships or go to therapy with you. Each act toward building bridges and reaching for more understanding is a smart and courageous step. Also, if you aren't thrilled in your relationship, stop focusing on the other person. They aren't your solution. This might be strange, but unless you are going to leave right this second, then you are in it, so as long as you are in it, then be in it! What do you imagine doing differently if you were not in the relationship? Seeing your friends more? Do that! Drinking less? Do that! The idea is, don't let your relationship be the excuse for you not taking care of yourself now.

Things get harder and harder when we feel difficulty or distance but ignore it. Think of two boats that are meant to be sailing together and remain in parallel, yet they're traveling at a slight angle to each other. If caught early, while it is still a tiny drift, it is much easier to course correct. Letting the drift go on for years can lead to a massive gap between the two, making it far more difficult to steer back together. When we take the risk to ask, to reach out for opportunities to grow together, this shared effort can deeply impact you both.

13

Deepening Security
Among Us

There are many reasons to scoff at the idea of security among us.

In 2023 alone, we witnessed mass murders, inhumane retaliations, geopolitical tensions, and entrenched wars that have renewed fears of chemical and nuclear attacks. On the individual level, we are being incited toward division and malignant hate while effective political leadership in many areas has ground to a halt as elected legislators put personal interest and vendettas above governance for the people they represent.

We are also experiencing profound social upheaval and are grappling with fundamental issues of trust—everywhere. With divisive perspectives of reality, trust in long-established respected institutions—such as the free press, universities, and the scientific community—has eroded. American parents in particular wrestle with managing their mixed feelings caused by simply dropping their children off at school—a flashpoint of incomprehensible violence.

With intact families being an important base of security, children are being detained and separated from their parents at the border of Texas, only miles from where we write this today, perpetuating a cycle of trauma that effects an entire generation. Simultaneously, an uncontrolled invisible virus lurks—one that often inflicts lasting physical and mental damage that we don't yet understand and can't treat.

And as a lovely cake topper, this is all unfolding in the context of the perilous destruction of our environment and unprecedented devastating climate storms that impact even those who have been privileged and protected to date. Young people worry about their future in a way that has never rationally made as much sense as it does today.

Considering all this very real turmoil and unease, promoting the idea of contagious secure relating may ring false. How can we dare talk about collective security when the world is so unstable?

Our argument is—*how can we not*?

If we don't, we will stay in our bunker of defenses and retreat, collapse, get sick, and infight, all the while remaining powerless to effect real change. This will just feel normal, as will the apathy and hopelessness that justify inaction.

It doesn't help that many believe that things are worse now than they have ever been—but many historians would disagree. Perhaps some perspective is helpful. Imagine an eighty-nine-year-old in 2023. They've seen a lot in their lifetime: the Great Depression, World War II, the Cold War with the constant fear of nuclear attack, the Korean War, the Vietnam War, and the polio epidemic. Depending on where they live they may have experienced regime changes, devasting natural disasters with little aid, the HIV health disaster, and Ebola.

If she is a woman, a person of color, or identifies as non-heterosexual, life in 1945, 1955, 1965, or 1975 was certainly scarier and more restrictive. Back then, many people had far less control over who they could love and what kind of job or career they could pursue. It's strange in this divisive climate to realize this, but with this perspective, we've come a long way in terms of promoting equality, diversity, and individual freedoms in most areas of the world.

The point is, as life continues to be harsh, scary, and full of unpredictable chaos, it also contains the capacity to heal and change. This matters because what we believe influences our future. Studies show what we believe directly impacts how we engage in the world, where we put our energy, and even how our body physiologically responds to experiences.

For instance, there is a real psychological phenomenon where when we believe something will help us, be it a pill or an intervention, it can shift our body's response and lead to healing change beyond the effect of the intervention itself (*the placebo effect*). However, the reverse is also true. If we believe this same pill or intervention will cause undesirable and even health-diminishing outcomes, it can produce physical negative effects on our body and minds (***nocebo effect***). So, your (realistic) perception of hope and felt-security practically matters.

Researchers have been tracking collective perceptions of security for a long time. Rates of *feeling secure* have diminished over our lifetime, and they especially took a downturn after the Covid epidemic. When we feel problems are pervasive and insurmountable, we shut down or cut off. After all, one might think, what else can you do other than duck back under the covers? Yet we know that ducking perpetuates the problem and leaves you in a state of hopelessness or dissocation, so what is an individual to do about problems so large?

First, grab ahold of the idea that there is hope, because there is.

Even with something as daunting as climate destruction—if we look for what is working, paying attention to even small signs of good news, and turn our focus toward local or national places to jump in, we are much more likely to stay engaged and be part of the solution. Volunteering and altruism in general help our community, but our physical and emotional well-being is the largest beneficiary. If we feel we are part of something larger and are having a meaningful impact, we literally feel better. It helps us connect socially and gives us a sense of meaning and purpose; who wouldn't want that?

By focusing on your ability to stay in your green zone no matter the chaos around you, there is hope to improve even the stalest of relationships as well as the entrenched, but ultimately movable, systems in which we live. This structurally works because given a little care, human beings' fundamental goodness emerges.

As we've emphasized, at our very biological and spiritual base, we crave connection and belonging. **If given kindness, care, and emotional safety, our best self emerges.** Across cultures and over time it's been demonstrated that people are fundamentally caring, which flies against the cultivated story that if societal pressures were removed, people's underlying greed and selfishness take over.

Rutger Bregman is a Dutch historian and journalist whose 2019 book *Humankind: A Hopeful History* carefully analyzes the myth that without social controls, humans become selfish and even savage. By chronicling numerous surprising examples, he carefully debunks that accepted but dangerous social assumption.

For example, he contradicts the socially accepted narrative in the still-popular *fiction* book published in 1954, *Lord of the Flies* by William Golding. This book is often required reading for school children and is about boys stranded on a deserted island that ultimately become savage toward one another as social order degrades. Rutger tracked down a real example (nonfiction) of a group of men that as boys were marooned alone together on a deserted island for many months. He documented not only that this group of boys cooperated throughout their harrowing ordeal, but in fact remained lifelong friends.

Rutger draws on a large range of historical and scientific evidence that shows humans are inherently motivated toward kindness and collaboration. We recommend reading *Humankind* to inoculate yourself from ingrained cultural negativity about people and to fan those embers of hope in change and recovery. We have thrived as a species *because* of our need to connect, care, and work together.

It is likely this innate part of you, your desire for connection, that inspired you to choose a book about secure relating. By developing your most mature capacities and working to resist devolving into patterned dysregulation, you are shifting things inside you and, by design, around you. You are creating new neural connections and interpersonal possibilities by continuing to challenge and push yourself to stay engaged. We need one another, so joining in where you can and building networks where they don't exist make a difference.

The tiny neural connections you are making flow outward, creating change in the brains of those close to you. *These changes add up, creating little waves of hope and health inside and around you.* These waves remind us of the interconnectedness of all things and that every action, no matter how small, has the power to exert an impact far beyond what we can perceive. They shape your relationships and the world around you in subtle but profound ways. Neuroscience research shows that changing your brain changes your mind, which changes relationships. And it is through relationships that we can impact one another, build community, and best effect change in the world.

Empathy Is Great, and It's a Problem

The self-protective strategies we've been discussing get activated depending on how we perceive events and how we define "our" community. It's not that hard to imagine—just think of how you define the concept of "us." When our kids or nieces or nephews get threatened, we get activated because they are mapped as part of *us*. When our beloved team wins, we feel as if we win because we've mapped our team as part of *us*—and as a community we celebrate this win together regardless of our many differences (however, if our team loses we are more likely to say "they" lost). If Earth were attacked by aliens, our community would be all of us and our planet. Pre-colonialism, humans worked together and lived in close collaboration with nature because people and the natural world were seen as extensions of one another and thus mapped as one community. We were an *us*.

However, while loving and protecting those close to us has its important benefits, it can also be one of our biggest Achilles' heel if we are not careful. When we reduce our community to an *us* and *them*—favoring one group or community over another—it triggers our defenses to go into a sort of tribalism and to take action to defend *our* group. It is not uncommon for fights at athletic events to break out between fans from opposing teams who know nothing else about one another except they are part of the "other" community. This is where empathy, while normally thought of as a powerfully positive emotion, can get in the way of collective security. When we feel empathy for the harm caused to our group, and use this to justify retaliative harm toward another, this leads to waves of justified destruction, promoting ripples of fear and adding to a sense of defensiveness and insecurity.

The Power of Community— for Better and for Worse

While generally having a sense of group identity and belonging can be positive, our bodies' awareness that we need it for survival keeps our protective system humming below the surface. Just as we want to know what activates us in relationships, let's deep dive into what happens for us in social groups, because they can cause us to quite literally lose our minds.

It's clear that humans are naturally drawn to belong to a group or cause. According to research, once joined, we tend to amplify biases and form negative attitudes toward members of *other* groups to help protect the strength of *our* group. This phenomenon, *in-group bias*, has been studied widely in psychology and social science. Similar findings have been replicated in various contexts, such as sports rivalries, political affiliations, and even experiments where participants are assigned to groups based on random criteria, such as a coin toss. These studies show consistently that individuals favor their group and exhibit negative attitudes toward out-group members, often perpetuating stereotypes, prejudice, and even aggression.

If random group divisions can stir such vitriol, consider our divisions by political parties, religious beliefs, national identities, and cultural practices. These groups come embedded with inherent differences in experiences, traditions, beliefs, values, and principles that hit the core of each member's identity. For example, in the United States, you don't just vote Republican or Democrat, you *are* Republican or Democrat.

When our sense of belonging and identity feels threatened, it's human nature to buck up and want to protect and defend. And, as we've been discussing, once we activate our protection system, our ability to embrace differences, see nuances, and engage with our higher, more insightful self gets sacrificed to our instinct for self-preservation against the "other" looming threat.

Groupthink Versus Collective Intelligence

In-group bias can lead to groupthink, where individuals prioritize consensus and power over critical thinking and independent judgment. It occurs when there is high pressure to conform and often under leadership that is directive and discourages alternative viewpoints, causing members to suppress any reservations or personal disagreements. Add to that a negative and stereotyped view of those not in the group, and the chances of uniformity of thought increase. Emotions drive decisions, and critical evaluation is abandoned.

When given room and safety to explore how we feel about a given topic, it would be hard to get even a few people to totally agree on most ideas. If you allow for it, you can find a range of differences of thought and perspective that help flesh out the strengths and weakness of the proposal. Cultivating collaboration and encouraging differences of opinion create collective intelligence, the opposite of groupthink. Collective intelligence occurs when diverse perspectives are considered and valued, and decisions are based on collective wisdom. The group as a whole always knows more than any individual, including the leader, if you can tap into this collective intelligence.

This tendency toward groupthink is something that emerges even in group therapy. As a group therapy leader, Sue's spider senses get alerted when the group becomes too homogenous in thought. She might ask things like, *What's not being spoken right now? What's stopping those who disagree from speaking up? If you held a different view, does this group feel safe enough right now to say it?* Once someone can express ambivalence or hold a less popular opinion, Sue can relax a little—the group is back on a secure functioning track.

Another Dan Siegel-ism we love is the concept of FACES, his acronym for a healthy-functioning internal neural system and signs of interpersonal flow and well-being. FACES stands for flexible, adaptive, coherent, energized, and stable. We start many task groups reminding members of this secure flow state—we literally spell it out—as an aspiration for the group work ahead. We encourage you to adopt it as well—for family meetings, dinners, couples' conversations, political work meetings, civic discourse, and so on.

This kind of flow state helps each member consider various viewpoints, which will always put you in a better position to consider things you wouldn't have thought about, and it helps participants feel a sense of ownership in the project because their thoughts and feelings have been included. Groups operating in this style foster a sense of inclusivity and shared power. There is a free exchange of information, clear decision-making processes, and an iterative learning process, with new learning updating current thinking.

On the other hand, groupthink dumbs us down. We can't learn and update ideas because those that challenge the current norm are discouraged. When group members are overly optimistic about their decisions and believe they are inherently correct, the group can have a false sense of invulnerability. They often exert undue power over their members by making the stakes higher, as in "You are either with us, or against us." *Our survival need for belonging will often dominate over our individual needs and vulnerabilities due to our fear of rejection.*

As you know by now, threat activation shuts down our ability to listen, think clearly, feel compassion, and maintain curiosity and care. Now imagine the human nervous system—you likely can tell where the bulk of activation comes from in groupthink as opposed to collective intelligence. If collective intelligence fosters a sense of value and security for its members and thus is part of the higher ventral vagal complex (our PFC-dominated connection system), then the conditional aspects of groupthink can cause a sense of threat and thus a regression into our defensive protection system.

Conflicts between groups are a part of our collective history. Before the internet and the emergence of social media, we were more cloistered in our in-group pods. Conflicts were most often between groups that faced competition for resources or power. Now, with the proliferation of social media, we are much more aware of global issues worldwide and can more rapidly and efficiently unite with or band against one another.

These rapid pixelated interactions bring opportunities to build connections and promote community, but, more often than not, they promote echo chambers that serve to divide. Anyone can now curate content to magnify the differences among groups, grabbing our attention and promoting distrust of the out-group. Using algorithms that serve content based on a user's preferences, we've essentially created virtual platforms for tribal group formations. Lies are disguised as facts and used to attack our mental security and basic sense of trust.

Partisanship Serves as the Tribe

Regardless of political affiliation, political partisanship has increasingly become tribal in nature. Polarizing party leaders worldwide have grown adept at using these forums to amplify powerful group identity, stir threat of the "other," and villainize the out-group, so we remain activated in our protective defenses and groupthink vulnerabilities. In this state, it's easy to point to those guys' thinking errors and egregious behavior *over there* yet be clouded by our protection system and not see the biases of our own party's misgivings. In-group bias is so strong that we are willing to do almost anything to enhance our party's position, even if it means losing rights, principles, and resources that are core to individual values and needs.

For instance, we are more willing to believe theories of deception associated with an opposing party than the same accusations if they were made toward those not politically affiliated at all. In other words, we are primed and looking for information to disparage our "rival" and enhance our group's position. This in-group bias can be dangerous: those who believe in conspiracies that question or threaten their party's identity are more likely to support or engage in acts of violence to protect their group, even if they wouldn't otherwise be considered violent people.

The power of groups and our human nature to protect them at all costs requires us to increase our awareness of how our protective self emerges, what values fuel our choices, and what leadership styles we are willing to get behind.

Unmasking Insecure Leadership Strategies

Just as marketers know how to fire up a sense of urgency—"For a limited time only!"—to make a sale, politicians know that stimulating fear and then inciting anger increases turnout and promotes loyalty. A scared populace is a controllable populace if someone exploits that vulnerability. By fanning the flames of division, perpetuating a sense of threat, and channeling the resulting anger toward a designated other, authoritarian-style leaders establish a common purpose and swift need for action. Then they offer oversimplified answers to wickedly complex issues—answers that often serve their agenda rather than the good of the community. What a relief to our nervous system to find someone who speaks to our worry and disillusionment with clear answers to block the evil "others" who have been designated the source of threat to our safety, culture, and pride.

We are naming this because when highly activated, the allure of unwavering authority and oversimplified visions can act as a seductive life raft that *isn't in your individual or collective best interest.* By blaming problems on our perceived adversaries and then upping the ante by attaching the issue to our moral values, group members incorporate their team and its leaders into their nervous system as an extension of themselves.

Doubt represents weakness and moral corruption rather than higher cognitive independent thinking. Rhetoric shifts from policy discussions and intellectual debates to an emotionally charged battle of all right and all wrong. Notice the flip: emotion is often disparaged by authority, yet it is emotion over reason that brings this group together and fuels their reactivity. Reason and discourse will not affect this bonded team because the stakes of who they are and what they stand for are being threatened. Our party or group affiliation has become our identity, and standing firm is the only morally righteous thing to do. We've gone fully tribal, and the only people who win in tribalism are the ones calling the shots.

In this state of mind, the simpler the answers, the more soothing they are to our nervous system. Engaging and struggling with anything important and complex is emotionally taxing and likely involves negotiation and feelings of uncertainty, maybe helplessness. Your neuroceptive threat detector will be having a heyday. With this reality, giving in or giving up is a tempting option, and being offered a simple solution can feel like a much-needed relief.

Quick answers to calm our nervous system do little to resolve a complicated issue or our own struggle within it. It is like consuming empty calorie junk food to soothe ourselves when we feel stressed—it feels good in the moment but provides no substantive value and degrades our health.

When we come from a more secure relating state, we understand that pain is a natural part of the journey, both personally and collectively, and we make room for feeling overwhelmed, confused, and even helpless. We are more likely to slow down and tolerate these difficult feelings when we are invested in solving important and complex issues. We can ask hard questions of ourselves and our leaders. We can hold curiosity and a desire to integrate diverse ideas from those whose position challenge our world view.

Your Brain on Power

Unbridled power can be dangerous for the people being led *and* the person leading. Most people who are inspired to lead are not in it for personal gain alone; they often have a deep desire to make meaningful, lasting change. Regardless of aspirations, the impact of having that kind of authoritative sway has been found to change behavior and critical aspects of brain functioning.

Dacher Keltner, a psychology professor at UC Berkeley, has conducted extensive research involving lab and field experiments on power for more than two decades. He found that those who hold positions of power experience changes in their brain functioning and often exhibit behaviors similar to those who have experienced traumatic brain injuries. They show increased impulsivity, reduced awareness of risks, and a diminished ability to empathize and understand other people's perspectives. Their increased sense of entitlement and diminished self-awareness can lead to what Keltner calls "acquired sociopathy."

Neuroscientific research confirms that compared with the brains of low-power individuals, those with power have impairments specifically in their mirror neuron functioning. Remember from chapter 3 that when you witness someone else performing an action, such as tearing up, corresponding mirror neuron systems fire in your own brain. This is an essential communication process for all of us and helps us hold meaningful connections. Yet, reading and understanding others' intent and emotional state are reduced when you are in power.

Also, those wielding power are often surrounded by subordinates who don't provide accurate real-time feedback, which only exacerbates this power-induced impairment. If unchecked, you are disinclined to tune in to or mimic others as you rise in power. You no longer laugh when they laugh or feel tension when someone else is tense, leaving you relationally blind to your impact on others.

How does "acquired sociopathy" caused by unchecked power tie in to secure relating?

We believe this unchecked power problem happens in couples, families, workplaces, and communities as well. We've said repeatedly that *shared power is vital to secure relating.* We may not have the functional MRI images to prove that the husband who treats his wife as his subordinate and not his partner may have a degree of neural deterioration in the interpersonal department, but we can begin to recognize the signs. *If we lose our ability to see how we are impacting those close to us, fail to empathize with the plights of others, and lose our ability to hold different perspectives, then we are not in our wise integrated self.*

When we start to hold power for the sake of power—that is, exerting control and masking insecurity under the guise of authority—we are compromising ourselves and those under our influence. We all need real-time feedback to stay connected meaningfully to those we love and lead. Listening closely, maintaining interest, and having empathy are not just acts of kindness and certainly don't make us "soft." These are brain-wise skills that are smart, healthy for your mind, essential for effective leadership, and required for secure relating.

Secure relating means we accept influence and that we can be influential. Rather than submitting and taking your hands off the steering wheel, your close people need you to influence them—for you to find your voice. Holding your own means staying connected to your sense of self and your beautiful, unique mind. It means sharing your opinions and thoughts with the assumption that your voice is welcomed. It means listening to others' opinions and thoughts with the assumption that they have a great deal to offer.

Remember, though, we can't make anyone else relate from a grounded mutually safe place. (Oxygen mask on you first.) Tracking our thoughts and feelings will help us clarify if we are not in a mutually respectful relationship. You may be intimidated to speak up, but does that activation mean you are *actually* in danger? There is a huge difference if we are in actual psychological or physical danger; then our threat response is right. Pay attention: safety first!

However, if you are intimidated to speak up but realize it's not because you are in actual danger (this happens a lot!), then it may be any of the other things we've been discussing. Find out more about that intimidation you feel. Listen and learn. It can be your implicit attachment map misfiring, socialization, or other systemic dynamics that are impacting you. They all matter, but you want to dig a little and learn about your personal sentry system. Secure relating in that instance is about recognizing what stops you from speaking up, setting boundaries, and taking your fair share of the power. This is not just for you but for every one of us!

Secure Relating in the Community and Beyond

Everyone is welcome and needed for the "work to stay in your green zone and help others do the same" movement, no matter your identity or political or religious or social orientation. Our message wouldn't be consistent otherwise.

The key that makes this kind of diversity work is that we must all be pulling in the *same direction toward promoting secure relating* no matter who you are. If it's truly a shared goal—if you are united in your desire to dismantle your own defenses and raise the bar of security, equity, and compassion for everyone—then it doesn't matter who is at the oars. Your approach can be your own and will probably be different from what others want of you. There is no way to make everyone happy, but if you are working to help the world become safer for people you will never meet, then you are on the journey of secure relating.

If we all work to explore and dismantle the ways our limbic system runs the show, we'd create a quiet but unmistakable empowered collective group. Find something—anything—you can do to stimulate that squirt of oxytocin in others. That's what drives those ripples of security: compassion and connection and felt safety. Those who mock connection and emotional intelligence and refuse to look inward are caught in their own toxic invulnerability and they need us to resist joining in their defensive reactivity. Instead, let's make the collective choice to hold strong and challenge us all to engage more securely.

Do what you can do in your circumstances: stay engaged in the world, don't reduce others to one-liners, speak up as you choose, question groupthink, question your leaders, expect more from yourself and them, find the ways you feel different than others on your life raft, and make room for complexity and shared power.

We know this is not easy. We can and will fall into quick judgments, unconscious stereotypes, and stubbornness in our attempt to do the work. We will become activated when differences threaten our core principles and values. We are not saying that you should whitewash your emotions, and we should all hold hands and sing "Kumbaya." We *are* saying that we all need to roll up our sleeves, do our own work, and not succumb to the internal or external pull toward division, hate, and self-righteousness.

You can hold to your beliefs, but do the work to actually listen and take in the perspectives of others without the use of shame and moral indignation. It's messy, and the path isn't well marked, but that's why we need to find our secure selves and others on the same journey: to help one another stay engaged and keep moving forward.

Remember, these values and this process will rarely be visible to outsiders because it's such a slow, intimate process. Be kind to yourself, for this work is hard. Here is the good news: the more you do it, the safer it will be for those around you to do the same.

Become the Leader of Your Defense Department

To do the hard work of staying secure in an insecure world—and inspiring security in your greater community—we need to take all that we have learned about how your brain works, what your nervous system is trying to balance, what neurochemicals you want and when, and how to activate warmth and turn down the defenses in yourself and those close to you. Being committed to staying on the earning security journey is key—improving your relationship with yourself and your close others and applying it to your local, national, and worldwide communities. Being intricately aware of how your protective system gets activated and ways to promote your and others' connective systems is part of our journey and essential in the change process.

Being the leader of our protection systems means recognizing signs that we are activated and having agency about what we do next. We can feel intense feelings, but the goal is to steer back toward the green with mindfulness. Our biggest challenge in this process will be not only recognizing that we are activated, but also holding our ability to handle and reflect on the activation, and resisting letting our more primitive selves take the reins. The pause and reflection step is crucial when the threat bubbles up. We must remind ourselves that we can handle the internal discomfort and activation that emerge naturally without rushing in to dominate or shut down and cede to the other.

We have to be emotionally smart (whole minded) to be effective. We have to hold ourselves accountable for the natural or learned desire to shame or the temptation to stay in self-righteous anger or even the temptation to just give up and say "This is not my problem." All of these are signs that our more primitive protection system is active, and this is exactly when we don't give up or give in, but go deeper: *What is our desperation? What is our fear? What is our anger propelling us to change?* We then do whatever is necessary to soothe the intensity, feel our own self-compassion for how hard this is, and own it. This helps us gain clarity about what is important, reflect on what informs our beliefs and fuels our biases, and recognize how to go forward with connection and agency to make a difference.

Become the Leader of Your Connection System

To get to a place where we relate better to others no matter how different we are, we must cross the divide and really work together. When these differences send alarm bells throughout our body, it can feel almost impossible, but it is not. Consider what you have in common with the person across the aisle from you. Don't start with the obvious differences, especially those that we assume are in opposition to our core values. How we bring down the threat and amp up the communication depends on what we can find in common with another person. If we focus on our complexities and learn to tolerate the differences, we naturally induce curiosity and discovery. They can take an opposing view, and you can handle listening and feeling the challenge; you just want to understand what drives their passions.

The key is, when you are able—and you won't always be able—to stay engaged in those hard conversations, then do listen to their point both to learn what you may be missing but also to help disengage their protection circuit, increasing your chances of eventual influence. **Hard but respectful conversations continued over time can change the world.** It's not gender wars or Liberal versus Conservative; instead it is connection versus division, shared power versus power over others, caring for and protecting others as opposed to protecting our own group at any expense. It is holding leaders and systems accountable and not blaming the marginalized individual. It is remembering context, always, including for those you are having trouble understanding. Start with their context.

Loretta Ross' wisdom reminds us that we are but one link in the long chain working toward human rights and social justice. You don't have to carry the weight of the world on your shoulders or accomplish everything in one lifetime—there have been many before you and there will be many after you picking up where you left off.

What About You?

Consider:

What is an example of your in-group right now? (Think about your friendship circle, neighborhood group, faith community, activist group, political party, etc.)

What is the out-group? Can you find a compassionate reason people
belong there?

Challenge yourself—can you find any instances where you or others in
your group may have been swept up in groupthink? What thoughts or
feelings do you have that you wouldn't be comfortable saying in your
group? What are the consequences you are afraid of?

We invite this exploration not to change your stance on specific issues
but rather to encourage you to bring your wisest and most connected self
to the mix. Overly homogenous cliches can end up limiting our view or
even trapping us. It is essential to make sure we are liberated to have our
own mind and inclusive dialogue to get the best out of everyone involved.

It's also important to maintain our composure and hold on to the
support of like-minded individuals who are working toward the same
goal. Setting and enforcing healthy boundaries, while responding with
compassion and understanding, can go a long way in promoting a more
inclusive and compassionate community. By approaching such situations with emotional intelligence and resilience, we can help create
a more harmonious and understanding environment for everyone involved. Remember, we are inclined to see the source of threat as the
"other," whether that is our spouse across the table or the other religion,
gender, race, or part of the world. We then turn our tribal loyalty into a
reason to remain in our reactive and protective fight response.

We aren't saying our protective system is bad. We are appealing for it
to kick into gear to protect *all of us* against those committed to their toxic
invulnerability. Consider as your community all of those interested in
promoting connections over divisions, mutuality, lifting those who need
help, and being willing to receive help when needed.

There are people all over the world in this moment trying to do the
right thing in relationship with others and the natural world. And those
who insist on maintaining their power over others, refusing to hear their
impact or look at their harmful influence and instead stay stuck in their
self-protective destructive behaviors, who are the threat and what we need
to collectively defend against. This transcends politics, gender, and race—
and what matters is what your feet actually do, the actions that you

take—not what you say you are about. And for those you see refusing to budge, remember to put them in context, context, context. There are probably good reasons they are stuck—this isn't about bad people, it's about the systems that hurt us and we are about fostering systems that support our best human functioning rather than those that cause us to devolve.

Creating fear to maintain power is a sign of weakness that exposes a reluctance to confront one's own vulnerability and a desire to avoid facing the fear and pain that accompany it. *True strength lies in acknowledging our vulnerabilities, embracing them, and working through the associated fears and pain.* By embracing our messiness, and the messiness of those around us, we can connect more deeply with ourselves and others and access that superpower of strength through connection.

This Truth Has Always Been and Will Always Be

By being courageous enough to look deeply at yourself—puddles and all—and seeing the systems that cultivate domination over others, you are actively part of a larger resistance. We don't say this lightly, resisting being pulled out of your green zone is indeed a superpower, and you have good company. The legacy of those who believe in the power of interconnection stretches far into history and will extend well beyond our grandchildren's lives. We are simply naming the truth and helping you find your place of belonging.

This drive for deep connection exists in every one of us. Those with brain injuries that wipe out their negative self-talk have seen it and enjoyed the connected bliss that is already right there, under the anxious chatter. Those emerging from psychedelic experiences have experienced it. Those of deep faith and spiritual traditions have felt it. Indigenous dancers have danced it, monks have sung it, canyons have echoed it, and trees have whispered it. We just have to look and listen and be open to this intraconnectedness. It's right there, for and with all of us. Think of that deep, resonant sound that Tibetan singing bowls make when played—ethereal and transcendent. This is the sound of the truth of our deepest unity.

Why are we so confident?

Because we see evidence of it every day. People coming out of their chrysalis, cave, or gaming den, their eyes blinking at the light. As we connect and find collective meaning, depression wanes, and hopelessness transforms. People, animals, and nature do recover if allowed to. Look for this natural drive toward relational life, and you'll see it. This deep yearning for connection threads through the tapestry of our existence.

This profound inclination to connect goes beyond societal norms; it is a deep-rooted aspect of human nature, shaped by the forces of evolution. Our ability to form and nurture social bonds has been a cornerstone of our species' survival and prosperity. The warmth of shared joys, the strength of mutual support, and the depth of emotional intimacy all reflect the significance of connection in shaping our lives. In embracing this intrinsic drive for connection, we find solace, growth, and fulfillment.

We hope this book has helped you to diligently explore how our personal histories, relationships, and the systems we navigate influence our attachment maps and shape our journeys toward secure relating. By understanding the triggers that activate our internal threats and recognizing the external forces impacting our defensive self-protection, we gain empowerment to stand firm and anchor ourselves in wisdom and groundedness. This journey is not easy, nor should it be solitary.

Bringing It All Together: Contagious Action and Ripples of Security

We require love and a shared sense of purpose to propel us beyond our comfort zones, and to motivate us to take action that transcends convenience. They grant us agency and empowerment. When infused with the attachment molecule oxytocin, we become more selfless, generous, and inclined to extend help even to strangers and embrace those who are different from us.

Focusing on secure relationships is a stabilizing force, safeguarding our self-worth from the toxic rhetoric that seeks to sway our rationality. It cultivates critical thinking, emotional intelligence, and resilience, fostering empathic dialogue and independent, thoughtful assessment. Through a secure self-identity, we gain introspection, agency, and the strength to effect meaningful change.

Don't underestimate your personal power, your example becomes a catalyst that expands beyond what you can even imagine. Maintaining a self-possessed, ventral vagal–enhanced secure state of mind really does generate small ripples of impact. These ripples of security can jostle others out of their complacency, nudging them to break free from their self-imposed limitations and embark on their journeys of growth and self-discovery and inspired action.

Thank you for taking on the challenges this book offered. Any steps you take toward more self-honesty matters. No matter how awkward and cringy it was or will be, all of us moving forward together can be momentous: identifying our triggers, taking risks to have new experiences, just feeling hard and loving feelings without taking action, talking about feelings, updating old narratives, upgrading our sunglasses, paddling toward the green and helping others do the same, staying engaged while having hard conversations—these things are not for the faint of heart!

We are in this together; we have to be! This is quite the pilgrimage, and if we stick with it in our own personal ways, we can become the antidote to toxic divisiveness. Cultivating moments of authentic humanity, holding hope, doing our part to clean up our unconscious litter, and working collectively to dismantle systems that oppress may be our best way to make a difference inside our own body and in this beautiful shaky world.

Stay uncensored and true to yourself, those close to you, and those you'll never meet.

Appendix 1
Resources: Related Expert Interviews

Listed below are only some of the most prominent and published relational science guests we've interviewed and who have deeply informed our work. For those who would like to follow up and learn more directly from these and many other contributors you can find in-depth interviews and show notes on attachment, trauma, and interpersonal neurobiology at www.therapistuncensored.com—just use the search bar on the home page.

Frank Anderson

Susan Ansorge

Bonnie Badenoch

Jill Bolte Taylor

Dan Brown

Sue Carter

Debra Chatman-Finley

Lou Cozolino

Patricia Crittenden

Deb Dana

Ramani Durvasula

Bruce Eckher

David Elliott

Jessica Fern

Steve Finn

Carol George

Robyn Gobbel

Lori Gottlieb

John Howard

Amish Jha

Dacher Keltner

Joseph LeDoux

Sue Ludwig

Nancy McWilliams

Stacey Nakell

Kristin Neff

Laurel Parnell

Tina Payne Bryson

Sarah Peyton

Esther Perel

Gliceria Pérez

Bruce Perry

Liz Plank

Stephen Porges

Pat Ogden

Loretta Ross

Kat Scherer

Bethany Saltman

Julianne Schore

Arielle Schwartz

Dan Siegel

Alan Sroufe

Elizabeth Stanley

Elizabeth Sylvester

Stan Tatkin

Linda Thai

Jan Winhall

Appendix 2
Modern Attachment Regulation Spectrum (MARS) Key

(This key includes technicalities that will make the most sense after reading all of part I)

Spectrum arrow: the range of states of mind (not traits)

Focus is on ebb and flow of experience and natural movement over time.

Colors on the spectrum: basic nervous system activation

Green Zone: The Connection Circuit

thinking/feeling balanced, oxytocin-enriched ventral vagal activation

This zone represents the *state of security*, not necessarily objective safety.

Red and Blue Zones: The Crotection Circuit

Unconscious perception of threat activates a range of defenses in increments represented by color variations

Distance from green indicates higher defensive activation and decreased higher cortical connections, i.e., we lose our thinking and our compassion.

Spectrum arrow directional shifts

shifting up—maximizes attachment behaviors moving toward the threat

shifting down—minimizes attachment behaviors, avoiding threat (vulnerability)

Sunglasses: biological information processing distortions

Clear sunglasses (green zone) mean no distortions of incoming information.

red-shift—enlarges and exaggerates signals of threat and expressiveness

blue-shift—blocks out important emotional information, misses emotional recognition and expression

Attachment maps: embodied internal working model + biology and psychological impact of current and historical culture and context

Maps are more stable, set a trajectory from childhood if left unchallenged, new safe experiences can and do shift maps toward green.

Co-regulation: neural Wi-Fi syncs us up for better or for worse

> Red activation stimulates threat in others and often causes shifts toward blue; blue-zone activation stimulates threat in others and often causes shifts toward red.

> By holding your own and staying in a state of felt-security, you not only help yourself but you pull those close to you back toward green as well. This is why your journey toward earned security and growing your green zone can change you, your relationships, and—combined with others on this journey—the world.

Appendix 3
A Non-Exhaustive Selection
of Key Relational Science Contributors

Developmental Attachment Researchers

John Bowlby	Alan Sroufe
Mary D. Salter Ainsworth	Debbie Jacobvitz
Mary Main	Karlen Lyons-Ruth
Nancy Kaplan	Mary Dozier
Judith Solomon	Beatrice Beebe
Carol George	Howard Steele
Patricia Crittenden	Miriam Steele

Attachment Styles in Adulthood

Jude Cassidy	Chris Fraley
Cindy Hazan	Kim Bartholomew
Phillip Shaver	Mario Mikulincer

Relational Neuroscience Contributors

Dan Siegel	Lou Cozolino
Allan Schore	Ed Tronick
Stephen Porges	Ruth Feldman
Joseph LeDoux	Dan Hughes
Jaak Panksepp	Bruce Perry
Bessel van der Kolk	Marco Iacoboni
Antonio Damasio	Lisa Feldman Barrett
Ruth Lanius	

A Few Clinicians Publishing Excellent Original
Clinical Applications of Attachment Research

David Elliott	Sue Johnson
Bessel van der Kolk	Jon Kabat-Zin
Amir Levine	Marion Solomon
Dan Brown	Ed Tronick
Stan Tatkin	Laurel Parnell
Bonnie Badenoch	Linda Thai
Pat Ogden	Arielle Schwartz
Steve Finn	John Howard
Diana Fosha	Robyn Gobbel
Peter Levine	Gabor Maté
Peter Fonagy	Jon Allen
Janina Fisher	Patrick Luyten
Tina Payne Bryson	Patrica Crittendon
David Wallin	Dan Hughes
Deb Dana	Arietta Slade
Sarah Peyton	Kathy Steele
Julian Taylor Shore	Jan Winhall
Paul Conti	

A Few of Many BIPOC, GLBTQ+ Contributors
Working to Expand Eurocentric Perspectives
of Mental Health Delivery

adrienne maree brown	Cara Page
Kenneth Hardy	Loretta Ross
Prentis Hemphill	Sonya Renee Taylor
Leah Lakshmi Piepzna-Samarasinha	Erica Woodland
Melody Li	Maria Yellow Horse Braveheart
Resmaa Menakem	shena young

Also see: Inclusivetherapist.com/resources

Appendix 4
Resources for Bottom-Up Healing

Deep individual and group relational psychotherapy

Sensorimotor Psychotherapy

Somatic Experiencing (SE)

Therapeutic Assessment

Psychedelic-assisted therapy

Eye Movement Desensitization
    Reprocessing (EMDR)

Psychobiological Approach to
    Couples Therapy (PACT)

Internal Family Systems (IFS)

Memory reconsolidation therapy

Mindfulness-based practices

Mindful Awareness Research Center
    (MARC)

Emotion Focused Therapy (EFT)

Integrative Attachment Therapy

Ideal Parent Figure (IPF) protocol

Self-compassion practices

Accelerated Experiential Dynamic
    Psychotherapy(AEDP)

NeuroAffective Relational Model
    (NARM)

Expressive art, music, dance, writing,
    and literature

Therapeutic yoga

Therapeutic improv and drama

Equine-assisted therapy

Holotropic breathwork

Hakomi—mindful somatic psychotherapy

Play therapy

Safe and sound protocol

Endnotes

Where "TU Episode XX" occurs, there is a full-length podcast episode and show notes often with extra resources at www.therapistuncensored.com—just put in the episode number or author name in Search.

1: The Earning Security Journey

8   Attachment is a pivotal concept in human development: John Bowlby and Mary Ainsworth, *Patterns of Attachment: A Psychological Study of the Strange Situation* (Hillsdale, NJ: Lawrence Erlbaum, 1978); John Bowlby, *Attachment and Loss*, vol 1. (New York: Basic Books); Bowlby, *Attachment and Loss*, vol. 2, *Separation: Anxiety and Anger* (New York: Basic Books, 1982).

15   He also introduced the idea: Dan Siegel, *The Developing Mind: How Relationships and the Brain Interact to Shape Who We Are* (New York: Guilford Press, 1999); Pat Ogden Sensorimotor Psychotherapy Institute; Clare Pain, Kekuni Minton, and Pat Ogden *Trauma and the Body: A Sensorimotor Approach to Psychotherapy* (New York: Norton, 2006). Here is a client-friendly infographic from the National Institute for the Clinical Application of Behavioral Medicine (NICABM), https://www.nicabm.com/trauma -how-to-help-your-clients-understand-their-window-of-tolerance/.

3: Relational Neuroscience 201

43   mind is a self-organizing process that emerges: Dan Siegel, *Mind: A Journey to the Heart of Being Human* (New York: Norton Series, 2016).

44   the impact of security can be seen on an fMRI!: Eun Jung Choi et al., "Attachment Security and Striatal Functional Connectivity in Typically Developing Children," *Developmental Cognitive Neuroscience* 48 (April 2021): 100914, doi: 10.1016/j .dcn.2021.100914. Epub 2021 Jan 20. PMID: 33517105; PMCID: PMC7847968.

50   reliably associated with reductions in hippocampal and amygdala volume: Ziv Ben-Zion et al., "Structural Neuroimaging of Hippocampus and Amygdala Subregions in Post-Traumatic Stress Disorder (PTSD): A Scoping Review," *Biological Psychiatry: Global Open Science* (March 2023), https://doi.org/10.1016/j.bpsgos.2023.07.001; F. L. Woon and D. W. Hedges, "Hippocampal and Amygdala Volumes in Children and Adults with Childhood Maltreatment-Related Posttraumatic Stress Disorder: A Meta-analysis," *Hippocampus* 18, no 8 (August 2008): 729–36, doi:10.1002/hipo.20437.

50   Dr. Jill Bolte Taylor's suggestion to name and call upon the different parts of your PFC and limbic system: Jill Bolte Taylor, *Whole Brain Living: The Anatomy of Choice and the Four Characters That Drive Our Life* (Carlsbad, CA: Hay House, 2021); Jill Bolte Taylor, interviewed by Sue Marriott, "Whole Brain Living: Psychology + Neuroanatomy + Spirit with Dr. Jill Bolte Taylor," *Therapist Uncensored*, episode 164, December 6, 2021, https://therapistuncensored.com/episodes/whole-brain-living-psychology -neuroanatomy-spirit-with-dr-jill-bolte-taylor-164/; and episode 195 (replay), January 10, 2023, https://therapistuncensored.com/episodes/whole-brain-living-psychology -neuroanatomy-spirit-with-dr-jill-bolte-taylor-replay-195/.

51   Dr. Stephen Porges . . . clinical practice in the 1990s: Stephen Porges, *Polyvagal Safety: Attachment, Communication, Self Regulation* (New York: W. W. Norton, 2021); Porges, interviewed by Sue Marriott, "Polyvagal Theory in Action—The Practice of Body Regulation with Dr. Stephen Porges," *Therapist Uncensored*, episode 93, April 10,

2019, https://therapistuncensored.com/episodes/tu93-polyvagal-theory-in-action-the
-practice-of-body-regulation-with-dr-stephen-porges/; Deb Dana, *Polyvagal Theory in
Therapy: Engaging the Rhythm of Regulation* (New York W. W. Norton, 2018); Dana,
interviewed by Sue Marriott, "Story Follows State—Investigating Polyvagal Theory
with Guest Deb Dana," *Therapist Uncensored*, episode 110, December 5, 2019, https://
therapistuncensored.com/episodes/tu110-story-follows-state-investigating-polyvagal
-theory-with-guest-deb-dana/.

52   what we respond to at any given moment: Louis Cozolino, *Interpersonal Neurobiology
Integrating Science and the Human Experience.*

53   you feel safe and are in a secure state of mind: Stephen Porges, *The Polyvagal Theory:
Neurophysiological Foundations of Emotions, Attachment, Communication, and Self-
Regulation* (New York: W. W. Norton, 2011).

56   *mirror neuron system*: Luca Bonini et al., "Mirror Neurons 30 Years Later: Implications
and Applications," *Trends in Cognitive Sciences* 26, no. 9 (September 2022): 767–81.

60   implicit, "right-to-right" connections: Allan N. Schore is a prolific author and
considered one of the parents of affective neuroscience. His writing can be dense,
but it is well worth tackling for professionals. Begin with *The Science of the Art of
Psychotherapy* (New York: W. W. Norton, 2012).

4: Attachment Theory's Coming-of-Age Story

66   Harlow's first concept, *separation anxiety*: Suomi and Leroy, 1982; S. J. Suomi and
H. F. Harlow, "Social Rehabilitation of Isolate-Reared Monkeys," *Developmental
Psychology* 6, no. 3 (May 1972): 487–96, https://doi.org/10.1037/h0032545.

67   the rhesus monkeys who'd never been isolated from their mothers: Suomi and Harlow,
"Social Rehabilitation," 487–96.

69   (1) secure, (2) insecure avoidant, (3) insecure resistant also called insecure ambivalent,
and (4) disorganized: Ainsworth et al., Patterns of Attachment"; Mary D. Salter
Ainsworth and Silvia M. Bell, "Attachment, Exploration, and Separation: Illustrated
by the Behavior of One-Year-Olds in a Strange Situation," *Child Development* 41, no. 1
(March 1970): 49–67, doi:https://doi.org/10.2307/1127388; Mary Main and Judith
Solomon, "Discovery of a New, Insecure-Disorganized/Disoriented Attachment
Pattern," in *Affective Development in Infancy*, eds. T. Berry Brazelton and Michael W.
Yogman (Norwood, NJ: Ablex, 1986), 95–124.

77   reveals a less organized attachment strategy: Judith Solomon and Carol George, eds.,
Disorganized Attachment & Caregiving (New York: Guilford Press, 2011).

80   than the early relationship with the mother alone: M. H. van IJzendoorn et al., "The
Relative Effects of Maternal and Child Problems on the Quality of Attachment:
A Meta-analysis of Attachment in Clinical Samples," *Child Development* 63, no. 4
(August 1992): 840–58, doi:10.1111/j.1467-8624.1992.tb01665.x.

82   One highly referenced study: Cindy Hazan and Phillip Shaver, "Romantic Love
Conceptualized as an Attachment Process," *Journal of Personality and Social Psychology*
52, no. 3 (March 1987): 511–24, https://doi.org/10.1037/0022-3514.52.3.511.

82   Kim Bartholomew added . . . the fearful-avoidant category: K. Bartholomew and L. M.
Horowitz, "Attachment Styles Among Young Adults: A Test of a Four-Category
Model," *Journal of Personality and Social Psychology* 61, no. 2 (1991): 226; K.Bartholomew,
"Avoidance of Intimacy: An Attachment Perspective," *Journal of Social and Personal
Relationships* 7, no. 2 (May 1990): 147–78, https://doi.org/10.1177/0265407590072001.

82   attachment styles came down to two dimensions: anxiety and avoidance: R. C. Fraley,
N. G. Waller, and K. A. Brennan, "An Item-Response Theory Analysis of Self Report
Measures of Adult Attachment," *Journal of Personality and Social Psychology* 78 (2000):
350–65.

6: Organizing the Disorganized—Tie-Dye

105   the primary feature of this category is *dysregulation*: Carol George, Julie Wargo
Aikins, and Melissa Lehman, eds., *Working with Attachment Trauma: Clinical
Application of the Adult Attachment Projective Picture System* (New York: Routledge,
2023). Also, Carol George, interview with Sue Marriott, "Working with Attachment
Trauma Using Lessons from the AAP, Failed Mourning, Disorganized/Dysregulated
Attachment with Dr. Carol George," *Therapist Uncensored*, episode 210, August 1,
2023, https://therapistuncensored.com/episodes/working-with-attachment-trauma
-dr-carol-george-210/.

106   most notably, the hippocampus: M. Arancibia, M. Lutz, Á Ardiles, and C. Fuentes,
"Neurobiology of Disorganized Attachment: A Review of Primary Studies on Human
Beings," *Neuroscience Insights* 18 (February 21, 2023): 26331055221145681, doi:
10.1177/26331055221145681. PMID: 36844427; PMCID: PMC9947683.

108   increases the risk of disorganized and unresolved patterns: M. H. van IJzendoorn,
C. Schuengel, and M. J. Bakermans-Kranenburg, "Disorganized Attachment in Early
Childhood: Meta-analysis of Precursors, Concomitants, and Sequelae," *Development
and Psychopathology* 11, no. 2 (Spring 1999): 225–50, doi:10.1017/S0954579499002035.

108   kids identified as having disorganized attachment suffered from substance
abuse, depression, or their own unprocessed loss or trauma: Lars O. White et al.,
"Conceptual Analysis: A Social Neuroscience Approach to Interpersonal Interaction
in the Context of Disruption and Disorganization of Attachment (NAMDA),"
Frontiers in Psychiatry 11 (December 23, 2020): art. 517372, https://doi.org/10.3389
/fpsyt.2020.517372.

108   needed skills to express and manage their emotions: White et al., "Conceptual
Analysis."

110   Renowned trauma therapists: Bessel A. van der Kolk, *The Body Keeps the Score: Brain,
Mind, and Body in the Healing of Trauma* (New York: Viking, 2014); Peter Levine,
*Trauma and Memory: Brain and Body in a Search for the Living Past—A Practical Guide
for Understanding and Working with Traumatic Memory* (Berkeley, CA: North Atlantic
Books), 2015; Paul Conti, *Trauma: The Invisible Epidemic—How Trauma Works and
How We Can Heal from It* (Boulder, CO: Sounds True, 2021); Rich Simon and Bessel
van der Kolk, "When Is It Trauma? Bessel van der Kolk Explains," *Psychotherapy
Networker*, https://www.psychotherapynetworker.org/post/video-when-it-trauma
-bessel-van-der-kolk-explains.

110   laws being put forward to deny autonomy to people like you: https://translegislation.com/.

118   look to Dr. Kristin Neff's research: K. D. Neff, *Fierce Self-Compassion: How Women
Can Harness Kindness to Speak Up, Claim Their Power, and Thrive* (New York: Harper
Wave, 2021); Kristin Neff, interview by Dr. Ann Kelley, "Harnessing Fierce Self-
compassion to Speak Up and Hold Your Power," *Therapist Uncensored*, episode 175,
May 10, 2022,https://therapistuncensored.com/tu175/; Kristin Neff, interview by
Dr. Ann Kelley, "Building Grit Through Self-compassion," *Therapist Uncensored*, episode
23, March 1, 2017, https://therapistuncensored.com/episodes/tu23-building-grit
-through-self-compassion-with-dr-kristin-neff/.

119   mental health–related podcasts makes a significant difference: Naoise Ó Caoilte,
Sharon Lambert, and Raegen Murphy, "Podcasts as a Tool for Enhancing Mental
Health Literacy: An Investigation of Mental Health-Related Podcasts," *Mental Health
& Prevention* 30 (June 2023): 200285, https://cora.ucc.ie/bitstreams/c6dbe8c4
-7803-4f36-aa60-02b4cfb4552c/download. Also, see Sharon Lambert, interview by
Sue Marriott, "Attachment Stress, and Bootstraps—On the Intersection of Poverty
and Mental Health," *Therapist Uncensored*, episode 191, November 15, 2022, https://
therapistuncensored.com/episodes/tu191/.

7: When Systems Create Insecurity

125 reduces discriminatory and aggressive behavior toward those outside one's social group: M. Mikulincer, P. R. Shaver, "Enhancing the 'Broaden-and-Build' Cycle of Attachment Security as a Means of Overcoming Prejudice, Discrimination, and Racism," *Attach Hum Dev* 24, no. 3 (June 2022): 260–73, doi: 10.1080/14616734.2021.1976921. Epub 2021 Sep 9. PMID: 34499022.

126 collaborative of international researchers on implicit social cognition: Project Implicit was founded in 1998 by three scientists: Dr. Tony Greenwald (University of Washington), Dr. Mahzarin Banaji (Harvard University), and Dr. Brian Nosek (University of Virginia). Project Implicit Health (formerly Project Implicit Mental Health) launched in 2011 and is led by Dr. Bethany Teachman (University of Virginia) and Dr. Matt Nock (Harvard University), https://www.projectimplicit.net/.

129 and People of Color are deviations of that norm: Robin DiAngelo, *What Does It Mean to Be White?*

130 invisible wounds of racial trauma that accumulate over time for People of Color: We highly recommend Kenneth Hardy's book *Racial Trauma: Clinical Strategies and Techniques for Healing Invisible Wounds* (New York: W. W. Norton, 2023) as well this helpful infographic: "How to Effectively Talk About Race," https://traumatransformed .org/documents/Effectively-Talk-About-Race-Dr.-Ken-Hardy-11x17.pdf.

130 impact of subjugation as including: Kenneth V. Hardy, "Healing the Hidden Wounds of Racial Trauma," *Reclaiming Children and Youth* 22, 1 (Spring 2013), https://sfgov.org /juvprobation/sites/default/files/Documents/juvprobation/JPC_2014/Healing_the _Hidden_Wounds_of_Racial_Trauma.pdf, https://traumatransformed.org /documents/Effectively-Talk-About-Race-Dr.-Ken-Hardy-11x17.pdf.

130 "the unconscious idealization of characteristics of those in power": Linda Thai, interviewed by Sue Marriott, "Healing Intergenerational and Ancestral Trauma with Linda Thai," *Therapist Uncensored*, series SRIW, episode 5, 206, June 6, 2023, https:// therapistuncensored.com/episodes/healing-intergenerational-ancestral-trauma -with-linda-thai/. On her website, linda-thai.com, she offers a series of six free full sessions of somatic embodiment regulation strategies: Moving Breath and Sound on Transforming Grief, https://www.linda-thai.com/blog/trf-tuesday-movement-breath -and-sound-for-transforming-grief-collection.

131 A study from the Center on the Developing Child: "How Racism Can Affect Child Development," https://developingchild.harvard.edu/resources/racism-and-ecd/ Center on the Developing Child online, accessed September 12, 2023.

132 Security for BIPOC teenagers may look different than traditionally expected: Fantasy T. Lozada et al., "Black Emotions Matter: Understanding the Impact of Racial Oppression on Black Youth's Emotional Development: Dismantling Systems of Racism and Oppression During Adolescence," *Journal of Research on Adolescence* 32, no. 1 (March 2022): 13–33, doi:10.1111/jora.12699.

133 have measurable negative impacts on physical health and create signs of trauma: US Department of Health and Human Services Healthy People 2030, https://health.gov /healthypeople/priority-areas/social-determinants-health/literature-summaries /discrimination.

135 WEIRD acronym: Western, educated, industrialized, rich, and democratic (WEIRD): Joseph Henrich, Steven J. Heine, Ara Norenzayan, "The Weirdest People in the World?," *Behav Brain Sci* 33 (2010): 61–83, discussion 83–135.

136 Western middle class represents only about 5 percent of the world's population: H. Keller, N. Chaudhary, "Is Mother Essential for Attachment? Models of Care in Different Cultures," *The Cultural Nature of Attachment: Contextualizing Relationships and Development* (Strüngmann Forum Reports), Keller Bard, ed., (Cambridge, MA: MIT Press, 2018).

136   signed by fifty-five attachment researchers, to provide guidance: Tommie Forslund et
       al., "Attachment Goes to Court: Child Protection and Custody Issues," Attachment &
       Human Development 24, no. 1 (2022): 1–52, DOI: 10.1080/14616734.2020.1840762,
       https://www.tandfonline.com/doi/full/10.1080/14616734.2020.1840762.

136   implicit culture bias when devoid of context: Mårten Hammarlund et al., "Concepts
       Travel Faster than Thought: An Empirical Study of the Use of Attachment
       Classifications in Child Protection Investigations," Attachment & Human Development
       24, no. 6 (2022): 712–31, DOI: 10.1080/14616734.2022.2087699 https://www
       .tandfonline.com/doi/full/10.1080/14616734.2022.2087699?src=recsys.

136   "separating the rights of children from the family or community circle would
       be deeply and structurally—indeed, ethically—problematic": Gilda Morelli et
       al., "Ethical Challenges of Parenting Interventions in Low- to Middle-Income
       Countries," Journal of Cross-Cultural Psychology 49, no. 1 (2018): 5–24, 9, https://doi
       .org/10.1177/0022022117746241.

137   mental health for American Indian/Native Alaskan populations incorporate
       the damage those historical traumas have had in terms of culture, identity, and
       spirituality: Maria Yellow Horse Brave Heart et al., "Women Finding the Way:
       American Indian Women Leading Intervention Research in Native Communities,"
       Am Indian Alsk Native Ment Health Res., 23, no. 3 (2016): 24–47, doi: 10.5820
       /aian.2303.2016.24. PMID: 27383085; PMCID: PMC5737007.

137   Circle of Courage is a model of positive youth development: Larry Brendtro, Martin
       Brokenleg, and Steve Van Bockern, Reclaiming Youth at Risk (Bloomington, IN:
       Solution Tree Press, 2019).

137   gain from such wisdom: See this poster: https://www.edu.gov.mb.ca/k12/cur/cardev
       /gr9_found/courage_poster.pdf.

138   American children experience regular alloparenting care, and in some cultures that is
       the primary form of parental behavior: William M. Kenkel, Allison M. Perkeybile,
       and C. Sue Carter, "The Neurobiological Causes and Effects of Alloparenting," Dev
       Neurobiol 77, no. 2 (February 2017): 214–32, doi: 10.1002/dneu.22465. Epub 2016
       Nov 25. PMID: 27804277; PMCID: PMC5768312.

138   affords a parent the time and basic security to focus primarily on her children: Keller
       and Nandita Chaudhary, "Is the Mother Essential for Attachment? Models of Care in
       Different Cultures," in The Cultural Nature of Attachment: Contextualizing Relationships
       and Development, eds., Heidi Keller and Kim A. Bard, Strüngmann Forum Reports,
       vol. 22, series ed. J. Lupp (Cambridge, MA: MIT Press, 2017).

140   "a whole journey unto itself": Devon Price, Unmasking Autism: Discovering the New
       Faces of Neurodiversity (New York: Harmony, 2022), 125.

141   Providing material support for early childhood conditions is more effective and less
       costly: Jack P. Shonkoff, W. Thomas Boyce, and Bruce S. McEwen, "Neuroscience,
       Molecular Biology, and the Childhood Roots of Health Disparities: Building a New
       Framework for Health Promotion and Disease Prevention," Journal of the American
       Medical Association (JAMA) 301, no. 21 (June 3, 2009): 2252–59, doi:10.1001/jama
       .2009.754.

142   four times more likely to be a victim of violent crime than cisgender: https://
       williamsinstitute.law.ucla.edu/press/ncvs-trans-press-release/.

143   their chosen name was used decreased suicidal thoughts by 29 percent:
       Stephen T. Russell et al., "Chosen Name Use Is Linked to Reduced Depressive
       Symptoms, Suicidal Ideation, and Suicidal Behavior Among Transgender Youth,"
       Journal of Adolescent Health 63, no. 4 (October 2018): 503–5, doi:10.1016/j.
       jadohealth.2018.02.00.

143   7.7 times the rate of suicide attempts and 3.5 times the rate of suicide deaths: Annette
       Erlangsen et al., "Transgender Identity and Suicide Attempts and Mortality in

Denmark," *Journal of the American Medical Association (JAMA)* 329, no. 24 (June 27, 2023): 2145–53, doi:10.1001/jama.2023.8627.

144   The gender pay gap in the workplace has remained stable at 82 percent for the past twenty years: "Gender Pay Gap Hasn't Changed Much in Two Decades," Pew Research Center, May 2023, https://www.pewresearch.org/short-reads/2023/03/01/gender-pay-gap-facts/#:~:text=The%20gender%20gap%20in%20pay,%2D%20and%20part%2Dtime%20workers.

144   In a 2020 survey among opposite-sex couples: Megan Brenan, "Women Still Handle Main Household Tasks in U.S.," Gallup online, last modified January 29, 2020, https://news.gallup.com/poll/283979/women-handle-main-household-tasks.aspx.

145   "If you hate the Barbie movie, it's because you hate patriarchy": Liz Plank (@feministabulous), Instagram post, July 30, 2023, https://www.instagram.com/p/CvVBrOEpDt8/.

146   "everything is your fault": *Barbie* [Film], 2023, Greta Gerwig, director, Gerwig and Noah Baumbach, writers, Warner Brother and Mattel.

146   2023 comprehensive review of relevant studies on the subject: Vladislav Krivoshchekov, Olga Gulevich, and Ilia Blagov, "Traditional Masculinity and Male Violence Against Women: A Meta-analytic Examination," *Psychology of Men & Masculinities* (2023): published online ahead of print, https://doi.org/10.1037/men0000426.

147   learning gender scripts . . . and a key place for intervention: Lise Eliot, "Brain Development and Physical Aggression: How a Small Gender Difference Grows into a Violence Problem," *Current Anthropology* 62, no. S23 (February 2021): S66–78, https://www.journals.uchicago.edu/doi/epdf/10.1086/711705.

8: Warming Up Blue Activation

170   individuals with dismissing attachment tendencies have different neural processing patterns: Cinzia Perlini et al., "Disentangle the Neural Correlates of Attachment Style in Healthy Individuals," *Epidemiology and Psychiatric Sciences* 28, no. 4 (August 2019): 371–75, doi:10.1017/S2045796019000271.

170   they legitimately miss important contextual cues . . . including other people's emotions: Dahlén et al., "Subliminal Emotional Faces Elicit Predominantly Right-Lateralized Amygdala Activation."

170   trouble managing the real emotional difficulty of loss and chronic pain: María Teresa Frías and Phillip R. Shaver, "The Moderating Role of Attachment Insecurities in the Association Between Social and Physical Pain," *Journal of Research in Personality* 53 (December 2014): 193–200, https://doi.org/10.1016/j.jrp.2014.10.003; Madison Long et al., "A Functional Neuro-Anatomical Model of Human Attachment (NAMA): Insights from First- and Second-Person Social Neuroscience," *Cortex* 126 (May 2020): 281–321, https://doi.org/10.1016/j.cortex.2020.01.010.

9: Cooling Down Red Activation

197   Neuroscience confirms that those of us with preoccupied attachment strategies distort in specific ways: Long et al., "Functional Neuro-Anatomical Model of Human Attachment (NAMA)," 281–321.

10: Resolving the Unresolved

214   associated with disorganized attachment absent any parental abuse: C. Cyr, E. Euser, M. Bakermans-Kranenburg, and M. Van Ijzendoorn, "Attachment Security and Disorganization in Maltreating and High-Risk Families: A Series of Meta-analyses," *Development and Psychopathology* 22, no. 1 (2010): 87–108, doi:10.1017/S0954579409990289.

219   Prolonged isolation creates structural changes in the brain and negatively impacts stress response systems: Erika M. Vitale and Adam S. Smith, "Neurobiology of Loneliness, Isolation, and Loss: Integrating Human and Animal Perspectives," *Frontiers in Behavioral Neuroscience* 16 (April 8, 2022): art. 846315, doi: 10.3389/fnbeh.2022.846315.

219   high inflammation in the body and brain: Faiza Mumtaz et al., "Neurobiology and Consequences of Social Isolation Stress in Animal Model—A Comprehensive Review," *Biomedicine & Pharmacotherapy* 105 (September 2018): 1205–22, doi:10.1016/j.biopha.2018.05.086.

219   lack of social stimulation can lead to cognitive decline: Limin Wang et al., "Potential Neurochemical and Neuroendocrine Effects of Social Distancing Amidst the COVID-19 Pandemic," *Frontiers in Endocrinology* 11 (October 8, 2020): art. 582288, doi:10.3389/fendo.2020.582288.

220   Giving up in defensive avoidance or despair is *dirty* pain: Steven C. Hayes, Kirk D. Strosahl, and Kelly G. Wilson, *Acceptance and Commitment Therapy: An Experiential Approach to Behavior Change* (New York: Guilford Press, 1999).

11: Deepening Security Inside Ourselves

237   reports that novelty, challenges, and discomfort trigger neuroplasticity: Andrew Huberman, "How to Control Your Sense of Pain and Pleasure," *Huberman Lab Podcast*, August 9, 2021, https://hubermanlab.com/how-to-control-your-sense-of-pain-and-pleasure/.

239   develop a mindfulness-awareness practice: For free guided meditations and research, go to "Free Guided Meditations," UCLA Mindful Awareness Research Center (MARC) online, https://www.uclahealth.org/programs/marc/free-guided-meditations; "Self-Compassion Guided Practices and Exercises," Dr. Kristin Neff online, https://self-compassion.org/category/exercises/#guided-meditations; and "Guided Meditations," Tara Brach online, https://www.tarabrach.com/guided-meditations/. See also Kristin Neff, *Fierce Self-Compassion: How Women Can Harness Kindness to Speak Up, Claim Their Power, and Thrive* (New York: Harper Wave, 2021), and Neff, interviewed by Dr. Ann Kelly, "Harnessing Fierce Self-Compassion to Speak Up & Claim Your Power with Dr. Kristin Neff," *Therapist Uncensored*, episode 175, May 10, 2022, https://therapistuncensored.com/episodes/fierce-self-compassion-harness-your-power-with-dr-kristin-neff-175/; and Tara Brach, *Radical Compassion: Learning to Love Yourself and Your World with the Practice of RAIN* (New York: Viking, 2019).

239   has a significant and positive impact: Jinlong Wu et al., "Effect of Mindfulness Exercise Guided by a Smartphone App on Negative Emotions and Stress in Non-Clinical Populations: A Systematic Review and Meta-analysis," *Frontiers in Public Health* 9 (January 25, 2022): art. 773296, doi:10.3389/fpubh.2021.773296.

241   enhancing positive feelings and reducing negative ones: Angela C. Rowe, Emily R. Gold, and Katherine B. Carnelley, "The Effectiveness of Attachment Security Priming in Improving Positive Affect and Reducing Negative Affect: A Systematic Review," *International Journal of Environmental Research and Public Health* 17, no. 3 (February 4, 2020): 968, doi:10.3390/ijerph17030968.

241   automatic negative thoughts, or ANTs: Daniel G. Amen, *Change Your Brain, Change Your Life: The Breakthrough Program for Conquering Anxiety, Depression, Obsessiveness, Anger, and Impulsiveness* (New York: Three Rivers Press, 1998).

242   we fill in the blank that we were afraid because we were running (top-down): LeDoux, "Amygdala Unpacked," *Therapist Uncensored*.

248   sunglasses in the MARS framework represent information distortion: Patricia M. Crittenden, "Attachment, Information Processing, and Psychiatric Disorder," *World Psychiatry* 1, no. 2 (June 2002): 72–75, https://www.wpanet.org/_files/ugd/e172f3_fd15491dd3de42eea51c55f120eaa99c.pdf.

250 Bruce Ecker, co-founder of the Coherence Psychology Institute: B. Ecker, R. Ticic, and L. Hulley, "A Primer on Memory Reconsolidation and Its Psychotherapeutic Use as a Core Process of Profound Change," *The Neuropsychotherapist* 1 (2013): 82–99, http://dx.doi.org/10.12744/tnpt(1)082-099; "Memory Reconsolidation Understood and Misunderstood," *International Journal of Neuropsychotherapy* 3, no. 1 (2015): 2–46, https://www.coherencetherapy.org/files/Ecker_2015_MR-Understood-& -Misunderstood.pdf.

250 empirically reviewed process of transformational change: B. Ecker and S. K. Bridges, "How the Science of Memory Reconsolidation Advances the Effectiveness and Unification of Psychotherapy," *Clin Soc Work J* 48 (2020): 287–300, https://doi.org/10.1007/s10615-020-00754-z.

252 Ideal Parent Figure Protocol: Daniel P. Brown and David S. Elliott, *Attachment Disturbances in Adults: Treatment for Comprehensive Repair* (New York: W. W. Norton, 2016). See also Elliott, *Therapist Uncensored*, episode 34; and Daniel Brown, interviewed by Sue Marriott, "Treating Complex Trauma and Attachment with Guest Dr. Daniel Brown," *Therapist Uncensored*, episode 87, January 10, 2019, https://therapistuncensored.com/episodes/tu-87-treating-complex-trauma-and-attachment -with-guest-dr-daniel-brown/; and episode 157 (replay), September 24, 2021, https://therapistuncensored.com/episodes/tu157-treating-complex-trauma-and-attachment -with-guest-dr-daniel-brown-replay/.

252 stabilization for individuals with complex PTSD has found encouraging results: F. Parra et al., "Ideal Parent Figure Method in the Treatment of Complex Posttraumatic Stress Disorder Related to Childhood Trauma: A Pilot Study," *Eur J Psychotraumatol* 8, no. 1 November 16, 2017):1400879, doi: 10.1080/20008198.2017.1400879. PMID: 29201286; PMCID: PMC5700488.

253 evidence-based intervention developed in Zimbabwe: D. Chibanda et al., "Effect of a Primary Care–Based Psychological Intervention on Symptoms of Common Mental Disorders in Zimbabwe: A Randomized Clinical Trial," *JAMA* 316, no. 24 (2016): 2618–26, doi:10.1001/jama.2016.19102; Ruth Verhey, interview with Sue Marriott, "Grandma Heals: Community-based Mental Health Care from Zimbabwe with Dr. Ruth Verhey," *Therapist Uncensored*, episode 127, August 4, 2020, , https://therapistuncensored.com/episodes/tu127-friendship-bench/.

254 right-to-right syncing: Alan Schore, *The Science of the Art of Psychotherapy* (New York: W. W. Norton, 2012).

254 "by which health is created in mind, brain, body and relationships: Siegel, *Developing Mind*, 336.

12: Deepening Security Between Us

259 A US surgeon general's report released in May 2023: *Our Epidemic of Loneliness and Isolation: The U.S. Surgeon General's Advisory on the Healing Effects of Social Connection and Community* (Washington, DC: Office of the U.S. Surgeon General, 2023), https://www.hhs.gov/sites/default/files/surgeon-general-social-connection-advisory.pdf.

266 even as we remain happily monogamous: Jessica Fern, *Polysecure: Attachment, Trauma and Consensual Nonmonogamy* (Portland, OR: Thorntree Press, 2020); Jessica Fern, interview with Sue Marriott, "Attachment in Polyamory & Consensual Non-Monogamous Relationships with Jessica Fern," *Therapist Uncensored*, episode 176, May 24, 2022, https://therapistuncensored.com/episodes/attachment-in-polyamory-with-jessica-fern-ep-176/.

266 higher percentage of securely attached individuals in polyamorous relationships: Amy C. Moors et al., "Multiple Loves: The Effects of Attachment with Multiple Concurrent Partners on Relational Functioning," *Personality and Individual Differences* 147 (2019): 102–10.

270 Experiences in Close Relationships (ECR): https://www.web-research-design.net /cgi-bin/crq/crq.pl. A self-scoring version of the ECR-R is available online at Your

Personality (www.yourpersonality.net). Site run by Dr. Chris Fraley of the University of Illinois at Urbana-Champaign.

13: Deepening Security Among Us

285 they especially took a downturn after the Covid epidemic: Faith Hill, "America Is in Its Insecure-Attachment Era: Discomfort with Intimacy Seems to Be on the Rise— and No One's Quite Sure Why," *Atlantic* online, last modified April 27, 2023, https://www.theatlantic.com/family/archive/2023/04/insecure-attachment-style-intimacy-decline-isolation/673867/.

285 Volunteering and altruism in general help our community: C. E. Jenkinson et al., "Meta-analysis on Volunteering and Well-Being: Is Volunteering a Public Health Intervention? A Systemic Review and Meta-analysis of the Health and Survival of Volunteers," *BMC Public Health* 13, no. 1 (2013): 773.

285 2019 book *Humankind: A Hopeful History*: Rutger Bregman, *Humankind: A Hopeful History* (New York: Hachette Books, 2023).

286 changing your brain changes your mind, which changes relationships: Siegel, *Developing Mind*.

288 This phenomenon, *in-group bias*: B. A. Bettencourt et al., "Status Differences and In-Group Bias: A Meta-analytic Examination of the Effects of Status Stability, Status Legitimacy, and Group Permeability," *Psychological Bulletin* 127, no. 4 (July 2001): 520–42, doi:10.1037/0033-2909.127.4.520; C. Merritt Carrington et al., "The Neural Underpinnings of Intergroup Social Cognition: An fMRI Meta-analysis," *Social Cognitive and Affective Neuroscience* 16, no. 9 (October 2021): 903–14, doi:10.1093/scan/nsab034.

289 FACES stands for flexible, adaptive, coherent, energized, and stable: See Dan Seigel discussing this and the idea of neural integration: https://www.youtube.com/watch?v=0TK62FdzzTs.

291 more willing to believe theories of deception: Elizabeth Harris et al., "Psychology and Neuroscience of Partisanship," chap. 4 in *The Cambridge Handbook of Political Psychology*, eds. Danny Osborne and Chris G. Sibley (Cambridge, UK: Cambridge University Press, 2022).

292 party or group affiliation has become our identity: John T. Jost and David M. Amodio, "Political Ideology as Motivated Social Cognition: Behavioral and Neuroscientific Evidence," *Motivation and Emotion* 36, no. 1 (March 2012): 55–64, 37–50, doi:10.1007/s11031-011-9260-7; Spassena P. Koleva and Blanka Rip, "Attachment Style and Political Ideology: A Review of Contradictory Findings," *Social Justice Research* 22 (September 2009): 241–58, https://doi.org/10.1007/s11211-009-0099-y; Harris et al., "Psychology and Neuroscience."

293 extensive research involving lab and field experiments on power: Dacher Keltner, *The Power Paradox: How We Gain and Lose Influence* (New York: Penguin Books, 2016).

298 Hard but respectful conversations continued over time can change the world: "Intergenerational Conversation on Climate Change," *Therapist Uncensored*, Episode 202.

300 Those with brain injuries that wipe out their negative self-talk have seen it: Bolte Taylor, *Whole Brain Living*; "Whole Brain Living: Psychology + Neuroanatomy + Spirit with Dr. Jill Bolte Taylor," *Therapist Uncensored*, episodes 164 and 195 (replay).

300 Those emerging from psychedelic experiences have experienced it: Jason B. Luoma et al., "A Meta-analysis of Placebo-Controlled Trials of Psychedelic-Assisted Therapy," *Journal of Psychoactive Drugs* 52, no. 4 (September/October 2020): 289–99, doi:10.1080/02791072.2020.1769878.

301 In embracing this intrinsic drive for connection, we find solace, growth, and fulfillment: Keltner, *Power Paradox*.

301 love and a shared sense of purpose to propel us beyond our comfort zones: *Our Epidemic of Loneliness and Isolation: The U.S. Surgeon General's Advisory on the Healing Effects of Social Connection and Community* (Washington, DC: Office of the U.S. Surgeon General, 2023), https:// www.hhs.gov/sites/default/files/surgeon-general-social -connection-advisory.pdf. Even before training as a psychiatrist, he did volunteer work at a residential school for maladjusted and delinquent children, concluding that the complex behavior of these children—not only their delinquency, but their anger, unpredictability, and rejection even of those who tried to befriend them—was directly related to their early emotional deprivation. As a young psychiatrist, he believed that psychoanalysis emphasized the child's fantasy world too much and what actually transpired in the child's everyday life too little.

Index

Note: Page numbers in *italics* indicate figures.